C000301442

# LOSING ARAB HEARTS AND MINDS

STEVE TATHAM

# Losing Arab Hearts and Minds

*The Coalition, Al-Jazeera and Muslim Public Opinion*

HURST & COMPANY, LONDON

First published in the United Kingdom by
C. Hurst & Co. (Publishers) Ltd,
41 Great Russell Street, London WC1B 3PL
Copyright © by Steve Tatham, 2006
All rights reserved.
Printed in India

A catalogue record for this volume is
available from the British Library.

ISBN 1–85065–811–0

*To Kye and to Pop*

*and in memory of my friend,*
*the distinguished and award-winning*
*news correspondent, James Forlong*

# CONTENTS

# PREFACE AND ACKNOWLEDGEMENTS

In July 2004 I was invited, as the British Ministry of Defence representative, to attend the first Al-Jazeera world forum held in Doha,
Qatar. During the course of that forum I appeared on the channel's
flagship current affairs programme 'The Opposite Direction',
hosted by British-educated Dr Faisal al-Kasim.

While waiting to go into the make-up room I asked Al-Kasim
about events in Iraq. He considered my questions carefully, and in
quiet, articulate English told me that Saddam Hussein should now
be released from gaol, without charge. As a military officer who had
been intimately involved in the planning and subsequent operation
to remove Hussein from power I was stunned and asked if the
victims of Saddam's numerous crimes of torture, execution and
mass murder did not deserve justice? Al-Kasim again considered
the question carefully before answering. When he did, aston-
ishment replaced shock in my mind. This highly intelligent, influential and renowned broadcast figure told me with absolute
sincerity that Iraq's mass graves contained not victims of the regime
but victims of the Iran–Iraq war and that Halabja had been gassed
not by Saddam Hussein but by Iran.

When I returned to Britain I asked the world-renowned expert
on the region, Professor George Joffé, to apply some context to Al-
Kasim's comments. He replied thus:

'You have had the great Middle East self-denial experience! Arab intellectuals are so angry about Western behaviour and so trapped in their own

humiliation in the defeat of Saddam that they deny realities or invent new ones—which they then believe. It is part of the process of the mart-yrisation of Saddam—of course he did most, if not all, alleged against him but many Arabs need to deflect blame that might rebound on them. We all go through this experience and have to learn to listen in silence as the conv-ictions are so acutely held.'

Soon after this I was with a retired architect (a friend of my family), who told me that his son had been offered employment in Qatar, and that he had tried hard to dissuade him from accepting because Qatar was home to the terrorist TV station Al-Jazeera and he would therefore be personally at risk.

Over the last twelve years I have come to love the region and in particular Arab hospitality and friendship. On an individual level much of that still exists, yet my most recent visit, in March 2005, suggested to me that something had changed. In Arab streets and households: intellectuals and moderates now held profoundly anti-Western beliefs. How did the world's most powerful country, which after the horror of 9/11 had the sympathy of the world, and its small coalition of military partners so convincingly lose the battle for Arab hearts and minds?

## Acknowledgements

I am indebted to the following individuals who readily gave their time and advice in the writing of this book: Dr Philip Towle, Dr Brendan Simms, Dr Tarak Bakawi and Professor George Joffé (Centre for International Studies, University of Cambridge); Joel Campagina (Committee to Protect Journalists, New York); Jihad Ali-Ballout and Khaled Hroub (Al-Jazeera TV); Alex Gardiner (late 22nd SAS); Sultan Sleiman (LBC TV); Nart Bouran (Abu Dhabi TV); Andrew Maskell (MBC Dubai); Colonel Simon Diggins (RRF); Dr Azzam Tamimi (Islamic Institute of Political Thought); Vic Henderson, CMG (late British Ambassador Sana'a); Professor

Justin Lewis (University of Cardiff); Simon Wren and Marcus DeVille (British Government Information and Communication Service); Dr Ian Stewart and David Howard (Ministry of Defence, Press Office, London); Colonel Angus Taverner (Media Operations Group [Volunteers]); Ashraf Eissa (late Foreign and Commonwealth Office Media Monitoring Unit); James Wilkinson (The White House); Lieutenant Commander Mark Hankey RNR, Wing Commander Adrian Frost, RAF (Ministry of Defence, London); Ihab Osman (MBC, Dubai); Hugh Miles; Ashraf Fouad (Abu Dhabi TV); Ambassador Mark Hambly and Jim Kelman (US State Department); Steve Rendell (FAIR, New York); Paul Adams, Orla Guerin and Frank Gardiner (BBC); Sam Barnett (MBC, Dubai); Nick Pollard (Sky TV); Salah Nagm (Al-Arabiya TV); the BBC Monitoring Service, Caversham; Commander Mike Mason, Royal Navy (rtd), Joyce Charlesworth (Naval Staff, Ministry of Defence, London); Tina Weadick and Ian Walker (MECI).

Thanks are also due in particular to Rear Admiral Richard Leaman for taking a chance on me, without which none of this would have happened, and to Rear Admiral Charles Style for twisting his arm in the first place. It was an honour to serve them both. I am also indebted to Michael Dwyer and Christopher Hurst as the publishers in London for their support and advice.

There are others who for security reasons cannot see their names in this list, but to whom I am also extremely grateful.

This is the author's private work, and expresses only his views and opinions. It is in no way intended to reflect the opinions or policy of the British government or armed forces. The author received no financial remuneration from any of the media organisations discussed in the book.

*Winchester, England*, 2005 S.A. TATHAM

# ABBREVIATIONS

| | |
|---|---|
| BBC | British Broadcasting Corporation |
| CENTCOM | Central Command |
| CNN | Cable News Network |
| CCT | Combat Camera Team |
| DoD | Department of Defense (US) |
| DGCC | Director General Corporate Communications (British) |
| DFID | Department for International Development (British) |
| DTIO | Department for Targeting and Information Operations (British) |
| FAIR | Fairness and Accuracy in Reporting |
| FCO | Foreign and Commonwealth Office (British) |
| GCC | Gulf Cooperation Council |
| GICS | Government Information and Communications Service (British) |
| ICBM | Intercontinental Ballistic Missiles |
| IO | Information Operations |
| LBC | Lebanese Broadcasting Corporation |
| MEPI | Middle East Partnership Initiative |
| MBC | Middle East Broadcasting Company |
| MoD | Ministry of Defence (British) |
| MP | Member of Parliament |
| NBC(1) | Nuclear, Biological and Chemical |
| NBC(2) | National Broadcasting Company |
| NSC | National Security Council (US) |
| OIF | Operation Iraqi Freedom (US) |
| PAG | Public Affairs Guidance (US) |
| PAO | Public Affairs Officer (US) |

| | |
|---|---|
| PIC | Press Information Centre |
| PLO | Palestine Liberation Organisation |
| PNAC | Project for a New American Century |
| RAF | Royal Air Force |
| RN | Royal Navy |
| SDI | Strategic Defence Initiative |
| SECDEF | Secretary of Defense (US) |
| TV | Television |
| UAE | United Arab Emirates |
| UN | United Nations |
| UNSCR | United Nations Security Council Resolution |
| USAF | United States Air Force |
| USMC | United States Marine Corps |
| WMD | Weapons of Mass Destruction |
| WTC | World Trade Center |
| 9/11 | The Al-Qaeda attacks in New York and Washington on 11 September 2001 |

# 1

# INTRODUCTION

'Either you are with us or with the terrorists.'—President George
W. Bush, Address to Congress, 20 September 2001

Such was the violence of the atrocity perpetrated against the United
States on 11 September 2001 that the President issued an ultimatum to the world, an ultimatum that was to become a harbinger of
war. In the US Administration a long tradition of multilateral diplomacy was replaced, seemingly overnight, by a new unilateral 'Bush
Doctrine'[1]—an interventionist policy that allowed the United
States to use anticipatory force to pre-empt a threat to its security.
The doctrine found its roots in a vibrant but still (at the time of
writing) only intellectually tested movement known as neo-conservatism; within days, bombs would be falling on Afghanistan as the
United States began its war against terrorism. Eighteen months later,
unfinished business would be concluded in the Iraqi capital, Baghdad. Thus, the first few years of the twenty-first century would be
characterised by conflict and turmoil in that most important of
regions—the Middle East. To many, particularly in the United
States, it appeared that Samuel Huntington's prophecy of a 'clash of
civilisations'[2] might indeed be fulfilled. An indignant American
media did little to counter the perception, moving into overdrive as
it pored over the question 'Why us?'

The former US Army general and Thirty-Fourth President,
Dwight D. Eisenhower, once observed: 'Fundamentally, public

1

opinion wins wars.' In America's new strategy of righteous interventionism, US public opinion never appeared to be in doubt; the
audacity and savagery of the 9/11 attacks inflicted a deep and lasting
wound in the psyche of an American public largely ignorant of
foreign affairs. Yet if the US Administration were to succeed in its
ambitions for democracy and stability in the Middle East, it would
need to engage with, and ultimately triumph over, Arab hearts and
minds. As Edward Kaufman, a member of the US Broadcasting
Board of Governors, noted: 'Winning hearts and minds strengthens
the traditional triad of diplomacy, economic leverage and military
power and is the fourth dimension of foreign conflict resolution.'[3] A
former coordinator for US National Security, Richard Clarke, placed the idea in a more contemporary setting: 'One would have
thought that after 9/11, improving relationships with the Islamic
world would have been high on the US list of priorities.'[4] The
United States was already vilified across much of the Arab world for
its apparently unequivocal and uncritical support for Israel, and its
decision to topple Saddam Hussein (which would be referred to by
the US military as Operation Iraqi Freedom—OIF) was hugely unpopular on the 'Arab Street'.[5]

In its foreign policy in the Middle East America has long been
regarded by the 'Arab Street' as beholden to Israel, and close to
repressive and authoritarian Arab regimes, and was widely, if for the
most part inaccurately, seen as anti-Muslim. Certainly the first two
allegations are easier to substantiate than the third. It has long militarily equipped and politically bankrolled the Israeli government
during some of the bleakest moments of that troubled country's
history. Yet it has also enjoyed a close relationship with Saudi
Arabia's ruling élite. For many Muslims the US espousal of freedom
of speech and of democracy was difficult to reconcile with the
tightly-controlled and heavily-censored Wahhabi state. Yet this
street view does not quite paint the whole picture, for the United

States has also had much to commend it in more recent years. The 1991 Gulf War, fought to evict Iraqi forces from the tiny Arab state of Kuwait, by no means gained universal Arab support, yet balanced as it was with UN Security Council Resolutions it was seen by some of the more nuanced and educated members of the Arab Street as being both proportional and, most important, legal. More recently Muslims observed the US government applying pressure on the European powers to intervene in the Bosnian civil war. Admittedly, it was difficult to interest the United States at first; the world security consensus was more concerned at the break-up of the former Soviet Union; the plight of Yugoslavia seemed largely irrelevant. Indeed the US Secretary of State James Baker famously commented that the United States 'had no dog in that fight',[6] and indeed in the initial stages the United States shared the same principal aim as Britain, which was to keep Yugoslavia together for as long as possible while staying out of the fight. However, by 1994 the official position in the United States was changing and its relationship with Britain was to sink to one of its lowest-ever levels. Britain, apprehensive that military intervention might result in its forces becoming entrenched, and aware of how in Northern Ireland British troops found themselves the targets of the very community they had deployed to protect, prevaricated over intervention. The United States meanwhile pressed for a lifting of the military blockade of Bosnia and the use of airpower to protect the Muslim communities. Sustained pressure from the international media and concerted lobbying from political and academic élites forced the policy change. As the US State Department official James Rubin noted, 'the pressure coming from newspapers and media—it was relentless, it had an effect.'[7] So in the eyes of the wider international Muslim community US attempts to protect Bosnian Muslims did not offset the 'injustices' of the Palestinian situation, but did do something to modify the street view that US foreign policy was intrinsically anti-Muslim. But the United States was not without some, albeit minor, political capital when it came to marketing its intended response to Iraq's continued intransigence in the face of UN Resolutions and the threat posed by weapons of mass destruction (WMD).

Many of America's closest friends in the region were genuinely concerned that their regimes might not survive a war. The assessments of Egypt's President Hosni Mubarak and Jordan's King Abdullah were particularly apocalyptic.[8] With hindsight such concerns were clearly misplaced; Arab regimes have survived the subsequent conflict, and those protests that developed around the Arab world, though occasionally characterised by civil disobedience and rioting, did not lead to either civil or religious war. But in the immediate aftermath of 9/11 these were serious concerns. In the 2003 edition of *The Military Balance*, a yearly assessment of the world's military capabilities, the International Institute for Strategic Studies (IISS) observed the effect of 9/11 on the Middle East:

The Middle East and North Africa have been more affected by the consequences of 9/11 than any other region. The evident link between Al-Qaeda, citizens of the regional states and non-state groups, along with a widespread anti-US sentiment, has made the support of regional governments for the US war on terrorism problematic.[9]

There was certainly an element of celebration on some Arab streets (notably in the West Bank and Gaza) after the destruction of the World Trade Center. Pictures of burning US flags looked darkly menacing on television screens and had some resonance for wider Arab audiences, particularly those where an underlying sense of support existed for Bin Laden's sentiments, if not his actions. Yet, as Professor Fred Halliday of the London School of Economics notes: 'Much of this was on issues of nationalistic concern: Western dominance, the presence of foreign troops and solidarity with Palestine.'[10] While this is true, such a sophisticated approach will have little impact on the stereotypical images that many in the West hold of the Muslim and Arab world, which vastly oversimplify the situation. The 9/11 attacks horrified moderate Muslims around the world and an unexpected degree of solidarity appeared to flicker in the international community. The United States received expressions of regret and sympathy from world leaders that seemingly bridged previous political divisions. There was widespread speculation that the response to the attacks would also herald resolution of other longer-standing conflicts. The Arab world looked on in the particular hope that the scar of Palestine might begin to heal, perhaps stimulated by the new emphasis and enthusiasm from the United States, while in Pakistan a resolution of the issue of Kashmir and the dispute with India seemed likely to claim some sustained international and political effort. Even previously unfriendly states such as Iran, Libya and Syria all denounced Bin Laden's actions. Many opinion polls taken in Islamic countries immediately after 9/11 suggested that people actually thought that the United States *was* doing the right thing in its fight against terrorism; support for Al-Qaeda was disparate and, contrary to public perceptions, a majority of those polled actually had a favourable sentiment towards the United States and all that it stood for. Yet within two years those opinions had dramatically changed. The 9/11 Commission Report, whose contributors had been tasked to consider 'a day of unprecedented shock and suffering… [to determine how] it happened and how we avoid such tragedy again',[11] studied approval ratings for the United States in the Arab and Muslim world. In Indonesia, the world's most populous Muslim country, they had fallen from a high of 61% down to 15%; among the Muslim community of Nigeria they fell from 71% to 38%; in Egypt, the largest Muslim recipient of American aid, only 15% of the population had a favourable view of the United States.[12] As the military operation in Afghanistan rolled inexorably into action in Iraq, this brief moment of international accord, this opportunity for progress, appears to have been lost. Despite enormous efforts in New York, particularly by the British delegation, the UN was unable to agree on a second Resolution to authorise military action in Iraq, and the vaunted 'coalition of the willing' appeared a rather sorry substitute for UN legitimacy. Thus the subsequent invasion of Iraq, with its apparent disregard for the inviolability of nation-state borders, would, especially in the Arab world, cause much previously moderate opinion to turn against the West and in particular against the United States.

Although much was made of the 'coalition of the willing', without the authoritative UN mandate, only a small handful of countries were willing to commit military assets—those perhaps most conspicuous by their absence being Arab states. While Saudi Arabia and the United Arab Emirates had helped bankroll the 1991 war, this time they offered little public support but much restrained, covert assistance. Perhaps most striking was the refusal of the long-standing NATO ally Turkey to allow US troops access to Iraq across its borders. Indeed, so sparse was international support for the operation that one US Navy officer wondered if the operation should be called Operation Justice ('Just Us'), referring to US and British participation.[13] Given the prevailing diplomatic climate, a concerted and pro-active effort would be needed to explain the US diplomatic position to the wider international community in general and to the Arab world in particular. The mechanism for this would be the world's media, for which the war in Iraq would be the story of the year.

In times of crisis the media often become unwitting participants in the sometimes shadowy world of the 'Information Campaign'— an intellectual war embracing a series of varying disciplines, waged by governments to win over 'hearts and minds' and to demoralise the enemy. It is a campaign that governments are invariably uneasy about discussing. The most obvious public manifestation of the campaign is the direct interaction between the military and the media—referred to in British military terminology as media operations. It is achieved through the provision for the press of military spokesmen, the establishment of Press Information Centres (PICs) and the placing of journalists (referred to as embedding) with military units. Other ingredients to this campaign are discussed later in greater detail. They are referred to generically as Information Operations and embrace such diverse disciplines as the interception and re-broadcasting of messages across existing enemy radio stations, the implementation of active measures against the enemy's computer and information systems, and psychological operations.[14] This last item is always an area of interest to the media. It may involve targeted e-mails and text messages, as well as the more conventional leaflet-dropping campaigns that were conducted as long ago as the First World War. All of these additional measures hold a degree of fascination for the media, which may simultaneously ponder their morality—perhaps finding them somehow underhand or devious.

Conflict often presents the international media with difficult decisions; ideological or political beliefs may have to be offset against national interest, while an absence of clarity and detail will frustrate attempts at objective and accurate reporting. During the 1982 Falklands war, the British Ministry of Defence issued a guidance document to the embedded members of the media. This document neatly summed up the dilemma that faces both sides in the relationship: 'The essence of successful warfare is secrecy; the essence of successful journalism is publicity.'[15] Such an observation is as true today as it was during the South Atlantic campaign. The normal conflictual/cooperative relationship between media and governments intensifies. Susan Carruthers has considered the dichotomies that arise: 'Governments, mindful of their own popularity, generally seek to harness mass media in wartime, to persuade citizens of a war's justness and the enemy's implacability.'[16] And what do the media get from the relationship? Carruthers is succinct: 'War sells.'[17]

From the outset the need to use the media to harness domestic and international support was recognised on both sides of the Atlantic. In its 'Lessons Learnt' document the British Ministry of Defence (MoD) described the aims and objectives of its Information Campaign. These were 'to influence the will of the Iraqi regime, the attitudes of its security forces and civilians as well as the regional audience, and to inform international audiences'.[18] The US Assistant Secretary of State for Defense (Public Affairs), Victoria Clarke, issued detailed media guidance to the military in a signal of 10 February 2003, which stated that the media would 'shape public opinion now and in the years ahead'.[19] This was well received. Many senior US officers had direct experience of Vietnam and had been convinced by that conflict that television could lose wars. After the tragedy of 9/11 America could not afford to lose Operation Iraqi Freedom.

While domestic media were never really in doubt, the concept of wining over Arab hearts and minds was always hugely ambitious. An intellectual and innovative media campaign would be needed, and to stand any chance of success it would have to be waged in the organic Arab media. As we see below, this was a very different environment from that of the 1991 Gulf War. Unlike in that conflict, the medium for the Coalition's messages was not now exclusively CNN or the BBC; the Arab world had developed its own TV channels, and their reach and influence were to become an important dynamic in the conflict. The most influential of these were the big three pan-Arab satellite TV stations: Al-Jazeera, Al-Arabiya and Abu Dhabi TV. While Al-Arabiya was in its infancy, both Abu Dhabi TV and Al-Jazeera were known to the Coalition from their coverage of operations against the Taliban, and Al-Jazeera had particularly come to

US attention after the screening of interviews with Osama Bin Laden. However, both US and British senior government officials had appeared on Arab channels and there was a sense that they had received a generally fair hearing. Certainly the Afghanistan campaign did not see any of the public rhetoric that was to characterise Iraq. That is not to say that all was well. The unfortunate bombing of the Al-Jazeera bureau in Kabul was a precursor for the friction that would later characterise the relationship between the US Administration and Al-Jazeera in particular.

There is no doubting the size of the challenge that confronted the United States. Despite post-9/11 sympathy and some stock it had accrued from brokering the Dayton agreement on Bosnia, the US message would not be an easy one to sell. Indeed many observers believe that America had already lost the battle for Arab hearts, long in advance of the Iraq conflict. The failure of the July 2000 Camp David summit, the highly controversial visit of Ariel Sharon to Jerusalem's Temple Mount, and the subsequent reoccupation of the West Bank by Israeli military forces, in the midst of which President George W. Bush publicly declared that the Israeli Prime Minister Ariel Sharon was 'a man of peace',[20] had all taken their toll. Images on television sets across the Arab world did not appear to substantiate the President's words. Indeed, for many Arabs that single sound-bite came to symbolise the apparent inability of the United States to comprehend Arab sensitivities. However, the unpleasant nature of Saddam's dictatorship meant that while hearts may well have been lost, the battle for Arab minds might still be worth fighting. Despite support in some quarters, notably among displaced Palestinian communities, Saddam was generally regarded by Arab intelligentsia as a despotic and evil dictator. While his removal by force was unpopular, US ideals of democratic change for the region enjoyed a degree of critical support.[21] The UN sanctions against Saddam had long been unpopular, but many people also recognised the Iraqi leader's intransigence in dealing with the international community and in particular the UN, a body that enjoys particular authority and deference in the region. There were also a number of minority groups who with careful management might well have given their support to the United States. A significant number of vocal Iraqi exiles, mostly Shias, continued to campaign for the removal of Saddam, while in the north of the country the largely and now semi-autonomous Kurdish homelands had long pursued their own war against the Iraqi dictator. While it was predictable that the weight of Arab public opinion would be largely anti-conflict it is easy to forget, particularly in the maelstrom that is post-Saddam Iraq, that there were voices of support. What was needed was a way to make those voices heard, not ignore them.

While the Coalition's covert information campaign (the leaflet drops and radio broadcasts designed to dishearten Iraqi troops) was to prove largely successful, the Arab media campaign failed. Despite obvious good intent, the symbiotic relationship between the Coalition and the strategically important Arab media appeared never to evolve from the drawing-board. Far from an imaginative and targeted media campaign that would build on past US achievements, the American-led Coalition directed its effort almost entirely at its own domestic audiences and in particular the hugely patriotic US market. Such engagement with Arab media that did occur was characterised by allegations of bias—what one observer referred to as the 'new four-letter word'. Those few Arab media that did embed with US troops left within days, believing themselves not only to have been cut out of the briefing process—a US officer explained to an Al-Jazeera team that it would not be briefed because theirs was a 'channel with a reputation'—but in at least one instance to have been exposed to physical danger. In the words of Middle East analyst Lamis Andoni, 'The US [government] had no tolerance for any narrative other than the one disseminated by the

US media, which had come to reflect the official line.'[22] It is apparent that while Coalition forces may have been successful in their military objectives, the reality of the battle for hearts and minds was very different. Historical connections between the region and Britain made for a slightly better understanding between Arab and British actors, but Operation Iraqi Freedom (OIF) demonstrated an absolute failure of US public diplomacy in the region. Thus the Coalition missed a second opportunity to reap a moral advantage from the tragedy of 9/11. Indeed, such was the manner in which the US-led Coalition conducted its media campaign, largely excluding from the 'pack' journalists who were not American or British (or who were perceived to be 'off message'), that one wonders if the policy articulated in President Bush's speech to Congress on 20 September had now been extended to encompass the media.

## 2

# ATTITUDES TO CONFLICT

'How you can win the population for war? At first, the statesman will invent cheap lying, that imputes the guilt of the attacked nation, and each person will be happy over this deceit, that calms the conscience. It will study it detailed and refuse to test arguments of the other opinion. So he will convince step for step even there from that the war is just and thank God, that he, after this process of grotesque even deceit, can sleep better.'—*Mark Twain*

History may well record the 2003 invasion of Iraq as the most internationally divisive conflict ever mounted against a sovereign state. On 27 November 2001, even as the conflict against Al-Qaeda and its Taliban backers in Afghanistan was being waged, the US Central Command (CENTCOM) chief, General Tommy Franks, received a phone call from the Secretary for Defense, Donald Rumsfeld, in which Rumsfeld said: 'General Franks, the President wants us to look at options for Iraq.'[1] The directive followed a series of meetings of senior US Administration staff, in which possible connections between the Al-Qaeda hijackers and the regime of Saddam Hussein were considered. Richard Clarke recalls in his memoirs: 'Later on the evening of the 12th September, I left the video conferencing centre and there, wandering alone, was the President.... "Look", he told us, "See if Saddam did this. See if he is linked in any way."'[2] The President's interest stemmed from the long-running antipathy between the US and the Iraqi dictator, although in the wake of 9/11 Saddam's declaration on Iraqi television that 'the United States is reaping the thorns that its rulers have sown in the world... when God strikes, no one can stand in the way of his power'[3] will have done little to endear him to anyone. On 17 September the President ordered the US Department of Defense to be ready to deal with Iraq if Saddam should threaten US interests in the region.[4] In the President's own words, 'September 11th changed my thinking a lot about my responsibility as President.... Keeping Saddam in a box looked less and less feasible to me.'[5]

Thus began the revision of CENTCOM Contingency Plan, code number 1003, the invasion of Iraq, and for the US Administration the next step in its war against terrorism. Yet OPLAN 1003V, as it would finally be referred to, sharply divided the unity of the Coalition that had sprung to the aid of the United States after the 9/11 attacks. A large number of countries were providing military assistance for Operation Enduring Freedom, yet for most this support would not be extended to encompass operations in Iraq. Despite considerable US and British efforts at the UN, an authoritative second Security Council Resolution never materialised. When the first bombs and missiles struck Baghdad, in a decapitation move targeted directly at Saddam, of the fifty or so members of the 'coalition of the willing' only the United States, Britain, Australia, Denmark, Italy, Spain, Romania and Poland had committed combat troops. As the war developed the British and other Coalition elements focused their attention on the Shia-dominated south, while the Americans took the harder task of northern Iraq, Baghdad and the regime's tribal heartlands.

For many of the servicemen taking part in the operation the justification for the invasion of Iraq was clear. America had been savagely and unjustifiably attacked. Regardless of what the UN might or might not have decided, the US Administration believed that such an attack could not and must not be allowed to happen again. Pre-emptive action, such as the removal of Saddam's regime, was seen by many Americans as a sensible and logical extension of the President's declared war on terrorism; the absence of agreement in the UN was simply a symptom of that organisation's impotence. Certainly there were dissenting voices. Some British servicemen privately questioned the legality of the operation, and disquiet existed among some of the more worldly-wise and experienced US military officers. Others, however, were simply confused. The *New York Times* columnist Maureen Dowd showed an erudite consideration of the problem when she wrote:

The US was about to go to war against a country that did not attack it on September 11th, as did al-Qaeda; that did not intercept its planes, as did North Korea; that did not finance Al-Qaeda, as did Saudi Arabia; that was not home to Osama Bin Laden's lieutenants, as was Pakistan, and that was not a host body for terrorists, as were Iran and Syria.

What is clear is that as the build-up of troops in the region continued, the prevailing views and attitudes of the countries from which they originated travelled with them. Those views were largely expressed in their national media and they were to have an important impact both on the way the subsequent battle would be conducted, and on the way each side would view the other. Some consideration of the sentiments that fuelled these views helps explain why the Arab media felt so shut off from the Coalition and why many in the coalition felt that to be a sensible and necessary precaution.

## British views

Despite a massive outpouring of sympathy for the United States in the immediate aftermath of 9/11, subsequent presidential rhetoric failed to resonate in Britain. While the war in Afghanistan was seen to be a direct and not unreasonable response to 9/11, the subsequent move to war with Iraq enjoyed no such moral legitimacy. The Cambridge academic Stefan Halper noted in his book *America Alone*: 'Since 1956 a central objective of British foreign policy has been to avoid choosing between the US and the EU.'[6] Yet over the issue of Iraq it appeared that just such a choice might be made. France and Germany led the main opposition in mainland Europe, while Britain, Spain and Portugal attempted to bring the continent around to the US view. The leading American neo-conservative Robert Kagan sees fundamental ideological differences between the United States and 'old' Europe:

[I]t is time to stop pretending that Europeans and Americans share a common view of the world, or that they even occupy the same world.... The United States, they [Europe] argue, resorts to force more quickly, and compared with Europe is less patient with diplomacy. Americans generally see the world divided between good and evil, between friends and enemies, while Europeans see a more complex picture.... Americans generally favour coercion rather than persuasion, emphasising punitive sanctions over inducements to better behaviour, the stick over the carrot. Americans tend to seek finality in international affairs: they want problems solved, threats eliminated.[7]

The British Prime Minister Tony Blair had become increasingly isolated both in the British media and in his own party, where a large number of backbench Members of Parliament strongly resisted his calls for military action without a further UN Security Council Resolution. The very public resignation of the former Foreign Secretary Robin Cook and the public doubts of the International Development Secretary Clare Short embarresed him considerably. Some parts of the British media appeared to develop a personal distaste for Bush, and Blair's uncompromising support for him allowed plenty of opportunity to lambast the government. A popular analogy among some of the media was of Blair as Bush's poodle, while one of the best-selling British tabloid papers, the *Daily Mirror*, ran a series of inflammatory front pages, the most notable with a graphic depiction of the Prime Minister beneath a headline 'Blood on his hands'.[8]

Some British servicemen deployed to the Gulf expressed private reservations about the wisdom and legality of the operation that was to come. Following the House of Lords debate on 18 March 2003, when the legal basis of the conflict was questioned, some senior British military commanders requested additional legal guidance for dissemination to their units. Public statements by Members of Parliament, such as the veteran socialist Tony Benn, on the possible illegality of war deeply concerned many, and as a consequence some began asking questions of their commanders. Benn said: 'If Britain joins in, we will be guilty of conducting an act of aggression and committing war crimes against those innocent civilians who are bound to be killed.'[9] This caused many servicemen to think carefully about what was being asked of them. The need to establish internal lines of communication caused a flurry of clarified signals and e-mails between British commanders and service chiefs back in Britain.

Some senior figures in the British military had been swayed by the arguments concerning WMD; Major General Robin Brims, commander British Land Forces, told the *Guardian* newspaper: 'Our business is to remove the weapons of mass destruction, and in order to do that we're going to have to get the regime's hands off them.'[10] However, others were not persuaded. The Chief of the Defence Staff, Admiral Sir Michael Boyce, demanded 'unequivocal...legal top cover', in addition to that already provided by the Attorney General, before British troops could be allowed to fight. His demand, made on 10 March 2003, was finally met on 15 March, only five days before fighting began.

More than a year later Admiral Boyce gave an interview to the *Observer* newspaper, which reported: 'He [Boyce] was concerned that, without the legal cover from [Attorney General] Goldsmith, military personnel could be prosecuted for war crimes.' Boyce hinted that if Goldsmith had not provided him with this he might have resigned. This would almost certainly have precipitated a major political and military crisis, at the very moment that more than 60,000 British troops stationed in Kuwait were preparing for war.[11] Boyce further admitted in April 2005 that he had never seen the full thirteen-page legal advice provided to the Prime Minister by Lord Goldsmith. Public scrutiny of this guidance had been rigidly resisted by the government and was only finally, and reluctantly, released to the British public during the May 2005 election campaign after portions were leaked to the media. That the senior British military officer had not been privy to the complex advice of the Attorney General is surprising; that the British Cabinet had not seen it either was simply astonishing. Boyce also noted in his 2005 interview that he believed he did not have full cover for immunity from prosecution at the International Criminal Court (ICC): 'If my soldiers went to jail .... some other people would go with me,' he told the reporter Anthony Barnett, who asked if this meant the Prime Minister and the Attorney General. 'Bloody well right' was the Admiral's curt reply.[12]

As pressure grew on the government, the Stop the War Coalition, the Campaign for Nuclear Disarmament (CND) and the Muslim Council of Britain (MCB) organised a massive protest march through London. Although official figures quoted 750,000 protesters, the Metropolitan Police acknowledged that the total could well have been higher.[13] The march, stretching for three-and-a-half miles, was covered by all the major national television networks and was followed carefully by British servicemen already deployed in the region. Similar processions were held in capital cities around the world, leading the BBC to report: 'Between six and ten million people are thought to have marched in up to sixty countries over the weekend—the largest demonstrations of their kind since the Vietnam War'.[14]

Undoubtedly many servicemen were influenced by the debate, which was now being very publicly waged in the British media. There was some concern among senior military officers that if military action should develop, public support in the country would not be forthcoming. A long-standing and implicit rather than overtly stated tradition decrees that even the most cynical British media will support British forces once combat operations have begun. Indeed this is no more than Edward Herman and Noam Chomsky found in their seminal study of US mainstream media and their relationship to government. Arguing that most media outlets are now associated with or owned by large corporations, and that by extension the media cannot risk losing market share in pursuit of political expediency, they observed that a nation's media normally 'rallied around the flag in times of conflict'.[15] While this idea may have characterised coverage of the conflict itself, during the lead-up to the invasion it was by no means clear-cut, and contrary to the assertions of Herman and Chomsky there were large news outlets in Britain that were angrily anti-government in their editorial policy.

Among Britain's Muslim population of 2.5 million there was deep concern and not a little confusion. An e-mail submitted to the MCB on the eve of the war summed up the dilemma of many:

I am a British Muslim and a bit confused. Being British should I support British troops now that they have started fighting, or should I be loyal to the Iraqi Muslims? I took part in the Stop the War rally. I don't want to be called a traitor to this country. Please advise me of what to do as a Muslim. Thank you.[16]

The Muslim Council itself was robust in its condemnation of the war. In its press release of 20 March Iqbal Sacranie, the Secretary-General, said:

This war appears to be part of a plan to redraw the map of the Middle East in accordance with the agenda of Zionists and American neo-conservatives. A military victory against Iraq and subsequent celebrations will be short-lived as the peoples of the region begin to resist what will be seen as the start of a new colonial enterprise that will not be limited to Iraq. The true cost of this war will only be apparent in due time.[17]

The Christian community was less forceful in its public condemnation, although the question of legality also appeared to trouble its hierarchy. In a joint communiqué the Archbishop of Canterbury Dr Rowan Williams and the Roman Catholic Archbishop of Westminster Cardinal Cormac Murphy O'Connor issued a statement on the crisis:

War is always a deeply disturbing prospect; one that can never be contemplated without a sense of failure and regret that other means have not prevailed, and deep disquiet about all that may come in its train.... The events of recent days show that doubts still persist about the moral legitimacy as well as the unpredictable humanitarian consequences of a war with Iraq.[18]

Senior leaders of the Church requested, and were granted, a meeting with Foreign Secretary Jack Straw on 3 March 2003. The Catholic Bishop of Leeds, David Konstant, and the Anglican Bishop of Southwark, Tom Butler, both of whom had formal responsibility for international issues within their own churches, followed on from the 20 February statement by their principals. In a carefully-worded communiqué they drew attention to the Churches' outstanding concerns as to the moral legitimacy of any war against Iraq.[19] Although the minutes of that meeting are not publicly available, a further statement by the Church calling the meeting a 'critical dialogue' suggests that it may have been an uncomfortable moment for the government.

Elsewhere all was not going smoothly. For many years the diplomats of the Foreign and Commonwealth Office (FCO) had been regarded by many in the international community as being pro-

Arab, and by extension unsympathetic to Israel, in their outlook. Indeed a rather unkind nickname of the 'Camel Corps' had endured since the early twentieth century. Many long-term FCO Arabists did indeed have private reservations about the justification and validity of the war. Predictably, and to an extent reassuringly, these views were seldom expressed in public although it is apparent that privately the British government encountered robust objections to its decision to join the conflict. But the Civil Service remained steadfastly apolitical, and for an indication of the strength of feeling that might have existed one has to look to the retired community. The resignation in February 2004 of a senior FCO legal adviser, Elizabeth Wilmhurst, is indicative of the disquiet that existed within the King Charles Street headquarters. She issued a statement to the press stating that she had not wanted to continue as deputy legal adviser at the Foreign Office because she 'did not agree that the use of force against Iraq was lawful'.[20] Equally damaging was the open letter written to the Prime Minister Tony Blair by Oliver Miles, a former British ambassador to Libya, and signed by fifty-two other former British ambassadors. Writing about the government's Middle East policy they criticised its apparent unequivocal support for US policy in the region:

You yourself seem to have endorsed it [Israeli and US policy], abandoning the principles which for nearly four decades have guided international efforts to restore peace in the Holy Land and which have been the basis for such successes as those efforts have produced.

The letter further noted: 'We are portrayed throughout the Arab and Muslim world as partners in an illegal and brutal occupation in Iraq.' Many of the signatories had been contacted in advance of the military operations by representatives of the FCO and the Ministry of Defence (MoD) and asked if they would be prepared to serve as interpreters in a post-Saddam Iraq. It is not known how many, if any, accepted, but among some of those contacted there was a clear sense of irony that while their professional expertise was ignored where policy issues were concerned, their language skills were in demand.

With so many protests, both public and private, the British government needed to gain public justification for the country's participation, a need that many felt became almost obsessional. The lynchpin of the government's case was the apparent threat posed by Iraqi weapons of mass destruction (WMD). In a dossier that was later to cause large-scale controversy, the government stated:

As a result of the intelligence we judge that Iraq has military plans for the use of chemical and biological weapons, including against its own Shia population. Some of these weapons are deployable within 45 minutes of an order to use them.[21]

While the threat from international terrorism and a 9/11-type scenario was never under-estimated, the principal reason provided to the British public for war against Saddam was the destruction of his stocks of WMD, a premise later proved to have been based upon faulty intelligence as revealed in the Butler enquiry report, published in July 2004.

Commissioning opinion polls to determine the mood of the country became the favourite pastime of the British media. Channel 4 News commissioned the respected YouGov polling organisation to determine the effectiveness of the government's Iraq dossier on public perceptions. Between 7 and 10 February 2003 YouGov questioned a representative sample of 2,300 people through an online survey system. Their results suggested that the government had largely been successful in making its case for war. The poll asked if Saddam had chemical and biological weapons: 74% of the country believed that he did. It also inquired if he was hiding weapons, and 71% believed that was also true. Yet when asked about Saddam's connections to Al-Qaeda the poll revealed that the government had failed to make a substantive connection in people's minds: 33% believed that he did; 34% believed that he did not; the remainder said they didn't know. The poll then considered the recent declaration made by US Secretary of State Colin Powell at the United Nations. Were the British public convinced? The poll revealed that 62% of people did not think his evidence amounted to proof that Saddam possessed weapons of mass destruction, and nearly a quarter (21%) thought that the evidence he had presented was fabricated.

## The Arab world

In considering the reaction of the Arab world to the impending crisis it is necessary to differentiate between the opinion of the 'Arab Street' and the public and private opinions of the Arab regimes that hold power over that street. If the impending war was unpopular with the British public, then across twenty-two Arab countries it was generally greeted on the 'Street' with hostility and anger. Across Arab borders there exists commonality in language, religion and consciousness. Arabic is spoken on two continents, across the breadth of North Africa, through the Arabian peninsula and into the Gulf. It is the official language of more than 120 million people, making it one of the ten most widely spoken in the world; its importance was formally acknowledged in 1973 when the UN recognised it as the sixth official language of that body. Its unbroken literary tradition extends back over thirteen centuries and it is the language of the Prophet Muhammad and of the world's fastest-growing religion. Its syntax and grammar are hugely evocative; it carries emotions, recollections, thoughts and inspiration. This linguistic and emotional solidarity is encapsulated in the Arab word *qaumiya*, an idea articulating commonality and nationalist ideals. It is based on a much older and basic concept of *asabiya* or 'blood solidarity'. Perhaps much more than in Western culture, poetry plays an extremely important part in the language, allowing feelings of 'Arabness' and unity to be described in eloquent and flowing classical stanzas, rich in meaning and historical context. Sandra Mackey, author of *The Saudis*, lived and worked in Saudi Arabia for many years, filing reports under a male pseudonym. In her book she notes the importance of poetry:

Traditionally there is a strong attachment to language, originating in the Spartan life of the Bedouin. The Bedouin poet was the repository of local tribal history. He expressed the ideals of manliness, gallantry, bravery, loyalty, generosity and independence of spirit...the richness of Arabic, combined with its cadence, transforms the language into an artistic instrument that provides great emotional satisfaction.[22]

As if to illustrate this point, two prominent Arab poets, Mahmoud Darwish and Abdel Rahman el-Abnoudi, worked together in advance of the Iraq invasion to produce three poems about Iraq, 'Nothing but Iraq', 'Salute to Baghdad' and 'Baghdad'. The poems, which called for Arab solidarity, were published widely in the Arabic press. 'Nothing but Iraq' connected the Mongol invasion of Iraq in 1258 with the coming invasion of 2003, thus appealing on a dual level to the Arab psyche, through the richness of the language and through an acute sense of historical injustice and persecution.

In considering the 'street view' before the war the BBC diplomatic correspondent Barnaby Mason noted: 'The idea of Arab unity is in practice often unrealistic, yet there is a consciousness that on some elevated plane, if not in everyday reality, all Arabs are one.'[23] Of course, there are regional differences, such as religion and state-based nationalism, which modify these ideas of unity. Some groups in the region may reject the Arab-based experience, but they are small and do not undermine the widespread and potent Arab collective of unity and understanding. In Egypt the journalist Hussein Amin observed the fascination with which the Egyptian public watched the news, seemingly compelled to switch between different news providers so as to maintain a continuous stream of reports. He too observed the concept of *asabiya*: 'Many Egyptians were compelled to watch or risk being accused of indifference and passiveness to their fellow Arabs.'[24]

Traditionally Arab rulers have influenced the minds of their people through a complex mixture of allegiances and patronage. Many of these ideas derived from the idea of the tribe which, after the family unit, is an important and compelling identifier. The values inherent in tribal process (discussion, consensus and ultimately decisions by a tribal leader) still resonate with many Arabs today. As a consequence an individual's loyalty is often defined outside the state's boundaries—be it in a larger context of religion, or in the smaller context of tribe, family or patronage.

But Arabs are also realists, and events in the United Nations were carefully and critically monitored. Ashraf Fouad, an influential media analyst based in Abu Dhabi, observed the move to war and reactions in the Arab world:

'The events, from the United Nations to going to war, were too fast a pace and that shocked people in the Arab world. It is because of the culture and the psyche in the Arab world. You want to get upset and talk and slam the door and come back in and have another meeting and try again. They could not take this boom boom boom—even if Afghanistan was not involved, and 9/11, in how we got to this point it would have still been a very unpopular war.'[25]

The absence of a definitive UN Security Council Resolution for military action, the open wound of Palestine, and the continuing UN sanctions against Iraq meant that the Arab community viewed events not only with anger but also with a considerable sense of shame—shame that once more a dispute in an Arab country could not be settled internally (indeed Arab attempts to resolve the problem had ended in farce). In the Arab mind the region's problems were again being resolved by external actors: Western military forces (forces that many viewed as 'crusaders'[26]) were plying their trade in the region. Given the Arabs' acute collective sense of historical context, President Bush's use of that word and his subsequent references to a fight between 'good' and 'evil' had much unhappy resonance. The term will not have been understood in the manner quite intended by the US President. For many Arabs the West, with its history of colonialism, is the evil party, not the good one. The United States, with its seemingly unshakeable support for Israel, its global industries and its status as the sole superpower, is in many Arab minds the most potent manifestation of this.

However, while most Arab governments loathed Saddam's regime (Syria's shock agreement to UN Security Council Resolution 1441 on 8 November 2002 was taken as an important signal of the Arab world's displeasure with him)[27] long-standing regional US allies were nervous. Many, such as President Hosni Mubarak of Egypt, counselled against attack, yet there was an element of duplicity in the way the Arab regimes presented their objections. Publicly many were highly critical of the United States (Saudi Arabia said it would not allow its military bases to be used in any attack, while Jordan's King Abdullah warned of a Middle Eastern Armageddon). Privately, however, national interests prevailed; most regimes decided that they were unwilling to risk direct confrontation with America. Diplomatically the Arab world appeared impotent; on 24 January 2003 officials from Syria, Jordan, Egypt and Saudi Arabia met in Istanbul in an effort to resolve the situation peacefully. However, they agreed only to call upon Iraq to continue cooperating with UN weapons inspectors, issuing a vague statement that Iraq should 'demonstrate a more active approach'. The inability to respond meaningfully to the crisis came as a disappointment to many. The former Jordanian Prime Minister Taher Masri told the media:

'The lack of results in the Istanbul summit shows that there is no Arab nation any more, only a collection of impotent countries.'

A second attempt was made at the Islamic Summit Conference held in Doha, Qatar, in March 2003. However, public divisions between the Iraqi delegation and the delegation from Kuwait had over-shadowed the summit. Far from demonstrating Muslim unity the summit became a laughing stock after Iraqi delegate Izzeat Ibrahim memorably said to the delegate from Kuwait: 'You monkey, you minion—shut up and sit down.'[28]

Jordan in particular typifies the dilemma that many Arab states faced. As the recipient of more than $400 million of US aid and an exporter of more than $300 million of goods to the United States under a favourable new free trade package, the Jordanians were compelled to act in their own national interests. Abdullah may also have recalled his late father's objections to the US-led coalition in the 1991 war and the subsequent damage this did to the country. But 60% of the Jordanian population are Palestinian and a large number of these believed that Saddam's regime was the only reliable champion of the Palestinian cause. The University of Jordan's Centre for Strategic Studies undertook a survey of public opinion in January 2003, which revealed that 98% of participants believed that war would be bad for Jordan and that only 2% believed that the United States should have access to Jordanian host-nation basing facilities. The Jordanian secret police were to become busy managing the wave of demonstrations and rallies that would follow. But even while the Jordanian foreign minister was at the Istanbul conference, the King himself was meeting CENTCOM commander General Tommy Franks to discuss areas of mutual military interest. Other Arab states followed a similar line. Bahrain continued hosting the headquarters of the US Navy's Fifth Fleet, the United Arab Emirates (UAE) continued to allow access to its bases and training areas, Syria voted for UN Security Council Resolution 1441,

Kuwait provided the staging post for the attacks, Qatar was to be home to CENTCOM's forward headquarters and Saudi Arabia would quietly allow use of some US facilities on its territory.

On Arab streets there existed a general suspicion of the Bush Administration and its aims. And here a paradox exists. Arab TV stations such as Al-Jazeera have demonstrated remarkable press freedom in criticising the actions of autocratic Arab regimes; some sympathy—in particular for US calls for democracy in the region—might have been expected. Indeed, long before 9/11 US neo-conservatives (hereafter also referred to as neocons) had been among the most ardent international supporters of the channel. But deeper-seated resentments were to prevail and the issue of Palestine remains paramount. For the Arab media the US-Israeli connection is always newsworthy, and conspiracy theories abound, perhaps with good reason. In 1996 three leading members of Bush's Administration had contributed to a discussion paper entitled 'A Clean Break: a New Strategy for Saving the Realm', published by the Jerusalem-based Institute for Advanced Strategic and Political Studies.[29] The paper, which was presented to the then Israeli Prime Minister Benjamin Netanyahu, made a number of recommendations. Chief among these was the removal of Saddam Hussein from power (a protective measure for the Israeli state), the adoption of a more robust neo-conservative line with Syria, and total abandonment of the Oslo peace agreements.[30] The report was twice widely reported in the media. At its inception it caused a flurry of interest in the US and Israeli press, and it appeared again in the lead-up to the Iraq war, this time in Arab and international media. The sense of a conspiracy was gradually gaining momentum.

There was also a sense that double standards were being applied. Iraq was often and roundly condemned in the West, yet the West appeared selectively blind to the terrible events in the occupied territories. As already noted, an added complication was Saddam's undoubted popularity with the Palestinians. For all his excesses, many admired the way that he, alone among Arab leaders, seemed prepared to stand up to the United States. These complex emotions are often misunderstood, not only in the West but in the Arab world as well. After the invasion of Kuwait in 1990 King Hassan of Morocco issued a public condemnation of Iraq's actions, yet he evidently misjudged the strength of feeling on his own streets; within ten days he was forced to make a further statement in which he significantly toned down his criticism: 'Over the question of Iraq our head lies in the Gulf but our heart lies in Iraq.'[31] As a consequence Morocco chose to provide troops only for the defence of Saudi Arabia and not as an offensive component of the international coalition.

Many Arabs believed that the impending 2003 conflict was not about WMD or human rights abuses by the Saddam regime, or even the establishment of a US-style democratic process. For many a single word summed up rationale for the US action—oil. The United States categorically denies this, although occasional crass comments did little to assuage Arab sensitivities: a US Air Force officer, Brigadier General William Looney, in charge of the CENTCOM no-fly zone air enforcement operations, was particularly indelicate when he spoke to the *Washington Post* some three years before: 'They know we own their country. ... We dictate the way they live and talk. And that's what's great about America right now. It's a good thing, especially when there's a lot of oil out there we need.'[32]

George Joffé has said of Arab public opinion: 'By the end of the 1990s and the Al-Aqsa intifada there was a feeling that Europeans and the US were fundamentally anti-Arab. Arab TV stations had to mirror public opinion—and indeed they did.'[33] The BBC security correspondent Frank Gardner, who has followed events in the Arab world for many years and was shot in 2004 while reporting on Al-Qaeda, said:

No amount of good PR and communications will undo the almost daily damage being done to the West's reputation by vivid footage of dead, injured and traumatised Palestinians being broadcast out of Gaza and the West Bank by the Arab media. However hard Her Majesty's Government works to explain our good intentions in the region the facts on the ground speak for themselves in most Arab minds. [34]

Anti-war protest demonstrations were held in some Arab cities, notably Damascus where more than 200,000 Syrian protesters marched. In Bahrain a candle-lit vigil was held outside the local UN offices (ironically, albeit unknown to the protesters, on the very steps of one of the accommodation blocks for US and UK troops based in the kingdom). Later violent disorder erupted on the streets of the tiny island state's capital Manama, aimed at the US and British embassy buildings. Perhaps unsurprisingly, protesters were particularly vocal in Baghdad, where the regime ensured that the world's media would capture images of crowds chanting their support for Saddam. However, in many Arab states the national security forces cracked down heavily, effectively preventing outward signs of dissent. This was apparently unnecessary; the protests, much to the surprise of Arab commentators, were on nowhere near the scale of those in the West.

This is not to say that the Arab world in any way supported the conflict; far from it. The absence of protest indicates not a lack of feeling but merely frustration. First, many of the regimes were determined to avoid massive demonstrations. In Egypt riot police outnumbered demonstrators. Secondly, and perhaps more important, a profound sense of futility permeated every layer of the Arab world and there was widespread feeling that demonstrations, even if tolerated by governments, would serve little purpose. The prevailing sentiment among many Arabs that their views were ignored and apparently unimportant in the international arena was to prove hugely advantageous to the more extreme Islamist elements of society. Indeed it is apparent that there has been a cultural shift in the region. Today the importance of religion has become the primary motor for change. In the 1960s the ideals of Arab nationalism drove Arab sentiment and ambition; opinion-formers in the Arab world were secularists and nationalists. Now they have been replaced by Islamic scholars, academics and extremists such as Bin Laden and Al-Qaeda. In the Arab collective the ideals and aspirations of nationalism have been replaced by concern for the defence of Islam.

Al-Jazeera's communication's manager, Jihad Ali-Ballout, neatly summed up Arab feelings: 'There is no doubt that a vast majority of our audience is not sympathetic to Saddam; they are sympathetic to the cause of Iraq. The vast majority of Arab public opinion is against the war. They believe it's an unjust war. They have not been convinced by the arguments put forward by the Americans.'[35]

## The United States: evil empires and an axis of evil

In the United States the events of 9/11 finally gave prominence to the ideology of neo-conservatism, the proponents of which felt that their time had come. Neo-conservatism was not a new phenomenon; it originated in the 1930s when a small group of intellectuals at City College, New York, would gather in an alcove of the college refectory to debate social and political issues. One of those was Irving Kristol, today regarded as the godfather of neo-conservatism. Over the years this group considered and debated a wide range of issues and was associated with both Democratic and Republican administrations. Today it is its tight relationship with George W. Bush's administration that has caused it to rise to international prominence and scrutiny. Advocating a policy of righteous interventionism, neo-conservatives believe in the supremacy, and primacy, of the United States and its right to launch pre-emptive attacks as an acceptable extension of foreign policy. The key to this is a strong US military. In neo-conservative thinking the US military needs sustained funding if it is to retain its position of pre-eminence.

The movement's influence grew gradually during successive administrations as its advocates gained increasing seniority and influence. Yet it was not until the Republican Ronald Reagan presidency of the 1980s that neo-conservative ideals would gain ground in political consciousness. Appealing to the Evangelical right, dismissive of previous liberal US domestic policies and alarmed at the perceived spread of Communist influence, the movement offered simple yet compelling rhetoric. The Soviet Union was portrayed as an evil empire[36] which had achieved military superiority over the world's guardian of freedom and democracy, the United States. The rhetoric seemed to be substantiated by events in the real world. In Iran the Islamic revolutionary Ayatollah Khomeini overthrew the pro-US Shah, and shortly afterwards the new Iranian regime appeared to demonstrate its contempt for the United States by allowing its diplomats stationed in Tehran to be captured and held as hostages. Concern at the instability in this strategically vital part of the world intensified in 1979 when Soviet military forces moved into and subsequently occupied Afghanistan. It seemed that the neo-conservative message was developing wider resonance. Reagan dramatically and publicly expanded the funding of the US military. Equally relevant, he engaged in an interventionist and largely under-cover foreign policy against Communist and Marxist-inspired insurgent operations in South America, North Africa and East Asia. In Nicaragua, El Salvador, Angola and, more publicly, Afghanistan the United States went to work. Neo-conservatism appeared to be on a roll and Reagan's announcement of plans for a Strategic

Defence Initiative (SDI)—a space-based defence system designed to combat the threat of Soviet Intercontinental Ballistic Missiles (ICBMs) and thus achieve military superiority over the USSR—was 'icing on the cake' for the neo-conservatism doctrine.

Yet Reagan's decision to engage with the Soviet Union in a programme of détente came as a blow to the ideology, and its supporters gradually drifted from the fold. His plea to the Soviet Premier Mikhail Gorbachev to 'tear down this wall'[37] and its unexpectedly successful outcome would mean that the United States, as the sole remaining superpower, would struggle to find a neo-conservative focus in the international community. Its older thinkers found the new international environment a difficult one in which to exert influence. Ronald Reagan was succeeded by George H. W. Bush, who was keen to capitalise on the Cold War defence dividend and began significant reductions in military spending. Between 1985 and 2001 the number of military personnel dropped from 2,151,600 to 1,267,700. Defence expenditure correspondingly dropped from $390,290,000 to $322,365,000. In 1986 it had formed 6.5% of US GDP—by 2001 it had halved to 3.2%.[38]

Saddam's invasion of Kuwait and the 1991 Gulf war provided a spark of interest to neocons as the Coalition moved against Saddam's armies; however, the subsequent decision not to remove him from power and, more important, not to support the Kurdish uprising in the north of the country caused dismay among its proponents. Bush believed that the United States should promote international stability and that pursuing Saddam all the way to Baghdad would be a destabilising and entrenching act that would serve little purpose. Such statesman-like moderation did not fit the neocon agenda of transforming the Middle East and 'defeating evil'.

In 1993 the Republicans lost the White House. As 'it's the economy, stupid' became the mantra of President Bill Clinton's Democrat administration, the neocons now found themselves excluded from closeness to power. In the latter half of the 1990s a new generation of intellectuals took over the mantle and began developing their ideas, adjusting their sights away from the evils of Communism. Domestically they focused their efforts on discrediting Democratic liberalism, and partnering the religious Right to highlight the perceived loss of morality in US society. Discrediting Clinton personally became a cherished objective for the neocons, who seemingly engaged in a concerted effort to discredit him and his administration. They were busy in the international arena as well. New think-tanks were developed, and articles and publications written. Much of this new thinking was articulated in the Project for a New American Century (PNAC),[39] created by William Kristol (Irving Kristol's son) in 1997. Among the many issues PNAC considered was the relationship between US homeland security and the need for democracy in the Middle East. 'Part of the drive to reshape the Middle East', wrote John Gray, 'comes from the Christian fundamentalist belief that a major conflagration will fulfil biblical prophecies of a catastrophic conflict in the region.'[40]

For its advocates, evicting Saddam Hussein from Iraq would trigger a cycle of American-style reform that would break the vicious circle of terrorism, dictatorship and poverty.[41] The 'clean break' document previously described provides much of the thinking behind this. The long-running issue of Iraq's defiance of the UN was a key element in this discourse and as William Shawcross explains, 'the neocons had one over-riding objective...the removal of Saddam Hussein'.[42]

The surprise election of George W. Bush in 2000 did not immediately provide *carte blanche* for the neo-conservative hawks and their policies. Bush initially appeared to lack the robust support for Israel advocated by the ideology. He also chose to adopt a more conversational than confrontational policy with the People's Republic of China. Whether or not he subscribed to the ideas advanced by the

'Blue Team' (the informal name given to those in the Administration and academia who believe that China is the pre-eminent
threat to US security and world interests), Bush was at first cautious
in his foreign policy pronouncements, no doubt prompted by his
almost complete inexperience in international affairs. Yet the
destruction of the World Trade Center and the simultaneous attack
on Washington changed his mind. Thus, when the President declared on 11 September 2001 that 'someone is going to pay'[43], the
neocons were ready with their plans. Perhaps most striking was the
use once more of the good and evil analogy. Reminiscent of the
intellectual battle against communism, Bush and his senior representatives used the terms liberally—the most striking being the
2002 State of the Union address in which President Bush declared
that: 'States like these [Iraq, Iran, North Korea], and their terrorist
allies, constitute an axis of evil, arming to threaten the peace of the
world.'

In support of their objectives, neocons such as Paul Wolfowitz
advanced their ideas in an array of sympathetic media outlets,
including Fox Television, the *Wall Street Journal*, the *Washington
Times*, Talk Radio and the *Weekly Standard*. Fox Television, in particular, had enthusiastically presented a neocon-type agenda after
9/11. In his book *America Alone* the Cambridge University academic
Stefan Halper considers the role of the US media in maintaining an
air of insecurity throughout the country, such that affirmative
military action, sold as it was to defend the US against future
threats, would receive widespread support.[44] He cites in particular
the FoxNews terror alerts which he believes 'took place with a fre-
quency that, by any reasonable calculation, went beyond the facts.
Americans now watched FoxNews in fear of an impending catas-
trophe as much as for informative coverage.'[45] We see later the way
in which Arab media became demonised by the United States, cited
as being anti-US and anti-Coalition. If Arab channels such as Al-

Jazeera did have an anti-Western agenda, and this is by no means certain, then the markedly right-wing activities of FoxNews must also be heavily scrutinised.

### The Fox factor

If there is one media organisation more than any other that has become associated with neo-conservatism and the US Republican Party it is Rupert Murdoch's Fox Television. By any rational measure the channel's coverage was at times so uniformly subjective, ultra-patriotic and hugely biased in favour of the President's actions that its strap line 'We report, you decide' appeared almost comically disingenuous. A selection of the thoughts on the war from its correspondents and anchors more than adequately illustrate this point. On anti-war demonstrators the co-anchor for Fox's live morning newscast 'Fox and Friends', Steve Doocy, told viewers: 'There are so many pictures of protesters out there... we want to show pictures of *pro*-Americans.' As if to reinforce the point, on 27 January 2003, Fox's afternoon anchorman John Gibson described anti-war protesters in Davos, Switzerland, as 'knuckleheads'. On the Iraqi people 'Talking Points' presenter Bill O'Reilly: 'Talking Points is distressed to see some American reporters doing sympathetic pieces about the Iraqi people... I don't have a lot of sympathy for the Iraqi people.' To make quite sure that viewers understood the channel's direction the 'Your World' presenter Neil Cavuto told viewers: 'Am I slanted and biased? You damn well bet I am.'[46] Anchor Bob Sellers described France as a member of the axis of weasels, while 'Fox News Live' anchor David Asman, asked if he had sympathy for the Arab view that Americans were invaders, said: 'There is a certain ridiculousness to that point of view.'[47]

Despite the apparent confessions of his presenters, the head of news gathering at Fox, David Rhodes, denied that the channel was anything other than an objective news organisation. Although Fox is the only TV channel that refused to assist in the research for this book, Rhodes did attend the first Al-Jazeera world forum in July 2004, where he told an invited audience that all media have their biases which they try to subdue every day. His answer was unconvincing and certainly not supported by the weight of evidence. One well-used defence often deployed by the channel considers the nature of the criticism, maintaining that those left-leaning observers who believe the channel to be biased are merely noting a lack of *liberal* bias. Consequently, they say, Fox is perceived as being 'right of centre' only because it is not 'left of centre'.

Perhaps it is no surprise that critics of the channel have developed variations of its strapline. 'We distort, you decide'[48] is one; another is 'We report, we decide'. This actually received tacit endorsement from Fox presenter Bill O'Reilly who, when asked if it was fair replied 'Probably'. So why is the bias of a New York-based television channel so important to the debate? The answer is simple and relates back to the studies of Herman and Chomsky—market share. Fox TV has now surpassed CNN as the leading cable news provider in the United States. This means that for a significant proportion of the American population it is the primary source of news. More interesting still has been the way in which Fox has become the adopted TV station of the US military. The author observed this manifestation at first hand in the US Navy's Fifth Fleet headquarters in Bahrain. In the cafeteria areas the huge wall-mounted plasma screen was tuned permanently to Fox News and, with exceptions made only for movies and basketball games, remained that way from November 2002 to April 2003. Every US serviceman passing through the cafeteria could not help but listen to Fox's highly patriotic and supportive interpretation of the war. Yet cable TV has yet to overtake terrestrial networks for viewer share. More people watch news from networks such as ABC and NBC than from Fox.

Why then should the reach of Fox be so influential? The Pew Research Centre has considered American viewing habits since 1993, and two particular trends are apparent. The first is that Americans are watching significantly less network news than ever. The second is the perception that the American public have of their news providers. The survey reveals that people tend to think of cable news more highly than other forms of television. When asked in early 2002 'Who has been doing the best job of covering news lately?', 38% of respondents said cable—more than twice the number that said network TV (16%) and nearly three times the number that said local television (13%). Only 10% said newspapers. Cable is the only medium that saw its confidence index grow in recent years, rising from 31% in 1999. Network news, by contrast, declined from 21% in 1999 and a full 50% in 1996.[49]

Elsewhere in the US media all was not well. The influential *New York Review of Books* carried a long critical article in which, among other topics, the media coverage of the alleged Iraqi stocks of WMD was carefully dissected by the journalist and media critic Michael Massing. He considered the US media holistically:

In the period before the war, US journalists were far too reliant on sources sympathetic to the administration. Those with dissenting views—and there were more than a few—were shut out. Reflecting this, the coverage was highly deferential to the White House. This was especially apparent on the issue of Iraq's weapons of mass destruction—the heart of the President's case for war. Despite abundant evidence of the administration's brazen misuse of intelligence in this matter, the press repeatedly let officials get away with it.[50]

A particular example of this emerged during the incident in which aluminium tubes were discovered. On 28 September 2002 the *New York Times* published an article in which the sentence 'The smoking gun may be a mushroom cloud' was used to argue the case for pre-emptive action and the possible consequences of not doing so. Some days later, on the *CNN* live discussion programme 'Late Edition', the National Security adviser Condoleezza Rice told the show's host, Wolf Blitzer, that the tubes 'are only really suited for nuclear weapons programs, centrifuge programs'. She then added a warning: 'We don't want the smoking gun to be a mushroom cloud'—a coincidence, or had the phrase been lifted directly from the *New York Times* article?

Many Americans meanwhile were seemingly intolerant of articles critical of the President. Whenever the *Washington Post* ran such pieces, reporter Dana Priest recalled, 'We got tons of hate mail and threats, calling our patriotism into question.' Fox News, radio 'jock' Rush Limbaugh, and the *Weekly Standard*, among others, all appeared ready to pounce on journalists who strayed, branding them, at best, liberals and at worst traitors—labels that could permanently damage a career. It was unsurprising therefore that some journalists opted instead for self-censorship.

It was not only the press that contributed to this feeling of unease and insecurity. Many US radio stations appeared to have a significant conservative bias, in no single individual more obviously than the immensely popular leading commentator Rush Limbaugh, whose show consistently attracts more than 10 million listeners and who has been syndicated by nearly 650 radio stations across the country. As well as being an established broadcaster Limbaugh is a regular contributor to journals around the country. In an opinion piece in New York's *Wall Street Journal*[51] he argued that a resolution passed by Congress in response to the 9/11 terrorist attacks[52] authorised war against Iraq. He thus established in the minds of his readers and listeners a direct connection between the events of 9/11 and Saddam's regime.

It is apparent that a close relationship exists between the US mainstream media and government—be it Republican or Democrat. Many organisations are owned, wholly or in part, by large

US multinationals. For example, General Electric, one of the world's largest defence contractors, owns NBC. The chairman of Fox TV, which is broadcast from New York City to more than 80 million subscribers, is a former political strategist for the Republican Party, while the presenter Tony Snow is the former chief speechwriter for the Administration of President George H. W. Bush. CBS News anchor Dan Rather considered his channel's coverage when he gave an interview to CNN's Larry King: 'I am an American. ... when my country is at war I want my country to win, whatever the definition of "win" might be. Now I can't and don't argue that that is coverage without a prejudice. About that I am prejudiced.' Other media outlets have their own allegiances—some to the Republicans and some to the Democrats, who were themselves broadly supportive of the war.

The influence of the major news networks in shaping public opinion is a subject of considerable ongoing academic debate. However, it appears that the Bush Administration, with its neocon leanings, had little difficulty in making a case for war with the American public through mainstream media outlets. The shock and anger of the attack on the WTC still resonated strongly with the US population. As David Frum said, '9/11 broke the country's heart, anthrax shook its nerve.'[53] The President and senior Administration officials regularly and publicly connected the war on terrorism to the regime of Saddam Hussein. Richard Clarke observed: 'Americans believed it because the Bush Administration had implied it.'[54] In October 2002 President Bush said:

'We know that Iraq and the Al-Qaeda terrorist network share a common enemy, the United States of America. We know that Iraq and Al-Qaeda have had high-level contacts that go back a decade. We've learned that Iraq has trained Al-Qaeda members in bomb-making and poisons and deadly gases. And we know that after September 11 Saddam Hussein's regime gleefully celebrated the terrorist attacks on America. Confronting the threat posed by Iraq is crucial to winning the war on terror.'[55]

The Secretary of State Colin Powell carried the theme over into the international community. On 6 February 2003 he took the US case to the floor of the United Nations, and in his presentation, entitled 'A threat to international peace and security', he told the assembled delegates that there existed a 'sinister nexus between Iraq and the al-Qaeda terrorist network'. With such forceful rhetoric, backed by seemingly incontrovertible intelligence, few voices of dissent were heard in the mainstream media. The many anti-war protests across the country failed to find national media outlets. For example, some 2,000 protesters marched on the New Mexico home of Donald Rumsfeld, declaring him to be a war criminal. There was no national media coverage. In San Francisco demonstrators stretched for a nearly a mile in their march on City Hall. Again there was no national outlet coverage. Indeed opinion polls appeared to confirm US public support: when asked if there was a connection between Saddam Hussein and 9/11, those answering 'yes' ran from a high of 70% to a low of around 45%. Americans were so trusting of the White House that 57% of respondents to a CNN/USA *Today* Gallup poll said the invasion of Iraq and the war on terrorism that began after 9/11 were the 'same war'.[56] Steve Rendall, senior analyst at New York-based Fairness and Accuracy in Reporting (FAIR), said 'these polls suggest that the US is one of the only places on the planet where large numbers of people believe that such links exist.'

Some US correspondents feared that the country would *not* go to war. On 27 February 2003 the prominent NBC journalist Andrea Mitchell expressed concern that Iraq might actually destroy its alleged stocks of WMD. She told her 12 million viewers: 'For the US it's a nightmare scenario. If Iraq destroys the WMD it will be much harder to get support for the war.'

This is not to say that there were no voices of dissent, merely that the US public did not hear them. In a survey conducted by FAIR between 20 March and 9 April 2003, 71% of all sources quoted across the highest-rated national news shows were pro-war,[57] while only 3% were anti-war. The survey also found that not one anti-war campaigner was ever invited to a television studio for an interview, and the only anti-war sentiments expressed on the CBS network were by the documentary-maker Michael Moore during his Oscar acceptance speech.

Of course there were dissenting voices,—they just never enjoyed the same level of prominence as the 'hawks'. Even big networks struggled against the tide of neocon rhetoric. A leading CNN correspondent said: 'My station was intimidated by the administration.'[58] At a Cambridge University conference Steve Rendall summed up the situation: 'While there was a broad debate in US society, it was virtually invisible on US television.' The public would have to look hard among the alternative, smaller media outlets and on the internet if they wanted to find a counter, dissenting view.

As the operation progressed into the post-conflict stage, and in stark contrast to Britain, the US media hid from public view the regular transport flights of USAF aircraft filled with the bodies of dead servicemen. As the death-toll mounted and exceeded the number killed in the initial stages of the operation, the usual pomp and ceremony of the return of the fallen seemed to be quietly ignored. At the time of writing the US President had not attended a single repatriation ceremony or funeral. Although commander-in-chief of the US armed forces, President Bush has seemed publicly to distance himself from the emotions and heartache of the repatriation process. Indeed when secret photographs of the interior of US transport aircraft filled with the flag-draped coffins of dead soldiers finally appeared in the US press, there was a massive outcry not over the number of deaths but at the apparent insensitivity of the press in allowing the photographs to be printed. Although this may not have made much impact in mainstream US media, it was not ignored by the US military press. In an October 2005 article entitled 'No Witness to Sacrifice' the US Navy's newspaper, *Navy Times*, opined:

The Army leadership, which grew up in Vietnam and its wake, still blames the media and their pictures for the loss of public support. They view 'Sustaining the national will' as part of the mission, so they discourage the creation of photos portraying Americans in death, which they equate with defeat.

The article suggested that US mainstream media should be asked a simple question: 'Have you considered you are... serving the White House's political goals by not publicising the pictures?'

The President's mother Barbara Bush appeared on the ABC network's 'Good Morning America' show on 18 March 2003. She considered the reality of war thus: 'But why should we hear about body bags, and deaths, and how many, what day it's gonna happen, and how many this or what do you suppose? Or, I mean, it's not relevant. So, why should I waste my beautiful mind on something like that?'[59]

Yet the American public were not entirely blind to the apparently one-sided nature of the public debate. In late February 2003 the respected Gallup polling organisation produced a survey that suggested that the US public *were* aware that the argument was not entirely balanced. Although on the whole satisfied by their media's reporting of possible terrorist threats, the poll revealed broad doubts as to whether the media were entirely accurate in their reporting of world events; almost six out of ten Americans told Gallup that they believed their news stories were inaccurate.[60]

The renowned British journalist Robert Fisk summarised the thoughts of many:

American journalism is, I think, I'm sorry to say, becoming increasingly neutered. You only have to look at the cozy relationships now between journalists and power in Washington. The relationship is very evident. If you go to a press conference it's, "Yes, John." It's "Mr President, can I ask you..." It's first name terms for the journalists and Mr President. The journalists in many ways have become mouthpieces. I remember pointing out in lectures in the United States before the invasion of Iraq that the *New York Times*, everytime it had a major story, the first paragraph always ended with the words 'according to American officials' or 'American officials say'—often by Judith Miller at the *New York Times*. Over and over again we have seen a failure of American journalism, who should—I mean the fourth estate should be out there for the people to ask the serious questions and challenge power. I go back to Amira Hass, the brilliant Israeli journalist, who once defined journalism to me as monitoring the centres of power. I think by and large, with the exception of a few newspapers and small television and radio programs, yours for example, by and large major American news organizations are neutered. They have neutered themselves. They will not monitor the centers of power. They will not challenge authority.[61]

Given President Bush's well-publicised Christian beliefs, the political muscle of the Evangelical Right (who believed that liberalism had eroded US society) and the importance with which the Christian church is still regarded in present-day American society, it is useful to consider briefly the view of the US churches while the country was moving towards conflict in Iraq. On 30 January 2003 the National Council of Churches (an organisation representing thirty-six Protestant, Episcopalian and Orthodox denominations, in all an organisation with more than 50 million US citizens as members) wrote to President Bush requesting a meeting 'to convey face-to-face the message of the religious community that we represent on the moral choices that confront this nation and your Administration. You are no doubt well aware of our activities to slow the rush to war and our continuing uneasiness about the moral justification for war on Iraq.'[62]

They were not afforded their meeting; the fiercely Evangelical President had been unable to alter his schedule.

Yet how did this translate itself on the ground? Surveys have shown that nearly 60% of those who attended a church service heard their clergy talk about the war, yet far fewer, less than 22%, heard a definite stand taken on the war. Where opinions were expressed from the pulpit they mostly followed the national stance of their respective faiths: white Catholics and African Americans were hearing strong anti-war messages, while white Evangelical Protestants were listening to a pro-war point of view.

Paradoxically it is apparent that some senior figures in the US military, both serving and retired, had reservations which since the end of the war have increasingly crept into the public domain. General Franks's predecessor at CENTCOM, US Marine Corps General Anthony Zinni, who was appointed as the Bush Administration's Peace Envoy to the Middle East, has been particularly vociferous in his criticism. In his book *Battle Ready* he recalled passing a warning to Congress about the timing of the impending war: 'This is, in my view, the worst time to take this on. And I don't feel it needs to be done now.' His comments resonated with other former 'big hitters': Norman Schwarzkopf, who commanded US troops in the 1991 Gulf war, former army Chief of Staff Eric Shineski, and former National Security Adviser Brent Scowcroft all spoke against the conflict. Schwarzkopf in particular was hugely distrustful of Donald Rumsfeld, whose management of the war he publicly referred to as 'plain scary'. In the words of *The New Yorker*, he 'uttered what many Army officers had long felt. Not since the Vietnam war had there been such a pronounced dissonance between the military and civilian leadership in a time of war.'[63]

General Zinni meanwhile described the war as 'one that the military did not want to engage in, but that the civilian staff in the Pentagon did.'[64] He believed that Saddam had been more than contained by the extensive no-fly zones and the UN's oil-for-food programme. What remained in the balance was the ongoing fight against the Taliban and Al-Qaeda in Afghanistan. He did not want military forces engaged on two fronts. Zinni told CBS that somebody had 'screwed up...those who foisted this strategy on us... ought to be gone and replaced'. Zinni was almost certainly referring to the neo-conservatives. General Wesley K. Clark, former Allied Commander, Europe, considered how everyday Americans viewed the impending conflict: 'It has been extraordinarily difficult for Americans even to ask critical questions about this war. In the aftermath of 9/11 some simply sought strong American leadership and supported it without question; others feared being labelled as unpatriotic if they dared ask why.'[65]

As in Britain, retired diplomats provided a measure for the feeling that might exist in the State Department through the publication of an open letter to the President. Drafted by Andrew Kilgore, a former US ambassador to Qatar, the letter directly criticised Bush's Middle East policy:

Your unqualified support of Sharon's extra-judicial assassinations, Israel's Berlin Wall-like barrier, its harsh military measures in occupied territories, and now your endorsement of Sharon's unilateral plan are costing our country its credibility, prestige and friends.... A return to the time-honoured American tradition of fairness will reverse the present tide of ill-will in Europe and the Middle East, even in Iraq.

While the former British diplomats had made the headlines in the home media, the letter achieved almost no mainstream media attention in America. 9/11 had significantly altered the national psyche; voices of dissent, even from known patriots such as Kilgore and his colleagues, were coolly received. And in one sense this is understandable, for despite numerous Al-Qaeda-linked attacks on US interests, including Ramsi Yousef's attack on the World Trade Center in 1993, the 9/11 attacks took the majority of the US population completely by surprise. While not ignoring the threat, the US government had failed to draw together the many strands of intelligence that pointed to the likelihood of such an act and to warn the public about it. The 9/11 Commission Report noted the possible effect of this administrative 'silence' on the domestic and international community: 'We believe that American and international public opinion might have been different, and so might the range of options available to the President—had they been informed of these details.'[66]

### The other Coalition members

President Bush declared that nearly fifty countries had joined the Coalition of the Willing to support the war in Iraq, but this was nowhere near the level of support established in advance of the 1991 conflict. As the British political commentator John Kampfner observed: 'For the first time since Vietnam, US forces were engaging in a big military conflict without the support of several of America's most important European allies.'[67]

Although the State Department listed states such as El Salvador, Eritrea and Ethiopia among the Coalition members, few offered any tangible military assistance. Indeed some countries, such as the Netherlands which offered broad support to the war, explicitly withdrew any Dutch personnel serving in the region, including those on exchange with the American and British forces. In particular the late removal of two foreign-exchange officers left one Royal Navy warship in the region temporarily without experienced warfare personnel in two key roles on board and necessitated a rapid redeployment from a ship in British waters. Aside from Britain few countries contributed military support: Australia, Poland, Spain and Denmark, of which Australia was by far the largest, all contributed forces, as did Romania (which suddenly and beneficially saw the US State Department upgrade its official national assessment of the country to 'functioning market economy').

In Australia it appeared that a clear majority of the electorate was against the war and believed that without a UN Security Council resolution it would be an unjust conflict. Like Britain, Australia was a long-standing ally of the United States and, also like Britain, its armed forces enjoyed a close relationship with US military and were already operating in support of Operation Enduring Freedom in Afghanistan. Australia's Special Forces were operating on the ground in Afghanistan and in the northern Arabian Gulf, its warships were regularly operating as part of the Coalition. Indeed immediately before the Iraq war, the commander of the multinational Maritime Interdiction Operations Force (the term applied to the maritime enforcement of the UN oil-for-food embargo programme) was a senior Australian naval officer. Finally, like Tony Blair, the Australian Prime Minister John Howard believed that Iraq possessed stocks of WMD: his intelligence agencies assured him that this was so and the decision to commit military forces was easily made. However, once Howard had made the decision he did not come in for quite the same derision and scorn as the British Prime Minister. Despite a vigorous politically motivated campaign by the opposition, polls revealed that most Australians believed Howard had committed troops in good faith. An opinion poll commissioned by the the *Sydney Morning Herald*[68] revealed that a majority believed Howard's motivation to be honest despite the majority also believing that the war was unjustified. Howard's subsequent re-election as Prime Minister in October 2004 may have offered the beleaguered Bush and Blair some encouragement, perhaps leading them to believe that while their campaigns might be dominated by the issue of Iraq they might actually be decided by domestic issues.

One of the first actions of the coming war would be the capture and securing of the highly important offshore gas and oil platforms which jutted from the Iraqi Al-Faw coastline, an action that would be undertaken in part by Polish Special Forces commandos. Poland would seem an unlikely ally for the United States; it had witnessed centuries of European wars, so there was little appetite for conflict among the population. Also, the opposition of the Vatican to military action would have carried considerable weight with the staunchly Catholic Polish public.

It was perhaps paradoxical that this proud country, formerly a member of the Warsaw Pact, had developed a reputation as an American Trojan horse[69] based on its rock-steady and unwavering support for the United States. Some of that solidarity is based on the family connections that continue to exist in the large American Polish expatriate community. There is also a continuing feeling of gratitude for the part America played in defeating the Nazis during the Second World War and the battle against communism that followed it. The coming conflict therefore stirred a series of emotions in the hearts of the Polish public, and across the population concern grew over the morality of the attack on Iraq. A poll published in the *Los Angeles Times*[70] noted that 50% of Poles were against the war, regardless of what the UN's inspectors might or might not find. 62% of those polled believed that Poland should not support America if it launched military action. However, Polish President Aleksander Kwasniewski appeared not to share the reservations of his countrymen. He visited the United States in January 2003 and met the US President for talks at the White House. In the press call that followed, George Bush declared: 'I've got no better friend in Europe today than Poland.' While Tony Blair might have felt that this accolade was more rightly his, Kwasniewski was clearly delighted with the praise, and replied that Poland would stand by America even if diplomatic methods of disarming Iraq failed. In all, it sent around 200 troops to the conflict.

In Spain public opinion was firmly against military action yet Premier José-Maria Aznár stood firm with the United States and Britain, playing a particularly prominent role at the pre-war conference held in the Azores. Politically, however, he had severe problems. This was clearly illustrated when the Spanish warship *Glacia* arrived in the newly-captured Iraqi port of Umm Qasr on 28 March 2003. Both America and Britain wanted substantial press coverage of the arrival of another Coalition country's armed forces arriving in-theatre, and a clear directive was passed to the military media operations staff to gain as much coverage as possible. But the Spanish liaison officer to the British headquarters in Kuwait could not have been more explicit in his refusal to entertain any kind of press facility, which he felt would be highly insensitive given the prevailing political climate in Spain. Aznar's subsequent defeat at the Spanish election was regarded by many commentators as punishment by the Spanish electorate for his involvement in the war. Much to American and British concern, the new government quickly withdrew all Spanish forces from the region.

## Preparing for the 'hearts and minds' battle

So the views and opinions of the major participants in the conflict were by no means clear-cut. How then are we to view the prevailing attitudes towards war and, more fundamentally, how did these affect the attitudes of the protagonists on the ground towards the Arab world? It is quite apparent that in the United States there was considerable disagreement over the war, yet it is also clear that little mainstream public exposure was afforded to the anti-war movement. 9/11 had become the baseline for public discussion, be it analysis of what went wrong, introverted examination of 'Why us?' or the ruthless determination that such an event should and would never be repeated. In the immediate aftermath of the 9/11 attacks President Bush himself asked the question that was on many American lips: why was there such 'vitriolic hatred for America in some Islamic countries'?[71] This absence of understanding led many

Americans to believe that their President had responded strongly and positively to the crisis; Al-Qaeda and its Taliban host had after all been largely expelled from Afghanistan. The President appeared to enjoy the trust of the US public and, despite the small protest fringe, to most mainstream Americans there seemed no reason to doubt the integrity of the Administration's plans for Iraq or the apparently strong intelligence that the CIA was developing on the evolving threat of Iraq's WMD. An article in the *New York Times*, retrospectively considering the trust the nation placed in its President, quoted a US general as opining:

Why is this man in the White House? The majority of Americans did not vote for him. Why is he there? And I tell you this morning that he's in the White House because God put him there for a time such as this.[72]

How did these attitudes affect US service personnel? One had only to visit a US military unit to experience the strength of feeling. On the giant nuclear-powered aircraft-carrier USS *Carl Vincent* the author witnessed sailors' mess decks bedecked with US flags and images of the World Trade Center and New York fire-fighters. Soon to be used ordnance, coated in spindly graffiti linking Al-Qaeda and the regime of Saddam Hussein, adorned the flight deck. At the headquarters of the US Fifth Fleet in Bahrain the outdoor eating area was surrounded by Stars and Stripes, signed and sent by well-wishers back home in America. Inside the sailors' communal areas Fox TV held court. Even the CENTCOM commander Tommy Franks travelled round the Gulf in a personal helicopter with a World Trade Center silhouette on its side.[73] There can be little doubt then that the US armed forces felt unambiguously entitled to the action they were about to take part in, and that in the minds of the majority an undouted link existed between the 9/11 attacks and the regime of Saddam Hussein. A consequence of this was that in the battle and post-conflict reconstruction phase that was to come,

PROAVIS SUIS JOANNI & CATHARINÆ
KEURINCKX AVIS JOANNI & CATHARINÆ
LUYUNA SCHUT PARENTIBUS JOANNI
SIGISFRIDO & MARIÆ MAGD. SCHENAERTS
UXORI JOANNÆ MARIÆ DE CONINCK
POSTERISQ: & SIB: HOC MON. RENOVAVIT
JOANNES BAPT. JOSEPHUS VAN DEELEN
ANNO 1775

**ANTWERPEN O.-L.-VROUWEKATHEDRAAL**
P.SCHEEMAECKERS (1652 - 1714)
Grafmonument Keurlinckx - Van Delft ( 1688 )

© **A.V.M.** B-8400 OOSTENDE Tel.: (059) 70.86.22

**AVM**
V.N. 92
1308

many US troops would regard Iraqis in particular and Arabs in general not as innocent people but as enemies—enemies who, the US media had told them, had collaborated with Bin Laden and Al-Qaeda to mount the horrific attacks on the World Trade Center.

This story was not repeated in the other countries of the Coalition. The British people certainly had considerable sympathy for the United States after the 9/11 attacks; the indiscriminate murder of so many civilians resonated with the collective memory of IRA attacks in Deal, Omagh, Brighton and a host of other locations around the country where innocent bystanders had been killed by terrorism. They largely supported the often hard line of the British government during the Northern Ireland Troubles and there appeared to be a collective acknowledgement of the validity of the US-led Coalition operation in Afghanistan, which was a war to which the British public could relate. They had seen the results of the attack, they did not doubt the duplicity of the Taliban, and they supported the response. Yet Iraq did not make the same connection in the minds of a large proportion of the British public, and the harder the government made the case the more uneasy and suspicious the British public became. The Prime Minister's address to the country on the first night of the war acknowledged the deep divisions it had caused but also asked the audience to support the troops. Whether they did so because of the Prime Minister's speech, or in spite of it, is debatable. Many commentators believe they did so because the British public have always supported British troops and their families once military action has begun. But an important distinction between support for the troops and support for the war clearly existed. For the troops going out to the war, many of them reservists, the prevailing sense of unease travelled with them on the trooping flights. British commanders realised this and travelled around theatre addressing units. Considerable effort went into the internal communications operation: Defence Secretary Geoff Hoon made a trip to the region just before the war began, addressing naval personnel in Bahrain and Marine and army units in the deserts of Kuwait.

In Spain, Australia and Poland similar feelings existed, although only in Spain was there the same sense of personal distaste for individual politicians that Tony Blair seemed to generate in Britain. All countries would send forces, although the numbers were substantially smaller than the British contribution. Indeed the Polish contribution of Special Forces Commandos, highly successful though it was, passed the majority of the Polish population by.

In the Arab world analysis was much simpler. Feelings of dismay, suspicion and resignation blended together in an environment already deeply distrustful of the world's last remaining superpower. Four key issues emerged in the Arab collective. First, Arab populations developed an enormous concern for the potential fate of Iraqi civilians, who were regarded with considerable sympathy. Here was an Arab people, in the very cradle of civilisation, who had suffered for many years under the brutality of the Saddam regime. But there was an inevitability about the death and injuries that would result from any military invasion. This was an issue of paramount importance and became a major focus of pan-Arab satellite TV stations' coverage.

Secondly, the Arab world was unable to understand how Israeli aggression against Palestinians in the occupied territories could continue, and seemingly with US support. Arabs regarded the Israeli government in much the same way as the Americans regarded Saddam Hussein. The much publicised visit of the Likud leader Ariel Sharon to Jerusalem's Al-Haram Al-Shareef (Temple Mount) on 28 September 2000 had caused great offence and is cited by many as the event that triggered the riots of the Second Intifada. Their often brutal suppression, as well as the building of the wall dividing the two communities, was met with fury and despair.

Thirdly, the Arab world was hugely concerned at the legitimacy of the Coalition's actions. The absence of a definitive UN Security Council resolution, the refusal to allow the UN weapons inspectors to continue their work, and the tenuous connections between Saddam's regime and the 9/11 attacks also raised serious doubts in Arab minds.

Finally, many Arabs questioned the future intentions of the United States, believing that the forthcoming war was to be fought either as unfinished business left over from the Administration of the President's father, or over the issue of oil. The Arab world simply did not trust or believe the Administration when it said that Iraqi oil was for the Iraqis.

The Lebanese newspaper the *Daily Star* summed up the concerns of the Arab world: 'To Washington and London this week's attack against Iraq is part of a historical process to promote Arab peace, liberty and democracy. To most Arabs it is a cruel reappearance of demons that have haunted them for centuries.' Unsurprisingly there was no such concern in Israel, where the Foreign Minister Silvan Shalom told the media: 'Israel stands together with the American people and their allies in their campaign to destroy the threat posed by Iraq's weapons of mass destruction.'

The preconceptions with which the major participants went to war were fundamental to the hearts-and-minds battle. From the outset Coalition troops were regarded as illegal, immoral and unjustified invaders and this would be how they were portrayed in many of the Arab world's newspapers and TV channels. Despite the unpleasantness of Saddam's regime, the Arab media's reaction to the failure of his armies to repel the Coalition forces was one of considerable shame and anger. For the forces of the Coalition, and in particular those from the United States, Arabs were inextricably linked to terrorism. In many minds the Arab world would benefit from a large injection of US-style democracy.

## Ali Baba and the Forty Thieves?

The influence of television and movies on real life is widely debated in society. Do movie scenes of extreme violence promote or influence real-life action? While a member of the US National Rifle Association might disagree with this proposition, the parent of one of the children murdered at Columbine High School might take the opposite view. Yet there is strong empirical evidence that the way in which individuals and cultures are portrayed does influence audiences, particularly those who do not themselves travel much beyond the borders of their own country. Despite the massive wealth of the United States and its sizeable and ethnically diverse population, only a tiny minority actually hold a passport[74] and therefore have the ability to travel and experience cultures apart from their own if they so wish.

As we have already seen, the national US media networks are at times questionable in their portrayal of events, and while there are newspapers of substantial standing and quality, the size of the country inhibits the production and distribution of a national daily newspaper of quality. As a consequence many American citizens take their news and views from local or regional papers, in which international news will not be given the same attention or coverage as local issues. Despite the multicultural heritage and tradition of diversity of the United States, understanding of international issues is, in comparison to the European average, weak.

One area in which the US undoubtedly excels is the production of entertainment films, and despite recent increases in European and Indian film output it remains the world's largest producer of entertainment movies and is the home of the 'Hollywood block-buster'. Is there any correlation between the way the Arab world has been portrayed in films and the prevailing attitudes of the audiences that watch them?

The Palestinian intellectual Edward Said devoted much work to the way that the Arab world was regarded in the West. He even assigned it a specific term: orientalism. Said believed that orientalism was essentially a bi-polar phenomenon; the world was either good, developed, civilised and superior—terms he felt were commonly attributed to the global West—or it was inferior, chaotic, corrupt and violent—terms more often applied to the orient and global East. He believed this to be reflected in the film and television imagery of Arabs; he noted that there existed a significant number of films in which the 'all-American hero' would launch a raid into the Middle East, perhaps to break up an Arab terrorist group or rescue US hostages. There are many examples to choose from. The 1982 film *Wrong is Right* portrayed an evil Arab sheikh providing terrorists with two nuclear bombs—to target Tel Aviv and New York. *Protocol* (1984) was set in the fictional Arab state of El-Ohtar—which spells 'rat hole' when read backwards—and again dealt with the 'evil' intent of shadowy Arab figures. In the highly successful *Delta Force* (1986) Arabs hijack a civilian airliner and torture US hostages; *Navy Seals* (1990) sees the 'good guys' recovering sophisticated US weaponry from Middle East terrorists; in *Executive Decision* (1996) a group of radical Islamists hijack a planeload of chemical weapons; *Death Before Dishonour* (1987) portrays a US marine captured by Arab terrorists. Finally there is the '*Iron Eagle*' series, which sees the aerial rescue of the US military hero from a Middle Eastern state. Said believed that the demonisation of the Arab world in Western media had become so pernicious that it was comparable to the way in which Jews were demonised by the Nazis in the years before the Second World War: 'The anti-Semitic images current from before World War 2 have been transferred from the Jews to the Arabs.' Stephen Prince makes similar observations in *The Media and the Persian Gulf War*: 'The brutal Arab terrorist, who does not flinch from practising violence but welcomes it enthusiastically, is a characteristic feature of Hollywood war films.'[75]

These themes remain popular today. In April 2000 the top box-office attraction in the United States was *Rules of Engagement*, the story of a fictional attack on the US embassy at Sana'a in Yemen and the resulting actions of a US Marine Corps officer. One reviewer noted: 'The audience I saw the film with cheered when the Marines slaughtered the [Arab] civilians.' Yet not all reviews were positive. The American-Arab Anti-Discrimination Committee described the film as 'possibly the most vicious anti-Arab racist film ever made by a major Hollywood studio'.[76] When the book *Rules of Engagement* (by James Webb, a former official in the Reagan administration) first appeared, it was set in an unnamed South American country. But when Paramount bought the film rights it was inexplicably switched to Yemen. Could one possible reason for the switch have been that the studios believed the film's rhetoric would upset the large Spanish-speaking community now resident in the United States? Arab anger was possibly easier to bear than that of the Latino population.

The US armed forces provide assistance to many film-makers, either through the provision of specialist advice and even equipment, or by affording access to US military facilities and personnel. The benchmark for offering assistance is always that the US military should be portrayed realistically and fairly. And so it was for *Rules of Engagement*. The Pentagon spokesman Kenneth Bacon explained that the United States would assist in production provided that the movie was an 'accurate portrayal of the military'. The Yemeni ambassador to the US did not agree: 'All of a sudden Yemenis have become terrorists and want to kill Americans. This is outrageous.'[77] The ending of the film, when credits roll telling what subsequently happened to the imaginary characters after the incident, helped reinforce the belief among cinema audiences that this had been a true story. The Yemeni ambassador later told the media that he was being asked by US citizens when the event had actually happened. Godfrey Cheshire, a critic at the time with the weekly *New York Press* magazine, wrote: 'Arabs are the only vicious stereotype that not only are still permitted but which are actively endorsed by Hollywood.'

*Rules of Engagement* was but one film in a long list of disobliging and inaccurate portrayals of the Arab world. So prolific has been the output that the subject has itself generated academic consideration in its own right. In 2001 Jack Shaheen wrote *Reel bad Arabs: How Hollywood vilifies a people*; the word 'Arab' had become Hollywood shorthand for 'bad guy', and he summarised this study of more than 900 films by saying that 'film-makers have collectively indicted all Arabs as Public Enemy No. 1'.

One has to wonder what effect such pejorative images, set in an entertainment format, have on an audience that is largely ignorant of the problems of the Middle East. Hussein Ibish of the American-Arab Anti-Discriminatory Committee is in no doubt: 'These negative stereotypes are rooted in the very aggressive role that the US plays in the Middle East. These stereotypes emerge from popular culture that informs government policy and reinforces the willingness of producers of popular culture to promote stereotypes and so on. It's a spiral.'

Such observations suggest that Edward Said's polar model is as relevant today as ever. Yet these often immature and ill-formed ideas of good and evil exist beyond the realm of cinema and appear to exist in US political rhetoric. Indeed, the connection with the Evangelical right and the connotations of good and evil have been recurring features of neo-conservatism. President Ronald Reagan often referred to the 'evil empire' in his dealings with the Soviet Union, while the invasion of Kuwait by Iraq led President George H. W. Bush to engage in a programme of demonisation of Saddam Hussein and his regime. Such rhetoric clearly resonated with the wider US public, and after 9/11 much stronger statements were made by George W. Bush—the most notorious being his 'axis of evil' phrase, in the January 2002 State of the Union address. Identifying Iran, Iraq and North Korea as regimes that 'sponsor terror', the US President contrasted their seeming evil intent with the willingness of the United States to defend tolerance, free speech and the rule of law on a global scale. The whole concept of America and its allies acting as a global 'force for good' was to become one of the key British messages of the Iraq war, which senior commanders and spokesmen were encouraged to voice at every opportunity.

Indelicate public statements from senior administration officials have added to the problem. Although his office has subsequently observed that his words were taken out of context, US Attorney General John Ashcroft has never denied telling an investigative journalist that 'Islam is a religion in which God requires you to send your son to die for him; Christianity is a faith in which God sends his son to die for you.'[78] Condoleezza Rice has commented on the need for Arabs to 'change their behaviour', Under Secretary of Defense Douglas Feith has observed Israel's 'moral superiority over the Arab world', and the policy adviser Richard Perle has described the Egyptian government as 'barely managing their own country'. Thus we see the demonisation of the Arab world not only in cinemas but also in the presentation of news.

Perhaps one of the most striking examples of this public demonisation was the 'heroic' rescue by US Special Forces of Private Jessica Lynch, a US servicewomen captured by the Iraqi military. The media portrayal of the event was of the brave and heroic Private Lynch, injured in the fighting and then imprisoned by her evil Iraqi captors. The reality of the story was a little different, however. Her 'captors' were Iraqi civilian medical staff who had attended to her injuries and who got word to US troops of her location after they themselves had tried to convey her back to the US lines. The former account of heroism and bravery is of course a better story than the reality—a frightened young woman being looked after by sympathetic and caring Iraqi medical personnel. The simplicity of the situation simply did not suit the US media and their audience, nor did it fit the stereotype that the media had built of the Arab world over many years.

## 3

## TOWARDS FREE ARAB MEDIA

'It's not a matter of what is true that counts but a matter of what is perceived to be true.'—Henry Kissinger

Article 91 of the Universal Declaration of Human Rights Convention, adopted by the United Nations in December 1948, proclaims: 'Everyone has the right to freedom of opinion and expression; this right includes freedom to hold opinions without interference and to seek, receive and impart information and ideas through any media and regardless of frontiers.' While the Convention idealistically encapsulates the desirability of universal press freedom, this remains an elusive and sometimes unwelcome principle in many countries. The annual and independent *Freedom of the Press* survey notes: 'The region with the worst conditions for the media in 2003 continued to be the Middle East and North Africa.'[1] George Joffé believes that many regimes in the Middle East regard the media as 'the vehicle by which governments impress order upon their populations'.[2] In *The Multiple Identities of the Middle East* Bernard Lewis considers the issue thus: 'They serve the State.... The State, more often than not, meant the ruler and the small group of people helping him in the exercise of his autocratic power.'[3] Jihad Ali-Ballout, communications manager for the pan-Arab TV satellite station Al-Jazeera, is more direct: 'The media environment in the Middle East has been characterised by the supremacy of the censor.'[4]

60

The development of the press in the Middle East is a comparatively new phenomenon and sees its roots in Arab nationalism, first in the decline of the Ottoman Empire and latterly in the struggles for independence from the great European colonial powers. Indeed, nationalists were often journalists, who used the media to rally public opinion. Yet independence did not bring a free press. Egypt, which had been in the vanguard of free expression, nationalised its press under Gamal Nasser; Iraq and Syria followed suit. While North African states such as Tunisia and Algeria were more tolerant of journalistic expression, what was and was not acceptable (so-called 'red lines') had to be understood. To misinterpret those rules could lead to an extended period of incarceration. Unsurprising therefore that a habit of self-censorship should develop among the region's journalists that endures today.

In many Arab states the media are closely monitored, if not controlled, by the regime; the mechanism for this is invariably the omnipresent Ministry of Information that exists in most of these countries. To a visitor, particularly one accustomed to Western practice, the output of state media can at times appear almost comical—certainly it lacks maturity and modernity when compared with organisations such as the BBC. In the press much of the space on the front pages is taken up by photographs of members of the regime welcoming dignitaries or undertaking functions of state. Editorials may focus on the regime's achievements or particular events in the government's calendar. Criticism is rare and where it occurs it is either tame or focuses on external actors; investigative reporting and exposés of misbehaviour among the ruling élite is largely un-heard-of. These outlets are therefore often referred to as 'protocol' news—in essence a showcase for the regime. Almost all are controlled to a greater or lesser extent by the Ministry of Information and it is not surprising that many Arab media organisations have, over the years, chosen to develop and work outside the system, many basing themselves in London.

As we see in the next chapter, one of the defining features of the 1991 Gulf war was the almost complete absence of any form of organic Arab media. To escape the mediocrity and banality of state media, many English-speaking Arabs watched the war through CNN or the BBC, often on illegally-owned satellite dishes. In the comprehensive study *The Media and the Persian Gulf War* there is barely a single reference to organic Arab media in more than 300 pages. That such a cataclysmic event could occur with not a single regional media organisation capable of reporting it became in itself a stimulus for change. Yet there were others which superseded even this.

In 1996 a new news outlet was unveiled in the tiny peninsular state of Qatar. Al-Jazeera ('the island'), as the new channel was to be called, began broadcasting news, opinions and views worldwide with an Arab perspective. From humble beginnings it has grown in size and output, and today broadcasts twenty-four hours a day to an audience estimated at more than 35 million people. Its impact was not lost on the *Freedom of the Press* survey, which noted in its 2003 edition:

This glimmer of hope for expanding press freedom in the Middle East, a region long resistant to press freedom, was part of a small but significant series of signs of change in that region. Rulers of Qatar quietly funded Al-Jazeera, the television channel whose frank coverage of Arab and international affairs angered many neighboring regimes.[5]

Under its strap-line 'The opinion and the counter opinion' the channel has enraged nearly every sector of international society, while simultaneously being courted by all. Variously described as anti-Arab, anti-Jewish and anti-American, the channel and its increasing number of clones around the region have transformed civil society in the Arab world. As CNN became the face of the 1991 Gulf war, so Al-Jazeera defined the first conflicts of the twenty-first century—coming of age in Afghanistan (the only broadcaster officially allowed into the country by the Taliban government) and becoming a major influence in the US-led invasion of Iraq in 2003. Middle East media analyst Ashraf Fouad said of their impact:

'You cannot take away from Al-Jazeera what they have done—they really pushed the envelope at a time when there were only a handful of channels...showing music and dance and film. And then bam! You had this 24 hours a day and lots of controversy and they were saying it live.'[6]

But what was so radical? Essentially it was the absence of 'red lines', whether self-imposed or state-controlled. Journalists from the channel were actively encouraged to shed the shackles of censorship and to say what they thought and report what they saw. Suddenly Arab journalists seemed prepared to push and break the old taboos, asking previously unaskable questions and airing footage that might not previously have reached the public eye. In the West such coverage is of course not unusual. Politicians and public figures are regularly subjected to the most detailed and at times intensely personal questioning, often on issues to do as much with their private lives as with their professional responsibilities. Such impertinence and inquisitiveness were anathema in the Arab world, at odds not only with years of self- and state-imposed censorship but also culturally alien to a people who value privacy and discretion. The *New York Times* columnist Thomas Friedman wrote: '[Al-Jazeera] is not only the biggest media phenomenon to hit the Arab world since the advent of television, it is also the biggest political phenomenon.'[7] But it is even more than that. In his book *Unholy War* the American Middle East specialist John L. Esposito expresses the belief that 'the daily coverage from embattled Muslim frontiers has had a profound effect upon the everyday consciousness of Muslims around the world.'[8]

Why then this departure from the established Arab norm? Why and how did Al-Jazeera develop and why did it find its catalyst in the tiny and almost insignificant Gulf state of Qatar? Apart from a long-running dispute with its smaller island neighbour Bahrain, Qatar had done little previously to attract international attention. Many people would have been unable to find it on a map, sticking out for-lornly as it does from the eastern coast of Saudi Arabia and stretch-ing northwards towards Bahrain. Certainly its unobtrusiveness may in itself have been a motor for change; the origins of the channel form a tale of coincidence and intrigue that arguably says more about Qatar's international relations at the time than any altruistic desire for the establishment of a pan-Arab free press. Indeed it is questionable if the channel would ever have been launched had the Qatari government anticipated the difficulties it would cause on the international scene. With a hint of irony and a mischievous smile, Al-Jazeera's congenial, chain-smoking Lebanese communications manager Jihad Ali-Ballout told the author: 'I would be stretching it a bit if I were to say that the Al-Jazeera of today is what they [the Qatari government] had envisaged.'[9]

## Big voice, tiny country[10]

Like its larger next-door neighbour, the tiny country of Qatar, which at just 4,400 square miles is roughly equivalent in size to Jamaica, is a highly conservative and traditional Arab state. Although the majority of the 600,000 inhabitants are expatriate workers (less than one third are indigenous), Qataris themselves follow the ultra-conservative branch of Wahhabi Islam. The Wahhabi movement takes its name from the eighteenth-century Islamic scholar Muham-mad Ibn Abd al-Wahhab, who advocated a return to pure funda-mental Islamic values. The message gathered potency when al-Wahhab joined forces with one of the Arabian peninsula's tribal chiefs, Muhammad Ibn Saud, who used the ideology to unite the region's disparate families, leading ultimately to the creation of the Saudi state. Even today the Wahhabi religious establishment under-writes the continuance of the ruling family's monopoly on power but enforces adherence to a strict code of conduct by all who live within the vast desert kingdom. Qatar is the only other Arab country to adopt this version of Sunni Islam, although unlike Saudi Arabia it takes a relatively secular approach to religion, tolerating and even supporting small Christian and Hindu communities.

Qatar is wealthy. Although it contains oil reserves of more than 15 billion barrels, liquid petroleum gas (LPG) now underpins the vibrant and growing Qatari economy.[11] Indeed so substantial are these gas reserves that LPG makes Qatar, per capita, the richest country on earth. If this statistic were not startling enough, Qatar also has the world's fastest-growing economy. All of this helps gives Qatar great stability. *The Economist* correspondent Liesl Graz noted in her 1992 study of the region: 'Nothing, since the money started coming in, has had much effect upon Qatar..... Qatar's luck is perhaps to be found in its lack of grandeur. It remains something of a quiet backwater.'[12] This affluence affords the tiny state a considerable degree of self-confidence and autonomy vis-à-vis its large and powerful neighbour. Her at times uneasy relationship with Saudi Arabia is a testament to this. A long-running border dispute existed between them over the precise delineation of the Khofous border post—driven by shared interest in the large natural gas field that lies under it.

Since June 1995 the ruler of Qatar has been Sheikh Hamad bin Khalifa Al-Thani, who seized power from his ageing father Sheikh Khalifa Bin-Hamad Al-Thani in a bloodless and carefully negotiated coup. Considered by many to be a reformist, Sheikh Hamad almost immediately began a modernisation programme, instituting long-delayed elections and, almost uniquely for the region, undertaking formal, albeit low-level relations with Israel. He also chose to abolish the Ministry of Information, an unusual move for an Arab state but one which would facilitate the development of the fledgling new channel. In April 2003 a new constitution separating the judicial, legislative and executive branches of government was over-whelmingly accepted in a national referendum. As a result two-thirds of the governing Shura Council are now elected by popular vote. Qatar may well be moving, albeit slowly, towards establishing the region's first constitutional democracy. Unsurprisingly these reformist policies have caused the Saudis and their Wahhabi sup-porters to regard Sheikh Hamad with suspicion, and their public support for the return of his father has proved an irritant to the new Emir.

For conservative states, particularly those in the Gulf region, disputes are rarely conducted in public; that a satellite television network should be an indirect consequence of just such a dispute is remarkable. In 1994 the BBC launched a TV news channel in Ara-bic, hosted by the Orbit Satellite network which was administered and broadcast from inside Saudi Arabia. The relationship did not prosper, and in 1996, with the contract barely twenty months old, it was severed after the BBC refused to accede to a Saudi government request to censor a proposed documentary about executions inside Saudi Arabia. The service collapsed and in consequence nearly 250 Arab media professionals, all of them trained by the BBC, became unemployed[13] and thus available to participate in the new Qatari Emir's bold new media project—a project that would banish Qatar's sleepy backwater image and not only place it firmly on the world map but also provide it with a welcome opportunity to rile the sensibilities of its large omnipresent neighbour.

The intricacies of the channel's relationship with the government of Qatar can only be guessed at, yet there is no doubting the impact of Al-Jazeera not only across the Arab world but also in the West. The words 'This is Al-Jazeera television from Qatar' are heard every day by millions of Arab viewers world-wide, in turn bestow-ing tremendous prestige upon the tiny state. This is not to say that the channel is an instrument of Qatari foreign policy. The Qatari government likens the relationship to that between the British government and the BBC. And like the BBC, Al-Jazeera has had disagreements with the Emir's government. In particular it has developed a largely critical view of US policy in the region. The channel has questioned the bilateral security arrangement and generally close military and political relationship that Qatar has carefully built with the United States since 1992—in particular the hosting of the giant US air base at Al-Udeid and its involvement in UN sanctions operations and ultimately the 2003 war against the Saddam regime. Such coverage cannot have been comfortable for the Qatari Emir.

Satellite TV stations are expensive and Sheikh Hamad had to invest heavily in order to satisfy his media ambitions. Al-Jazeera's Jihad Ali-Ballout explained the relationship at a meeting in Doha: 'There is an unwritten charter for Al-Jazeera that stipulates the creation of Al-Jazeera as an independent media organisation plus sets the seed money for the budget to the tune of $150 million for the first five years; after that, Al-Jazeera would be self-financing.'[14] However, it is a charter that has been only partly fulfilled. More than eight years after the channel's launch it still relies heavily on the Emir for survival. Although free to air in the Arab world, it has developed a subscription base in the United States and in Europe, particularly during the Iraq war when more than 4 million new subscriptions were taken out in Europe alone.[15] But this has not been enough to sustain its growth, and the channel continues to chase advertising revenue. Although its desirability to multinational corporations would seem obvious, actually securing new revenue has proved difficult, the intricacies of the region's international relations intruding upon business. Ali-Ballout is frank in his consideration of the way in which the region's hegemon, Saudi Arabia, has subtly yet decisively strangled the channel's advertising revenue:

'If you know the Saudis you will know that nothing is explicit! Everything is done is a subtle way—back-room chats. I recall two and a half years ago there was a summit for Ministers of Information from the GCC [Gulf Cooperation Council] and there was a proposal by the ministers put forward to officially boycott Al-Jazeera—don't give them official access to buildings and so forth. I think it was wise of the ministers to drop the proposal and it was decided that no official boycott would take place and it would be up to individual members of GCC to do what they wanted. It was clear however that Al-Jazeera was a prime target.'[16]

In short Saudi Arabia has put the brakes on any company with business in the kingdom from advertising on the channel. And here is the 'catch-22'. To attract and retain its large audience many commentators feel that the station has had to be outspoken and controversial by playing to the Arab crowd. In perfecting such attributes large commercial advertisers, particularly those with connections to the Saudi royal family, have become wary of causing offence and the revenue has thus failed to materialise. Yet it is precisely this willingness to court controversy that has seen Al-Jazeera's popularity with Arab audiences rise.

To many Arab regimes this phenomenon is viewed as a considerable problem. In May 2002 the government of the tiny state of Bahrain banned Al-Jazeera from reporting inside its borders. A government spokesman told the BBC: 'We will not deal with this channel because we object to its coverage of current affairs—it is a channel penetrated by Zionists.'[17] The Zionist reference is undoubtedly a smokescreen for the real reason for Bahraini protest—the channel's coverage of anti-US protests in the kingdom triggered by ongoing Israeli military action in the West Bank. But Bahrain is by no means alone. In July 2003 Reuters reported an unnamed Qatari governmental official as saying: 'Al-Jazeera is a headache—we need to sort it out as we are one [Gulf Arab] family and share the same destiny.'[18] This followed the airing of Saudi dissidents on one of the channel's prime talk-shows who criticised the Al-Saud regime. Qatar's Foreign Minister Sheikh Hamad bin Jassim Jabr al-Thani offered to visit Riyadh to resolve the dispute but pointed out to Reuters: 'Al-Jazeera is not an official channel; we just help it financially, like Britain helps the BBC.' It is evident that Saudi sensibilities have been repeatedly offended by the channel's output and even today there remains no senior Saudi representation in Doha—a direct consequence of Al-Jazeera's critical coverage. The recall of ambassadors from Doha has developed into a regular occurrence: Tunisia, Morocco and Libya have all recalled their diplomats in response to Al-Jazeera programmes. The Algerian government famously cut power to several of its major cities, including its capital Algiers, in an attempt to silence an Al-Jazeera programme about that country's civil war. Even the PLO has been embroiled in a dispute with the channel. The airing of an interview with the late Hamas leader, Sheikh Hamad Yessin, reportedly incensed the then PLO leader Yasser Arafat. The Palestinian bureau was all but taken over in March 2001 by PLO security personnel, angered when the channel considered the role of the PLO in Lebanon's civil war. Egypt's President Hosni Mubarak has been a regular critic of the channel. When he visited the station's Doha headquarters he was quoted as saying: 'All of this noise from a tiny matchbox.'

In the West the channel's existence remained largely unknown. Its focus on the Arab world and in particular on the Palestinian crisis was only of passing interest to Western news organisations which had their own correspondents covering events. That was to change in the wake of 9/11 as America began asking itself 'why us' and started looking for alternative views of its role in the world. On the night of 7 October 2001, when the US launched its attack on the Taliban regime in Afghanistan, Al-Jazeera was the only news channel allowed in by the Taliban government and showed in graphic detail the effect of ordnance landing in the already war-torn city of Kabul. The imagery contrasted sharply with that shown by the largely supportive Western news-providers and immediately caused

US Administration officials to question the allegiance and integrity of the channel.

But it was the airing of Osama Bin Laden's videotapes that was to rocket Al-Jazeera to international prominence and earn it the unfortunate and undeserved sobriquet 'Bin Laden TV'. In one of his first interviews Bin Laden stated that he had 'high regard and respect for the people who bombed [US barracks in Saudi Arabia]' while in a later tape he accused America of 'violating our land, occupying it and stealing Muslim possessions'. These tapes marked the beginning of an uneasy relationship between the channel and the United States and are almost certainly the reason for much of the anti-Al-Jazeera sentiment that many US servicemen demonstrated during operations in Iraq the following year. Yet by 2003 Al-Jazeera was no longer the only TV channel in the region. Arabs now had a considerable choice.

## The politics of clones and copies

Al-Jazeera has been widely acclaimed as the Middle East's first free media organisation. It is impossible to quantify the extent of that 'freedom' definitively, but inevitably allegiances and alliances will exist which will continue to cloud the discussion. The absence of 'red lines' is obvious, but what control is exerted behind the scenes? With little advertising revenue forthcoming the station remains reliant on the Emir, and while considering new revenue-earning opportunities, such as floating on the Stock Exchange, it is clear that the station has to maintain its relationship with the Qatari royal family in order to survive. It is equally clear that it causes that family considerable problems in its international relations. Confidential sources in Qatar admit that there are elements in the Qatari Foreign Ministry that wish to see Al-Jazeera closed down. While the Qatari government and the channel have robustly defended editorial inde-

pendence, the *Freedom of the Press Survey* for 2003 has noted: 'Although Al-Jazeera's critical coverage has angered a number of Arab
regimes, the station tends to shy away from covering sensitive
political issues within Qatar.'[19] What is undeniable is that Al-Jazeera
has stimulated the growth of free expression in the region and as a
direct result has spawned the development of other pan-Arab news
and current affairs networks. The most successful have been Abu
Dhabi TV and Al-Arabiya.

## Abu Dhabi TV

Abu Dhabi TV is not new, having been established in 1969 as part of
the Abu Dhabi Ministry of Information, nor is it a bespoke news
channel. However, in 1998 the channel was completely re-
launched, becoming the flagship of Emirate Media Group, a public-
private finance initiative chaired by the son of the President of the
United Arab Emirates, Sheikh Abdullah Bin Zayed. The channel
actually consists of three outlets—the Emirates Channel, which is
focused almost exclusively in the Gulf Region; the Abu Dhabi
sports channel, a very popular revenue-driven subscription service;
and the Abu Dhabi channel itself, with its focus on news and current
affairs.

Before 9/11 the channel had been particularly proactive in its
coverage of the Palestinian crisis. Ordinarily it had offices in Jerusalem, Ramallah and Gaza, but since the start of the intifada it has
greatly increased its presence across the occupied territories. This
was not without incident, and like many other media organisations
operating in the disputed lands the channel had experienced considerable difficulty working with the Israeli Defence Forces and in
ensuring the safety of its journalists and staff. The channel's comic
series 'Irhabiyat' (Terrorism), a satire on the Israeli Prime Minister
Ariel Sharon, will not have helped the relationship. The channel has

also run telethons for the Palestinian cause; one in April 2002 raised in excess of 210 million UAE dirham (roughly equivalent to US$57 million). The channel has also had difficulty with Arab governments, its news coverage angering various regimes. Like Al-Jazeera, Abu Dhabi TV has taken a firm view in this respect. The deputy director of the channel, Mohammed Dourrachad, recalled in an interview with the online Arab media magazine *TBS Journal*: 'We report to governments what their people think. A huge shift.'

The issue of footage and the imagery that Arab channels chose to air proved to be particularly contentious during the Iraq conflict. Many in the West criticised it for being 'inappropriate' while others applauded it for addressing the true cost of the conflict. Abu Dhabi TV has not shied away from this controversy and believes that such imagery is a necessity if the channel is to tell the true story of events. The channel had certainly recorded its share of graphic images in the occupied territories—'footage of civilians killed, civilians being treated like animals'.[20] This clearly resonates with Arab audiences. Before 9/11 Abu Dhabi TV believed that it had captured the majority of the Arab news market share. Surveys undertaken by both the channel and academic organisations such as the Palestinian Birzeit University concluded that the channel was in pole position in terms of credibility. After 9/11 that ranking may have dropped slightly as Al-Jazeera was afforded access to the Bin Laden tapes. Unlike its rival, however, its market share has been largely unaffected by Saudi sensitivities, and with the patronage of the Emirate royal family it has not experienced quite the same difficulties of income generation as its newer rival.

The channel's links to the Abu Dhabi regime and in particular its connection to the Ministry of Information may cause some to question just how editorially independent it can ever actually be. The government may not now impose the 'red lines' but does self-censorship remain? Nart Bouran is the channel's director of news, and like his colleagues at Al-Jazeera he has taken a common-sense approach over the issue of editorial influence:

'Everyone has editorial consideration. You always make calls on your editorial content to make sure you are understood properly, and that you are not taking sides on a story. The few editorial control cases involved not having the full picture or not having proper credible sources, that is when we tend to ignore or scrap a story. Apart from that, one should never claim full editorial freedom, as editorial considerations always play a part.'

When asked his view of the way that Abu Dhabi TV covered the war in Afghanistan and the move towards conflict in Iraq Bouran is forthright. Some observers have suggested that Abu Dhabi TV was the voice of moderation and common sense. His succinct reply is 'Absolutely'. However this is not to say that the channel has adopted a markedly different style of news-gathering from Al-Jazeera. Like its bigger counterpart Abu Dhabi TV adopted the strapline 'War on Iraq' for its coverage, and aired the images of captured Coalition troops that so enraged the US and British governments. What distinguished Abu Dhabi TV was the innovation that it applied to its war coverage. As will be seen in a later chapter they used the services of a former British Special Forces officer as their frontline, embedded reporter. It was an innovation that was to see them portray almost exclusive coverage of the Coalition forces in the frontline to their audience—something that not one of the other major Arab channels was able to sustain for more than a few days. Hardly surprising therefore that the channel is now one of the preferred outlets for news footage from military media teams in the region.

## Al-Arabiya TV

Al-Arabiya is a very different organisation, and it enjoys none of the heritage of Abu Dhabi TV. Part of the Middle East Broadcasting

(MBC) media group based in Dubai's Media City, it was established as a direct competitor to Al-Jazeera. Englishman Sam Barnett is the channel's director of operations and explained how the channel came about: 'There was a perception that Arab media was dominated by Al-Jazeera and that they had a certain line that was populist, heading towards sensationalist, and that there was a gap for a more considered and less sensationalist approach.'[21] Established only one month before the Iraq war the channel provides a diet of news, current affairs and discussion programmes. Like its two older competitors, Al-Arabiya also enjoys royal patronage. Though not prepared to state on the record, a number of Al-Arabiya staff privately confided that the station owed its very existence to the disputes between Saudi Arabia and Qatar. Tired of what the Saudis regarded as malicious and trouble-making reporting, the Saudi Sheikh Walid al-Ibrahim, brother-in-law of the late King Fahd, became the driving force behind the new news channel, hiring in experienced staff from across the region. Interestingly many were previously with Al-Jazeera or the BBC; one example was the head of news, Salah Nagm, once head of the BBC Arabic Service news and current affairs division, and who also previously worked at Al-Jazeera. Sheikh Walid told Paul Martin of the *Washington Times* that one of the channel's major objectives was to get rid of the 'Taliban mentality'. The paradox between his country's desire for an 'independent' news outlet and its fundamentalist Wahhabi teachings, which form the core of Taliban belief, is evidently ignored. Perhaps fired by the success of Al-Jazeera, Sheikh Walid sees the channel playing a key role in the Arab world, supporting a 'move towards democracy and freedom and against dictatorship, repression and Islamic extremism'. These ideals appear laudable, but they mask the channel's financial backing and the Saudis' reluctance to allow criticism of the kingdom and its ruling élite. Launched with an initial investment of $300 million from

MBC, the channel has undoubtedly gone from strength to strength, although its launch was far from smooth. In April 2003, just weeks after going live, its Kuwaiti investors withdrew their funding and the Kuwaiti government threatened closure of the station's office in Kuwait City. This was in response to what the Kuwaiti government called 'an absence of objective war coverage'.[22] Like its rivals, Al-Arabiya was broadly anti-war, a position that did not sit easily with the long-time enemies of Saddam, the Kuwaiti Al-Sabr ruling family. Despite these early setbacks, there is no denying that today, Al-Arabiya has captured a massive market share and is a very real rival to Al-Jazeera.

*Lebanese Broadcasting Corporation (LBC)*

There are other large networks that provide similar services. LBC is a privately-owned company, established in 1985 as a local commercial channel, but which in the 1990s evolved into a pan-Arab satellite channel. Although it has audiences around the Arabic-speaking world, it targets in particular the populations of the Gulf states. Unlike Al-Arabiya and Al-Jazeera, LBC is entirely self-financing, relying mainly on advertising revenue to sustain its growth. However, the company has recently entered into a partnership with the leading Arab newspaper *Al-Hayat* (based in London), which is owned by the members of the ruling Saudi royal family. However, its news editor and senior international correspondent, Sultan Sleiman, believes that this causes the company no difficulty at all: 'This partnership has no effect on the independence of the editorial decision-making process.'[23]

As well as the mainstream news broadcasters, two other channels are worthy of mention. Both have definite aims and their objectivity is open to question. These are Al-Manar, based in Beirut, and the US-funded Al-Hurra, based in the United States.

## Al-Manar: the station of resistance

Al-Manar (translated as 'the Beacon') is the TV station of Lebanon's Shia community and in particular of Hezbollah (party of God), a militant Islamic resistance movement that refuses to recognise the right of Israel to exist as a state. Al-Manar began as a terrestrial broadcaster in 1991 amid the devastation of the Lebanese civil war and the Israeli occupation of the southern part of the country. Its website explains its development:

There had to be a TV that committed itself to put out images of the suffering of our people in the occupied territories, the victims of Israeli arrogance, and that of those living in areas bordering the occupation who suffer its semi-daily aggressions.

In 1997 the channel was officially sanctioned by the Lebanese government and began broadcasting via satellite in 2000. Its focus is on Lebanese, Palestinian and, as a propaganda tool, Israeli audiences, and it targets them via Arabic, English and Hebrew broadcasts and websites. Its informal title 'the station of resistance' is an indication of its output. The channel is quite open in its editorial policy, which has at its core a mix of anti-Semitism and, by association, anti-Americanism.

The channel is also extremely loyal to Hezbollah leader Sheikh Hasan Nasrullah, who has called the United States 'the most ugly, the most deceptive democracy in the world'. He has also singled out American television programmes for criticism: 'The interviewer will sit with you for thirty or sixty minutes, after which he will cut your words and display only three minutes that condemn you and serve your enemy.' For Hezbollah the media constitute 'one of the most important weapons in the conflict' against Israel. Its role is clear: 'to support the Palestinian people and the intifada'.

Al-Manar's stated aim is to be 'the Lebanese TV station that aims to preserve the Islamic values and to enhance the civilising role of

the Arab and Islamic Community', and as 'the first Arab establishment to stage an effective psychological warfare against the
Zionist enemy'. It is taken very seriously in the Middle East and its
growth has allowed it to branch out into radio, sports and children's
channels. Its quiz shows have proved particularly popular, not least
for the large cash prizes offered on the popular game show *The
Mission*. In this programme contestants have to answer questions
that gain them virtual steps toward Jerusalem. The person who
'enters' the holy city wins up to 5 million Lebanese pounds
(US $3,300) 25% of which goes to 'support the Palestinian people'.
Questions include asking the names of the latest suicide-bombers.

Its employees are all committed Muslims, and its message is un-
ashamedly partisan. Its news presenters, women in headscarves and
men without ties in keeping with Shiite Islamic tradition, refer to
Israel as 'the Zionist entity' or simply as 'the enemy'. Its website proclaims: 'Most important is the struggle against the Zionist enemy.' It
broadcasts news bulletins on alternate hours and airs a variety of
programmes, including documentaries, game shows, political talk
shows and dramatic series produced in Egypt and Syria.

Al-Manar leapt to particular prominence in the media world in
the aftermath of the 9/11 attacks. A rumour had circulated on the
internet that on the day of the attack more than 4,000 Jewish office
workers had failed to show up for work. The rumour was unsub-
stantiated and most media organisations gave it no time at all;
however, Al-Manar broadcast it in its entirety to a believing
audience.[24] In a flurry of media excitement an Al-Manar reporter
told journalists: 'If we did not believe it, then we would not have
published it.' Strong words perhaps but words that are lapped up by
most of the channel's growing Arab audience. Al-Manar, they say,
makes a refreshing change from mainstream media; with its clear
and unambiguous political message and its Islamic ideology its
attracts an audience characterised by strong feelings about the Pal-

estine question. Salah Eddin Hafiz, the smartly-dressed managing editor of the newspaper *Al-Ahram*, sums up his own feeling with passion: 'The struggle is part of my spirit.' Al-Manar has tapped into that spirit, and seems to have done so very successfully. At the 8th Cairo Television and Radio Festival in July 2002 it swept the board of prizes.

### Al-Hurra (The Free One)

Although not an authentic Arab channel, a newcomer worthy of mention, and one that is examined in detail later, is Al-Hurra (The Free One). This is a pan-Arab channel funded directly by the US Congress, which began broadcasting from its US studios in Springfield, Virginia, in February 2004. Designed to present the US case, which many US observers feel is lacking in the organic Arab stations, the station hopes to replicate the success of the US-funded Radio Sawa station, whose mix of Western and Arabic styles has been popular with Arab youth across the region. However, serious media observers in the region regard it, like Al-Manar, with considerable suspicion and see it as little more than a clumsy propaganda tool for the United States. Rami Khouri, a journalist with Lebanon's *Daily Star* newspaper, wrote in its first week of broadcasting: 'Al-Hurra will be an entertaining, expensive and irrelevant hoax. Where do they get this stuff from? Why do they keep insulting us like this?' Hardly a ringing endorsement.

Thus the Arab world now enjoys a plethora of media outlets; no longer are viewers reliant upon Western media for real-time news and events. While in US-friendly states the big players enjoy the patronage of the hierarchy, their output is far from guaranteed and Arab viewers are able to hop from one channel to another for views and opinions in Arabic. It is important too that the Arab diaspora can also now watch events in Arabic-language programmes from their new homes in the West.[25]

# THE 1991 GULF WAR: WHO LEARNED THE LESSONS?

'George...this is no time to go wobbly.'—Margaret Thatcher, 1990

In his book *Military Lessons of the Gulf War* Bruce Watson considers the scope of war reporting during the 1991 Gulf War. While seeing it as apparently overwhelming in its breadth, he wondered about those aspects of the war which went unreported, notably:

... coverage of the wounded, POW camps and ground combat. Reporters state they were denied access to these stories. The result was a packaged, clean war, where smart weapons surgically destroyed bridges, military equipment and installations.... With only a few exceptions, the public were not privy to the dirty part of the war where people bled, were in pain and died.[1]

His conclusion was that access to the world's media was denied in order to maintain the public sense of euphoria at the speed and success of the Coalition operation. The deliberate ending of the war exactly 100 days after it began had the air of a Hollywood drama.

There may be some element of truth to the allegation, although such 'planned' mass deception seems rather advanced for the sometimes chaotic media management that typified the war. A more realistic explanation may be that Saddam Hussein was known to monitor Western media closely, in particular CNN and the BBC. It was therefore imperative that these channels should not reveal any information, either deliberately or inadvertently, that might compromise either the mission or soldiers' lives.

What is quite apparent, however, is that the dreadful coverage of the latter stages of the Vietnam conflict by what many senior US officers came to regard as partisan US media networks still resonated in the military collective. The US military were highly suspicious of the media and convinced that the media left to themselves would become an obstacle in the conduct of the war. President George H. W. Bush issued a warning note to the media, saying that 'US troops would not be asked to "fight with one hand tied behind their back".' Saddam Hussein appeared to understand the utility of the media much more than his Western antagonists. He extended a personal invitation to the US network CNN as well as to the BBC and ITN to cover the war from Baghdad. No doubt realising that the city would be bombed by the Coalition, he perhaps hoped that Western coverage of the results might have a coercive effect on public opinion at home.

As in all conflicts the need to maintain operational security became the imperative for the media/military relationship. General Norman Schwarzkopf, CENTCOM's larger-than-life commander, recalls watching a live report from CNN in which a pool correspondent explained that a major artillery barrage had just been undertaken by the US 82nd Airborne Regiment. Schwarzkopf recalls 'recoiling in horror at the report' and the huge effect it might have on operational security: 'Any half-competent Iraqi intelligence officer watching CNN ... would discover that the 82nd were positioned for a flanking attack, a fact that we had taken pains to conceal for some three weeks.' Even the need to maintain operational security cannot hide the very real difficulty that many senior military figures had over the presence of TV cameras broadcasting live from the battlefield. In his book *Storm Command* the British commander, General Sir Peter de la Billière, considers the press almost dismissively, particularly the importance that the politicians back in Britain attached to it:

> I had the CD [Chief of Defence Staff] on the phone for 40 minutes. We would have liked to have talked military matters but most of our talk was perforce about the press. Then Tom King came on for about an hour and I could only persuade him to talk about the war for 5 minutes. They are obsessed with [media] and Washington is the same, worse.

It had been nearly ten years since the British were last at war and the management of the media during that particular conflict had attracted enormous criticism.[2] If for no other reason than the significant leap forward in the use of digital and live technology, Operation Desert Storm was to prove a significant learning process for military and media alike.

While a small number of war correspondents were again embedded with military units, the major focus of the media management plan was in the provision of the pool and the daily briefings by CENTCOM staff. The United States appointed six of its public affairs officers to manage the media in theatre, including establishing the main briefing room in a Dhahran hotel. The military established a press pool in which members of the media were taken to and from units and to which the media were invited to add their footage, reports and photographs. This was then made available to other pool members who might not have been able to participate in a particular press facility. The pool was designed for three reasons. It ensured, first, that the American public would see coverage of US troops; secondly, that media were provided access to the front line; and thirdly, that military units would not be swamped by the press. But these arrangements did not suit everyone. A group of French photo-journalists in particular chose to operate outside the pool and as a result were able to capture some of the most striking imagery of the war. The team dubbed itself the 'Fuck the pool, pool'.

The pools attempted to provide the maximum amount of footage to the largest possible number of media outlets. During the war they came in for criticism as infighting and disagreements flared between news networks competing for footage and material. In turn the networks blamed the US military for instigating numerous layers of control over the footage. There was a belief that the news pool offered journalists very little first-hand action apart from what the military selected. Far from close-quarter combat many journalists found themselves on facilities watching aircraft on missions take off and land, or on board ships as cruise missiles were launched. The University of Ulster lecturer Craig McLaughlin believes that: the Gulf war was 'the first time in American history that reporters were essentially barred from accompanying the nation's troops into combat'.[3]

The media briefings came in for particular criticism; General de la Billière described them as 'the bane of our lives'[4]—a sentiment with which many of the journalists resident in Riyadh or Dhahran might have agreed. The Pentagon relied on slick video footage of smart bombs hitting their targets. Journalists were provided general information about the enemy attrition rates but casualty reporting was largely silent. McLaughlin again: 'Like entertaining a party of children, the briefers kept the journalists occupied and ... out of harm's way.'[5]

The Gulf war received more television coverage and press attention than any previous conflict. In general that coverage was broadly supportive of the Coalition operation to end the occupation of Kuwait, and its apparent lack of concern at Iraqi civilian suffering showed, in the words of the writer Miles Hudson, 'a surprising insensitivity'.[6] In the official view the media campaign was deemed a success; the US Assistant Secretary for Defense Pete Williams said it had been 'the best war coverage we have ever had'.[7] The media were much less enthusiastic, although curiously they were pleased with the access afforded them by the Saudi military under the joint force commander General Khaled Bin Sultan. In his memoirs the General related that US access granted by the Americans was problematic, but that he had been praised by a senior executive of *Newsweek* magazine because the Saudi military authorities were more accessible and more cooperative than American authorities.[8]

Undoubtedly the defining feature of the media war was the almost complete absence of any form of Arab media. The war was watched by Arabs either through the eyes of CNN, the ears of the BBC World Service, or Voice of America, or more commonly through the scanty and heavily-censored Arab state news-providers. Their coverage of course depended on their individual positions regarding the legality and desirability of US intervention. In the definitive *The Media and the Persian Gulf War* there is barely a single reference to Arab audiences in 300 pages. This is not to say that Arab journalists were not present during the conflict; there were many working for Western news organisations. However, even then issues of objectivity and reliability were being discussed. On 26 February 1991 ITN News broadcast a report about the effects of collateral damage—the euphemism for civilian casualties. The reporting team visited Baghdad hospitals and saw the effects of Coalition bombing on civilian housing areas. Yet ITN chose to prefix the report with the words 'The camera was operated by a Jordanian cameraman'. This was almost certainly a strong hint that the footage should not be considered completely 100% reliable since it was filmed by an Arab.

Samuel Huntington considers the issue of Western dominance of global communications as a manifestation of Western superiority: 'The extent to which global communications are dominated by the West is a major source of the resentment and hostility of non-Western peoples against the West.'[9] He notes that in the early 1990s CNN International boasted an audience of more than

55 million viewers, or nearly 1% of the world's population. Coincidentally this is the figure that, some ten years later, the first of the pan-Arab satellite TV stations, Al-Jazeera, would claim.

There were many lessons to be learned from the war, notably in perception management and the utility of the media pool. The presence of Western news organisations in Baghdad probably came as an unwelcome surprise to Coalition military commanders who would find questions about collateral damage and civilian casualties more awkward to answer, given the immediacy of reporting. Undoubtedly the 1991 Gulf war was a watershed in the military-media nexus and many of the lessons learned were used in the planning of subsequent operations, notably in the Balkans. But did the Arab world learn the lessons quicker then the US and British military? The obvious domination of news by Western network providers, the beginnings of a momentum for free expression, and the inequalities of the Palestinian-Israeli issue formed the catalyst for the explosion that was to come just five years later—the arrival of the Al-Jazeera pan-Arab TV station. Certainly the absence of a pan-Arab press was apparent to the Arab commander and Saudi Deputy Prime Minister, General Khaled Bin Sultan, who was despatched to London and Washington to 'ensure Saudi financial and political control of the Arab Press'.[10] The Paris-based newspaper *Al-Watan Al-Arabi* was the first to be bought out, and later the General succeeded in leasing the influential but commercially failing newspaper, *Al-Hayat*. He says in his memoirs that one of his over-riding objectives was the establishment of an independent pan-Arab daily. He certainly achieved the financial and political leverage that he wanted, although the ideal of independent media is debatable. In essence Khaled Bin Sultan succeeded in 'sewing up' the Arab press for the final years of the twentieth century, ensuring that Saudi Arabia and its autocratic regime would not be publicly criticised, and that the 'official' Saudi government view would become the primary voice of the Arab world. Although Al-Jazeera was to crack this mould, it was the events of 11 September 2001 that would break it open and finally, publicly and globally, expose the realities and divisions of Saudi society.

# WAR IN IRAQ: MANAGING THE MEDIA BATTLE SPACE

'In the First Amendment, the Founding Fathers gave the free press the protection it must have to fulfil its essential role in our democracy. The press was to serve the governed, not the governors. The Government's power to censor the press was abolished so that the press would remain forever free to censure the Government. The press was protected so that it could bare the secrets of government and inform the people. Only a free and unrestrained press can effectively expose deception in government. And paramount among the responsibilities of a free press is the duty to prevent any part of the government from deceiving the people and sending them off to distant lands to die of foreign fevers and foreign shot and shell.'—Justice Black, *NYT* v. *US*. 403 US 713[1]

While the world's media waited for the conflict to begin, both Britain and the United States had already begun planning their media-handling strategies months earlier. The US military have a dedicated uniformed Public Affairs Organisation which provides an entire military career structure, from Private to General, for Public Affairs Officers (PAOs). Most US military units have their own PAO and there exists a substantial support staff both in the Pentagon and in major US military commands around the world. PAOs come from all branches of the services, many having completed front-line tours before choosing to move to their new specialisation. The organisation has its own journalists and photographers, who are tasked with providing substantial material support for those officers whose job is essentially the promotion of the US military to the US public and taxpayers.

Britain, with a much smaller military, chooses to conduct itself differently. Public Affairs is given a much more operational and military focus. Media Operations Officers (as Britain prefers to call its PAOs) come from all disciplines of the service and will remain in the media operations world for no more than three or four years before returning to their source specialisation and career. As such British officers are able to offer substantial military experience but may be short of media operations know-how. Routine unit public relations activity is often conducted by Government Information and Communication Service staff. These are civil servants; although some of them are prepared to deploy for operations, the majority choose not to. Regular service officers are often supplemented by reservists, some of whom have been, or still are, employed within the media industry itself. While often highly enthusiastic for the task, their experience of the media is often tempered by their unfamiliarity with the military; Reserve officers are, after all, only required to undertake a few short weeks' attachment to regular units each year, and it can be difficult for them to retain currency. In short Britain has had an imperfect system of media operations management—which, in a world of immediacy and perception management, seems anachronistic.

Until the late 1990s being a Media Operations Officer was often seen as a rather dead-end appointment. However, through the lessons of Yugoslavia, Northern Ireland and Sierra Leone, the Ministry of Defence has gradually moved higher-calibre officers into these positions, particularly where they would be acting as spokesmen for senior officers, or for British policy. Media Operations Officers now undertake a formal training course in order to test the skills of the embryonic media operator; this includes a phase in simulated field conditions, with actors and real journalists appearing in scenarios such as the discovery of mass graves and the death of civilians—so-called 'collateral damage'—. However, British officers have a far smaller support staff to call upon than their US counterparts. A few military combat camera teams exist, which were used to great effect throughout Operation Enduring Freedom in Afghanistan. These are professional military photographers sent away to train, normally with the BBC, in the art of electronic newsgathering. They have proved an invaluable asset and their output is often out of all proportion to their small number. However, for most Media Operations Officers the major support is that offered by the MoD Press Office and its updated versions of 'Lines to Take' on particular issues, 'Key Themes and Messages' and 'Questions and Answer' material. These briefing notes provide the central government direction on what can and, often more important, what cannot be said. These factors explain why and how the calibre of such officers has been gradually improved. In a dynamic environment such as conflict it is inevitable that they will be required to construct their own material to react to a rapidly changing operational situation. Again, unlike their US counterparts, British Media Operations Officers are normally poorly equipped for the job. Lieutenant Commander Mark Hankey, the Royal Navy media officer in Kuwait, had no secure communications facilities and relied on a British-anchored mobile phone for communication. Similar problems beset nearly all deployed staff to a greater or lesser extent during Operation Iraqi Freedom. Another problem that seemed to bedevil British media operations staff was the attitude of some senior officers. The author witnessed this in Bahrain, where, in stark contrast to US Navy colleagues who seemed well attuned and receptive to the needs of the US media, one senior and influential RN officer continuously referred to all media as 'the enemy', regularly berating his media operations team in front of his other officers, as if it was directly responsible for the media's perceived shortcomings.

The British did have one highly effective weapon in their armoury—the so-called *Green Guide*. This flimsy and seemingly insignificant publication set out the agreed principles governing the activities and conduct of correspondents attached to British forces. As we see later in this chapter, that guide proved invaluable in prescribing the relationship between the military and the media. The United States did not enjoy the utility of any equivalent document.

These two groups of officers came together for Operation Iraqi Freedom. The way in which they conducted their relationship with the world's media proved to be very different, seemingly predicated on experience of their own domestic media, the prevailing state of domestic public opinion, and their familiarity with the region and its culture and customs.

From the two governments' viewpoints it would seem that the Americans started their Arab media campaign along more promising lines. Apparently recognising that the Arab channels had an important and influential role to play in the coming conflict, and noting in particular the reach and audience of Al-Jazeera, the US military assigned a military liaison officer to work directly with the channel. The Public Affairs Officer appointed, Lieutenant Josh Rushing, joined CENTCOM staff in Doha from the US Military Public Affairs Office in Hollywood, California. In a series of meetings he promised that the channel would have access to the US forces in any forthcoming conflict. 'We have gone to great lengths to reach out to Al-Jazeera', Captain Frank Thorp, one of the spokesmen appointed at an early stage to work within Central Command, told the *New York Times*. 'We have a very warm relationship and work with them [Al-Jazeera] on a daily basis.'[2] Yet Rushing himself had a slightly different angle: 'The overall conduct of the channel is highly politicized and confrontational towards us.'[3]

The *New York Times* piece went on: 'Several United States Central Command press officials accepted an invitation to a barbecue in this desert city at the home of its news director, Omar Beck.' This generated considerable interest and not a little fury in the US ultra-conservative lobby. Various websites carried condemnation of the US policy of embracing 'Bin Laden's station', and at the same time the channel laid itself open to criticism from its detractors in the Arab world. However, such developments appeared to bode well. The Americans were taking the Arab world and its sensitivities seriously in its planning—they had already shown consideration for Islam the previous year when the war against the Taliban and its Al-Qaeda lodgers was renamed from Operation Infinite Justice to Operation Enduring Freedom.[4] The change had been prompted to avoid upsetting Muslims, who believe that infinite justice could be dispensed by God alone. President Bush himself had already made attempts to distinguish between terrorists, who were the object of the war, and the Arab world as a whole. In his address to the nation on 20 September 2001 he said: 'The enemy of America is not our many Muslim friends; it is not our many Arab friends.'[5] However, it was unfortunate that this speech also carried the 'with us or against us' clause, since there were many in the world who felt unable to commit firmly to either option. Nevertheless it is apparent that in the early stages of the operation some consideration was afforded to Arab sensitivities.

Another indication of the apparent seriousness of US intentions was the willingness of senior Administration officials to appear on Arab channels, and Al-Jazeera in particular, for interviews. In the words of Al-Jazeera's communications director, Jihad Ali-Ballout: 'We will happily provide a platform for anyone in the US to expound their views.'[6] At first that was a platform that the US was happy to use, and after 9/11 nearly all of the senior figures in the Bush Administration had granted it interviews. The National

Security Adviser Condoleezza Rice did so during the operations in Afghanistan and again in March 2003. While much of this second interview was about the developing crisis in Iraq, the interviewer addressed what many in the Arab world saw as the duality of US policy—the apparent condemnation of Palestinian acts of violence while either condoning or offering no opinion on Israeli attacks:

'In every statement from President Bush and top US Officials… and in a way that creates discomfort amongst the Arab viewer or listener, whenever Israeli civilians are killed, there is clear and harsh condemnation. This is a duty. But very simple and vague terms are used when Israel kills Palestinian civilians in cold blood…. like "The US is worried." Why aren't clear condemnations issued whenever innocents are killed on either side?'

The National Security Adviser picked her words carefully:

'The loss of innocent life… whether Palestinian or Israeli or Arab or American.. is too much.'[7]

In the lead-up to combat operations in Iraq it was the Secretary of State (and former Chief of US Military Staff) Colin Powell who became the most prolifically engaged with the channel. In a live interview on 8 November 2002 he discussed the unanimous and surprise agreement to UN Security Council Resolution 1441. The interviewer was particularly interested in the discussion that led to the unexpected agreement of both France and Russia. Although the interview was short, Powell had been well briefed by his staff, ending the interview by wishing the interviewer '*Ramadan Karim*'.[8] Powell again appeared on the channel on 26 March 2003, just days after the outbreak of hostilities. He was asked if the United States would respond to a proposed call for a ceasefire by some Arab states. His answer was non-committal and referred to the UN Resolutions and the 'serious consequences' that flowed from them. The interview was short and once again Powell used it to his advantage, hammering home the Administration's message of liberation and not occupation: 'We come to help them, not to oppress them. We come to give them a chance for a better life, not to take away their freedom or in any way harm them.'[9]

The reception of this known Administration 'dove' contrasted with that of some of the more hard-line 'hawks'. However, this is not to say that Powell was not himself critical of the channel. He is on record as stating: 'When a particular outlet, Al-Jazeera, does such a horrible job presenting the news, and when it takes every opportunity to slant the news, present it in the most outrageous way, then we have to speak out, and we have.'[10] As the conflict dragged on, the animosity between the United States and the channel intensified (the trigger perhaps being the images of captured and dead Coalition soldiers) and it was not till June 2003 that Colin Powell again appeared on the channel. He was asked what the United States was doing to enhance its image within the Arab world. In a long and uninterrupted answer he explained that the world must judge the United States by its results:

'The people of the region will see that the Iraq people are going to have a better life; that their infrastructure is going to be repaired, their children are going to schools, that their press is free and that they are interacting with the rest of the world.... The people of the region will see over time that in the United States they have a nation that comes for no purpose other than to seek peace in the region and help the people of the region achieve a better life.'[11]

Secretary for Defense Donald Rumsfeld has been one of the channel's most consistent critics. His interview with the presenter Jamil Azer on 25 February 2003 started almost with an apology:

*Azer (Al-Jazeera)* 'Sir, there are lots of questions which we feel they might be sort of critical of the United States but we feel that Al-Jazeera's audience would like to know your views about. It isn't that we are trying to find fault or anything like that.'

*Rumsfeld* 'Fair enough. If I hear a question that has a premise in it that's inaccurate I'll state that and say that.... Good.'[12]

The long interview that followed focused on the UN Resolutions and the evidence of weapons of mass destruction: 'Well they do exist... it's a fact,' proclaimed Rumsfeld when their existence was questioned by Azer.

The apparent understanding and conciliatory tones of Colin Powell's interviews contrasted with the sharper and more direct exchanges with Donald Rumsfeld and caused some intellectual interest within the Al-Jazeera channel itself. Samir Khader is a forthright Jordanian journalist who moved to Al-Jazeera after many years working for French television. His views became famous as a result of the documentary-maker Jehane Noujaim's film 'Control Room', which followed the channel's fortunes through the Iraq war. The programme has proved enormously popular even in the West, and as a result some of the participants have developed a minor cult following. Khader was interviewed by the 'In these Times' reporter Kevin Kim in June 2004, and was asked how he reconciled his desire to send his children to America for their education (which he had stated in the film) when he himself was decidedly anti-US. His answer not only summed up the thoughts of a great many Arabs but also shed some light on the channel's view of Powell and Rumsfeld:

'We at Al-Jazeera try to make a difference between a country's government and its people. We try our best to explain to viewers that this US foreign policy has nothing to do with the American people's values, ethics, ideals and dreams. But people tend to confuse the government with the people, so we try to emphasise this is the policy of this particular administration, with discrepancies among its members. Take for example the position of the US Secretary of Defense [Donald Rumsfeld] and Secretary of State [Colin Powell]. Sometimes personally I wonder how these two men can exist in the same administration. In our coverage we make distinctions between them.'[13]

It would appear that US interests might be better communicated to the Arab world by the former General than the Defense Secretary! One notable absentee from the channel has been the President himself. Despite advice from the State Department, he has refrained from appearing on Al-Jazeera. When photographs of abuses against Iraqi prisoners at Abu Ghraib prison appeared in the US in early 2004, the President chose to address the Arab world through the US-funded and -based Al-Hurra television. Its limited reach (a result of its lack of credibility with the wider Arab audience) meant that the message was not well or widely received in the Arab world.

Britain also seemed willing to engage with the Arab world at a senior level. Tony Blair had first appeared on the channel in October 2001 to discuss the war in Afghanistan, and this interview will be best remembered for its very last question, in which the interviewer said: 'I have read, I think in *The Times*, that you read about Islam. What do you know about Islam?' The Prime Minister appeared to hesitate slightly before explaining that he enjoyed the message of the Koran. His clear lack of detailed understanding no doubt prompted the rider that he enjoyed it but only 'insofar as it can be translated'.

Perhaps most significantly, Alistair Campbell, the British government Communications Manager, met Al-Jazeera's managing director and chief editor on 10 January 2003 in the Cabinet Office complex in Whitehall. The purpose of the meeting was not clear, unlike the outcome. The channel believed that Campbell used the opportunity to express reservations about the channel's coverage of events. In particular the issue of Bin Laden's tapes was raised. Campbell was concerned that the channel was airing tapes that would incite killing, either overtly or through encrypted messages. The idea of 'secret' or 'coded' messages was an early mainstay of official criticism of the channel's output. Given the length and number of Bin Laden's videos[14] and the tiny amount of footage actually aired after an editing process, this seems an absurdity; nevertheless it became a stick with which the channel was frequently beaten.

The bulk of Arab media analysis and targeting was devolved to the Foreign and Commonwealth Office's Islamic Media Monitoring Unit, headed by the Arabist Gerard Russell. The small team, based in the FCO's London headquarters, is tasked with monitoring Arab media and advising the government on the Arab presentational implications of particular events. Russell regularly appeared on all of the channels—forward operating from an office in Jordan for much of the war—to explain the British position. His fluency in Arabic was appreciated by the Arab channels and added credibility to his case. The British forces also found a fluent Arabic speaker, Captain Hisham Hilawi, who for over eighteen months presented the view of the British military. His linguistic abilities too were well received by the Arab media.

Although Britain had had a small contingent of Media Operations Officers based for some time at Bagram airport in Afghanistan, the first British Media Operations Officers for the forthcoming Iraq War (what Britain would refer to as Operation Telic) were not deployed to the region till November 2002 when they were called forward to participate, alongside their American Public Affairs Officer (PAO) colleagues, in Exercise Internal Look. At a background brief held for the media in December 2002 a Pentagon official told reporters:

'Exercise Internal Look is designed to exercise the command, control and communications ability of Central Command Headquarters and all of our different component commands spread throughout our AOR [area of responsibility] in other parts of the world. This is going to be a very complex computer-based and assisted exercise that will not involve combat forces.... The CENTCOM battle staff and military personnel are going to participate in realistic but obviously fictitious military scenarios.

What this exercise is designed to do is to hone our battle staff's ability to command from a forward-deployed location while maintaining seamless connectivity with our folks back here in Tampa at the Central Command main headquarters.'[15]

While Internal Look was certainly a process management exercise, the fictitious military scenario referred to was actually the invasion plan for Iraq, codename OPLAN 100V. During the course of the exercise a series of 'vignettes' would be modelled, each one charting the progression of the Coalition invasion across different time periods. The first vignette considered the actual invasion phase while later ones considered the likely progress of operations—hours, days and weeks later. Curiously, given the importance of the information campaign, media operations did not form a major component of the exercise and, almost as an afterthought, the British directing staff threw in the rather lame Britain-only scenarios. The wider effects of the planned Information Operations (IO) campaign were briefly considered, in particular the leaflet drops designed to encourage mass surrender by Iraqi forces. For all its limitations, however, the exercise did present an opportunity for US and British media officers to meet and consider their strategy for the conflict to come. It would also be the first time that the different strategies for media handling became apparent. In their Public Affairs Guidance (PAG) signal of 10 February 2003 the US Department of Defense stated: 'Media will have long-term, minimally restrictive access to US air, ground and naval forces through embedding.'[16] Embedding was to become the cornerstone of the US media campaign. More journalists than ever before would be trained and embedded with US units. Indeed by the start of fighting in March more than 550 journalists were embedded as war correspondents with Coalition forces. As the build-up of US troops continued, many of the ideas disseminated by the US media travelled with them, as did the memory of a previous war against Saddam, when the world *had* united behind America.

For those who would look after the media the battle-lines began to take shape. The US media appeared to support the coming conflict unequivocally, and as their reporters began their preparations for embedding, the PAOs looked forward to a mutually beneficial working relationship. For their British colleagues the job would be a little more difficult. The British press was split down the middle; two of the country's biggest-selling tabloids had diametrically opposed views. Although TV channels were much less polarised, the challenge of catering for a much less respectful, far more inquisitive and largely distrusting and sceptical press could not be exaggerated. However, the British press was a known quantity to the MoD, and with the judicious selection of a heavyweight media manager the problem was not insurmountable. However, there was a third group with which the Coalition would have to work—the Arab satellite news media, which unsurprisingly had very different views from those of their US counterparts. Arguably the most influential of these channels was Al-Jazeera.

## *War correspondents*[17]

For the Coalition the story of the war would be told by those members of the media who had elected to embed with military units, sharing the discomfort, danger and realism of the servicemen and servicewomen alongside whom they worked with millions of viewers around the world. Although not a new phenomenon, the number of media places allocated was on an unprecedented scale. Yet even these did not meet demand; the British MoD's places were over-subscribed by a factor of five, and the Americans experienced a similar scramble for places. Knowing that the allocation of slots had the potential to develop into a combative and argumentative process, Britain handed it over to the press and broadcast associations, providing them with numbers and asking them to allocate individuals. As predicted, the process did not go smoothly. Many

British defence correspondents build up close relationships with the armed forces, and they now called upon their senior contacts to ensure they got the places they wanted. Most popular would be the Royal Marines, and the tabloid *Sun* newspaper, often (self-) billed as the forces' favourite, was angry to find that the Press Association had placed with the Marines not their correspondents but the defence correspondent from the rival *Daily Mirror*, the paper at the vanguard of the anti-war campaign. Other seemingly crass decisions included the placing of units of TV reporters with no cameramen and newspaper photographers with no copy-writers. As a consequence many media organisations, including those who had embed places, also positioned journalists in-theatre as unilaterals, who planned to move around the battlefield and remain outside military control and protection. Others, notably the Arab media, based themselves in Baghdad. Both were dangerous assignments. A noticeable omission was that of Arab correspondents, who were excluded from the British embed programme. An indication of why that might have happened, and where the British government's emphasis lay, is given by Squadron Leader Tom Rounds, who was the officer responsible for the management of the British embedding process. When asked why there were no Arab media he explained: 'The drives for the decision was due to the relatively small number of slots available.... We felt the primary audience was UK plc.... We had to win the media battle and public opinion for our forces and the government position.'[18]

Across the Atlantic, and for all the initial enthusiasm, only a handful of Arab media were provided places with the US forces, which in all but one instance failed to materialise. For the Arab media the news would be reported from Baghdad, from between the lines or from Coalition briefing centres.

The Coalition Press Information Centre (CPIC) established at the Hilton Hotel in Kuwait City became a hub for Coalition media management, and at the end of hostilities it had registered nearly 3,000 journalists. Similar centres existed in Bahrain to cover naval operations, and at CENTCOM forward headquarters in Qatar.

There were four levels to the British media strategy. It recognised that embedded journalists and unilaterals would gain the most interesting and dramatic news coverage, but because of their position this was always at the unit level. With so many embed reports flooding back it would be difficult for audiences to put them into context. Accordingly the British anticipated that the major focus of their efforts would be the PICs. These were established in Doha for the Coalition (headed by a New Zealander, Group Captain Al Lockwood), in Kuwait for British ground forces (headed by Colonel Chris Vernon) and for the Navy at the US Fifth Fleet headquarters in Bahrain (headed by the author, Lieutenant Commander Steve Tatham). The final layer was for the political briefings which would be made at the regular Downing Street press conferences and at the Ministry of Defence press briefing theatre in the old ballroom of the Metropole building (formerly a hotel) in Northumberland Avenue, London.

Yet all did not go according to plan. From the outset the two main Coalition partners regarded the conops (concept of operations) differently. The embeds were the major thrust of the US campaign and, as is described later, the Doha briefing centre achieved mixed results. More important, perhaps, the images that the war correspondents were able to record took on a life all of their own. Footage of minor skirmishes and fire-fights was irresistible to news editors, and therefore given prominence. While some imagery was of considerable merit, much was boring, and the sole reason for its being aired was that it came from the front lines of a major conflict. Networks showed tanks charging across barren desert landscapes, their onboard commentators trying hard to sensationalise otherwise drab and tedious visual images. Of course there were also moments of extraordinary realism and excitement. Sky TV showed again and again the moment a British unit engaged with and destroyed an Iraqi army tank with a Milan rocket-launcher. As in previous wars, the coverage was never quite extended to include a record of the aftermath of the attack—of the death and destruction caused by the missile. Nonetheless the imagery was such that no briefing officer in Doha or Kuwait could hope to match its stunning visual attraction.

The death of unilateral reporters, in particular ITN's Terry Lloyd, who was killed filming between the lines of battle, convinced many organisations that the risk was too great for the objective and neutral imagery stories that were returned. Consequently many unilateral correspondents were either pulled out of theatre completely or were latched on to British and Coalition units as surrogate embeds. This was particularly true of Sky TV whose commentator Jeremy Thompson would move between British front-line units and anchor the evening's news coverage from whichever unit he found. Thus the two major Coalition partners went to war with very different ideas about the management of the media; ideas that potentially and inevitably clashed as the war progressed.

David Howard, a civil servant, was head of the MoD Communications Planning Unit (CPU) in the Director General Corporate Communications (DGCC) office of the Ministry of Defence. He and his small team were responsible for coordination of the media operation across other British government departments, particularly the FCO and the Department for International Development (DFID), and the other Coalition partners. They were subordinate to the Strategic Communications Unit established by Alistair Campbell across Whitehall and in the Downing Street Cabinet Office. Throughout Operation Telic the CPU was tasked with providing detailed presentational advice on military posture and profile, often attempting to balance the requirements of politicians against the expectations of the military. It was a difficult job and not always managed successfully. In advance of the start of combat operations a virtual moratorium was imposed on British military media facilities. The public's gaze was directed towards the political and diplomatic efforts being made to avert the impending crisis. Howard described the strategy in simple terms: 'We did not want to appear that we were committed to go to war.'

This created significant difficulties in-theatre. Many British troops were already attaching to US military units, which had no such moratorium in place. Thus when US networks joined US units, the British detachments were required to hide away from view. This became particularly acute out at sea on the US aircraft carriers. The US Navy was running back-to-back media facilities from its Press Information Centre in Bahrain, yet the British team there was unable even to confirm that the Royal Navy had arrived in-theatre. Some senior RN officers had been loaned to these US ships to act as advisers and liaison officers. They regularly reported their difficulties with embarked US media, who were fascinated by their presence and hugely disappointed when they were asked to turn their cameras off. Matters finally came to head as frustrated British 'hacks' vented their spleen with a series of critical and at times comical articles about the level of preparedness of British troops. It was to be a hard-hitting and pointed e-mail from the senior British civilian media adviser in Doha, sent directly to Alistair Campbell in the 10 Downing Street strategic information centre, that finally caused a relaxation in the policy.[18]

Howard was categorical when he considered the target audience of his unit's output, echoing the comments of Squadron Leader Rounds: 'There is no doubt that the focus is the British media.' He of course acknowledged that the Arabic media were important, but he saw their utility from the angle of information operations—trying to influence and implant messages. For him this was a move away from media into information operations and was not an area in which he felt that he either should or could work. However, he was candid in his assessment of its success: 'Information strategy for the campaign was run by Director General Operational Policy in the MoD. It never seemed to work very well.'

The dissemination of advice and guidance to media operations teams in-theatre was a convoluted yet carefully managed process that originated inside Number 10. The working day began around 5.15 a.m. when the overnight planning team would come together to produce a planning grid for the briefing of the so-called 'O Group'—the Chief of Defence Staff and other key advisers. This planning grid would attempt to identify the key messages of the day (remembering that the theatre of operations was a full three hours ahead of London). The Prime Minister would be briefed between 8.30 and 9 a.m., and following this, and any amendments that were forthcoming, detailed guidance would be sent out to theatre by the DGCC. This would arrive in theatre by e-mail or telephone at around lunch-time and would be used for the daily briefings of the media. Although this is an oversimplification of a complicated planning process, there is an obvious omission—the link into the US strategy. Howard was asked where this was in the planning process, and once again was candid: 'There wasn't! We hoped to have the main links in Qatar. It did not work out as anticipated, as the US took a different approach to the way that we wished to run it. They did not brief.'

Howard believed that one of the fundamental difficulties between the two countries was the very different attitude towards the war taken by their media: 'The US had an incredibly compliant press.' He illustrated this with a discussion he had with the senior British civilian media adviser in Doha, Simon Wren. Wren had been asked by a member of the US press corps in Doha if they could interview the head of British forces, Air Vice Marshal Brian Burridge.

So that he could prepare Burridge properly, Wren asked them what sort of questions they wanted to ask, and the US correspondent replied: 'What questions do you want me to ask him?' Compliance such as this meant that the Americans, and the Pentagon in particular, had little understanding of the type of pressures that some of the other Coalition governments would face. However, he also acknowledged that there were more fundamental differences with the United States that should have been resolved earlier: 'We should have cemented relationships with the Pentagon. The Director General and the Director of News went out and met the top of the office but it never really developed.'[19]

The fragility of the relationship was borne out on the first three nights of the war. As Howard reported, 'We got caught out badly.' The first incident was the loss of a US helicopter in which British personnel were travelling. On the second night the two British helicopters from the aircraft-carrier *Ark Royal*, one carrying a US Navy exchange pilot, were lost. On the third night a British Tornado was hit and destroyed by a US missile battery. In all three incidents cross-Atlantic cooperation was lacking, with the two organisations putting out different lines on the loss of their personnel. Howard was frustrated by the absence of any clear dialogue: 'I spent 40 per cent of the time building relations to sort out a strategy. It was very much one-way traffic; we had to go to them. On the first night when the helicopter went down, we didn't want to say anything. Yet within half an hour of it happening the US had issued a statement saying that British personnel were on board and that there were no survivors.'

Howard believed that special consideration was given to the needs of the Arab media, although this came mainly from the British side. The Minister for Defence Procurement, Lord Bach, was asked to become the British government's focal point for ministerial briefings to Arab media. 'He gave lots of interviews', Howard recalled; 'not all were successful.' He believed that the interviews were often played fairly but that the commentary from the correspondent or studio anchor, after the interviews, was disappointingly negative—a point noted by Sky TV's Arab media logger. But how did Howard learn what was or was not being said? 'We got feedback from the BBC Caversham media monitoring unit to monitor channels.' That feedback disappointed people and to a certain extent, in Howard's view, expectations were lowered. It was not until the end of the conflict that the government made a substantial push for Arab opinion, by running a bespoke Arab media facility out of London, directly into Iraq. Yet again Howard noted that this was outside his unit's responsibilities.

For Britain the embedding process began in January 2003 when, as part of the contingency planning process, the three armed services were invited to consider how many journalists they would be able to accommodate should conflict occur. The entire process would be based on a document negotiated between the MoD and the major British broadcast and press organisations: the so-called *Green Guide*.[20] In its preface the *Green Guide* states its objectives: 'The practical arrangements for enabling media representatives to report events...including the MoD plans for representative numbers of correspondents to accompany British Forces in the front line.' The *Green Guide* is particularly important on issues of operational security. It recognises that sensitive and secret information may became known to journalists during the course of their embed, and its Annex provides examples of such information: military movements, casualties, place-names and tactics. Recognising that the list cannot be complete, the guide states: 'Correspondents will be advised on current restrictions—which will differ from operation to operation.'

Given the stated objectives of the Coalition campaign, an additional and important requirement for those journalists who would embed with its forces was to undertake biological and chemical weapon training. Those joining warships would additionally require training in survival at sea. This became an 'expectation management' problem in itself; the very attendance of journalists on such courses came to be seen as an indicator of likely military action. For media organisations this was a sign that conflict was inevitable, a message that conflicted with the one being sent from the Downing Street Press Office of continued diplomacy through the UN.

The deployment of media into theatre would present similar problems. If they appeared too early, this would send similar messages; if too late the media would miss the start of the war and claims of censorship would result. Their subsequent arrival in the early weeks of March was just in time; for the Coalition's military commanders it became an extra worry as they completed their last-minute plans. However, the *Green Guide* provided a welcome safety net, and paradoxically also proved advantageous to the embedded journalists. Commanders began entrusting information to the media, knowing that the regulations in the *Green Guide* would see it preserved. According to Nick Pollard, head of news at SkyNews, 'They [embedded Sky journalists] got very detailed briefings from their units and were told the grand plan in advance.'[21] In Doha, the BBC defence correspondent Paul Adams received similar information: 'Alerting me to developments that had yet to unfold, trusting me not to reveal them until reports from the field suggested that they were under way.'[22] Such briefings were soon regarded as mutually beneficial. For the media events did not come as a big surprise, and they were better able to shape their reports, while the military began to feel comfortable with their correspondents when they realised that the *Green Guide* actually worked.

The *Green Guide* became a vital tool in the management of British embedded media. Yet its contents had been negotiated only with British media, and with one (American) exception it catered only for the embed of British nationals from British media organisations. In hindsight the MoD has realised that this was a mistake.[23] Despite initial good intentions, operational security remained paramount, and officials were simply not prepared to risk engaging with media organisations of other nationalities, including the Arab media. This policy called for careful management on the ground. Lieutenant Colonel Sean Tully was managing one of the forward Press Information Centres. He recalls trying to be fair with the Arab media: 'I did not allow *any* of the media into our Ops tent to view the Secret Mapping, as I knew I could not be seen to exclude Al-Jazeera.... I waited until they left.'[24]

For all the enthusiasm at higher levels, on the ground the Americans were not much different. The Al-Jazeera correspondent Amr El-Kakhy had found a place with US troops, yet his embed was to end prematurely. He spent time with the US Marines, but became frustrated by the total absence of access to information. However, a much more sinister event was to herald his departure. Free Iraqi Forces directly threatened him—accusing his station of being a supporter of Saddam Hussein's regime. Concerned for his safety, he approached the Marines commanding officer who appeared unable or unwilling to help. El-Kakhy chose to end his 'embed'.

Al-Arabiya also secured a place with US forces, yet this too ended in failure when its correspondents became detached from their unit and were captured and imprisoned by Iraqi troops. Indeed for all the good intentions and hard work at senior levels, the relationship never developed properly on the ground. The failure of the Arab embeds was an obvious blow to the Coalition information campaign. Some far-sighted media staff did attempt to redress locally what was evidently an unsatisfactory situation. Recognising the importance of Arab media, the British military spokesman Colonel Chris Vernon had managed to circumvent the system and move a small Al-Jazeera team forward with the British army headquarters. Vernon worked hard to accomplish this because he viewed them as 'a key and credible conduit for [British] key messages'.[25] However, the subsequent decision not to brief them on the operational plan resulted in their departure early in the operation. Captain Roxie Merritt was head of US Navy public affairs at Fifth Fleet headquarters in Bahrain. In an e-mail on 11 March[26] she requested the US aircraft-carrier *Constellation* to embark Al-Jazeera journalists directly from Qatar—the normal embarkation point, Bahrain being closed to Al-Jazeera after a programme to which the Bahrain authorities had taken exception. The embarkation inexplicably failed to materialise.

Yet the Arab media were perfectly prepared to sign up to any of the Coalition's guidelines if they had been asked. Regarding Britain's *Green Guide* Jihad Ali-Ballout considered Al-Jazeera's position: 'Al-Jazeera realise that there have to be some rules of the game— we will try to get away with as much as we can, but as long as we can get a balanced picture we will play the game.'[27]

The issue of balance is important. A recurring criticism levelled at the embedding process is that journalists become so dependent on the military that they may lose their objectivity. This was a serious concern for those embedded with front-line infantry units; Nick Pollard of SkyNews believed that it did not happen with his reporters: 'Our embeds did not go native and report with a strongly pro-military stance.' It is debatable what influence, conscious or otherwise, of living, eating, sleeping and being shot at alongside front-line troops can have. The BBC commissioned Professor Justin Lewis of Cardiff University to investigate the whole issue of embedding and bias, and his study suggests that Pollard's observation is correct, at least for the British media. There is no similar study for US units, but one can speculate. Given the largely unconditional support for the war among many US media organisations, it seems unlikely that their experience of embedding was anything but positive.

The absence of Arab media with Coalition forces was clearly a wasted opportunity and served only to reinforce unhelpful ideas of marginalisation and lack of interest in Arab public opinion. Placing Arab media with forces would undoubtedly have been a risk, but there were also potential benefits. Arab audiences would have been able to view Coalition soldiers as individuals, rather than as an oppressive and invading presence. By building up a rapport, in the same way as many Western journalists, they might have been able to see the care and attention that the Coalition claimed was paid to selecting targets and the way in which captured Iraqi troops and injured civilians were attended to. Their presence would have required careful management; obviously Arabic-speaking Coalition minders with sufficient rank and stature to ensure the channels received the access they wanted were a pre-requisite. But the imagination and innovation needed to accomplish this were absent. An Arab journalist, writing in the Egyptian newspaper *Al-Wafd*, warned the official American media policy-makers that they would have to 'use Arab voices and pens ... since Arab audiences suspect any direct American media.'[28]

## Doha: the Coalition Press Information Centre

For the Coalition the centrepiece of the information campaign was the purpose-built Hollywood-designed press information centre at CENTCOM's forward headquarters in Qatar. It was staffed by US Public Affairs Officers, and a heavyweight Washington public relations strategist, James Wilkinson, was drafted in to help orchestrate the media campaign. With considerable experience of the White House, Wilkinson had the job of running the overall US media strategy, making sure the message was managed correctly, and that the embedded programme worked in the field. He worked directly with the CENTCOM commander General Tommy Franks on each of his media appearances. Franks had made it clear from the outset that he was no Norman Schwarzkopf and told the Defense Secretary: 'I do not deal with the media.'[29]

Wilkinson was accustomed to working with senior political figures, as well as explaining controversial US foreign policy. He had headed the Coalition Press Information Centres based in Washington, London and Islamabad during operations against the Taliban in Afghanistan. He had also acted as spokesman for the Defense Secretary, Donald Rumsfeld, during the presidential transition. Indeed it was Rumsfeld himself who asked him to be Franks's strategic communications manager—a job that Wilkinson embraced eagerly. He came from a military family and the operation would be highly personal; his brother was an officer in the US 101st Airborne and would see action on the ground in Iraq, while Wilkinson himself was a lieutenant in the US Naval Reserve.[30]

Conscious of the importance that the United States attached to the facility Britain decided to send its own 'big hitter' to mastermind its strategy. As the ex-Ministry of Defence chief press officer and the current press secretary to the Secretary of State for Transport, Simon Wren had ample experience for the job. Perhaps most important, he had earned the respect of the British media, to which he was not afraid to talk frankly and at times roughly, and which had previously nicknamed him 'the Bruiser'. He was the ideal choice; while he would orchestrate the British part of the campaign from behind the scenes, the spokesman would be Group Captain Alan Lockwood, the Royal Air Force officer already mentioned. A small British military staff was drafted in to assist, bringing the total Coalition staff of the Centre to around fifty people.

From the outset of the campaign the Americans and the British regarded the utility of the Doha centre differently. Colonel Paul Brook, the assistant director of Media Operations in the British

MoD, articulated a widely-held belief that the reports of the war correspondents on the ground would add to the picture being built by the Coalition staff in Doha.[31] But he and his senior British colleagues found the US view diametrically opposed to this concept: according to this view, war correspondents were the major, indeed primary source of information, and the Doha Press Centre was designed simply to supplement their reports. Certainly the principle that Doha was designed to provide a strategic overlay to the work of the embedded war correspondents was widely understood by British media operations staff, who soon became sceptical of the slick presentations of their US counterparts, which they felt were heavy on special effects and light on detail. Wren recalls the US presentational style: 'They were very reliant upon the stage-managed once-per-day press conference, where they put out as little information as possible—they would leave it at that.' He goes on to describe the relationship between the Americans and British:

'There was never enough detail or information.... This was an American strategy that we did not feel comfortable with at all and it was not what they said they were going to do.... We briefed the Brits [press] quietly around the back.... We could not do that with US papers because it would have kicked the legs out from under them.'[32]

The difference in strategy became a problem, and Wren recalls heated debates with the US staff: 'We tried to get them to change their tune, and in the end we just went our own way—we just had to. Our media would not have accepted the paucity of information that the Americans were giving out.'[33] In short, he says, the US had 'no strategy for engaging with the media—period.'[34]

Of course, it was not only the military staff who had difficulties—the resident journalists shared their frustrations. The BBC defence correspondent Paul Adams had been sent to Qatar to provide a strategic overview of the reports of embedded media around the battlefield, and he too was frustrated by the absence of information: 'The White House media relations hot-shot appointed as [General] Tommy Franks's chief spokesman was affable when you were lucky enough to run into him but was generally conspicuous by his absence.'[35] Adams refers to the behind-the-scenes briefings given to the British media by the British representatives: 'It was an adult way of doing things and one that the Americans could not, or would not, emulate.'[36]

Some elements of the normally complacent US media voiced their own displeasure. In one of the most memorable moments of the war's briefings the *New York Magazine* media critic Michael Wolf asked the US military spokesman General Vincent Brooks a series of quick-fire questions: 'Why are we here? Why should we stay? What's the value of what we are learning at this multi-million dollar press centre?'[37] Wolf got more than he had bargained for. The short put-down by Brooks was followed by a series of more than 3,000 hate e-mails, inspired by elements of the US media, who called Wolf a potential traitor.

Wilkinson has acknowledged that the media were dissatisfied with the Centre: 'A lot of reporters in Qatar were angry that I did not spend more time with them, but I was overseeing the media for the whole operation.'[38] Yet he was unconcerned by the criticisms levelled at his team:

'Frankly, I see that the reality of the situation is that with all of those embedded reporters the news has got to come from the front lines. People on news desks did not want to see someone from Qatar on TV. They wanted someone who was on the ground in Iraq. Our best spokesmen were the troops in the field. It almost made Qatar less relevant because the reporters in the field were ahead of the game.'[39]

He did not share Simon Wren's recollection of heated disagreements between the US and British staff, although he admitted that the first forty-eight hours of the operation, when absolutely no briefings were provided at all, caused them difficulties:

'When the war began we did not talk to the press for forty-eight hours because we did not want to give Saddam our war plan. We still wanted him to think that we were attacking from the West. It was part of the confusion and that was a tough forty-eight hours for me personally and for Simon and the Brits. They wanted to brief, but General Franks said no, he thought that he should be the first one, and then the Coalition should brief together. I was in the room when the senior British officer [Air Vice Marshal Brian Burridge] went to General Franks and said "I want to brief" and General Franks said "No".'[40]

Unlike the British practice, where strategic messages were developed and maintained by Whitehall and then passed through Qatar for dissemination to media operations teams around theatre, the US team in Doha was much more focused on the tactical events on the ground—leaving strategic messages to come directly from the Pentagon and the White House. Every day Wilkinson would meet General Franks and senior staff from the intelligence, current and future operations divisions of the planning staff, and receive their direction on the points they were to make in their daily briefings. Invariably these came directly from General Franks and, as Wilkinson recalls, were:

'His best guidance on what he knew about the war plan and what was coming. We showed a lot of television, we wanted to show the Iraqi people that we were not bad people... We were interested in the reality out there and the reality was [for example] "What about the Atropine that you found in Basra?" We would see the President's words and use them, or Secretary Rumsfeld's words and use them.'[41]

Again, in contrast to the British practice, Wilkinson did not issue any guidelines to US troops: 'With so many journalists in the field their guidance was what they were shooting at. We would send out talking points, we would say that we are going to talk on points a, b and c today—that sort of thing. I just did not have the time, and looking back I wish I could have done better.'[42] The absence of clear guidelines to units was highlighted by a former US Navy Public Affairs Officer, Lieutenant John Oliveria:

We received one set of communication points from the DoD [Department of Defense] about two weeks before the war. The day the shooting started, those communication points were basically moot. We never received any communication points after that…it was very disorganised.[43]

Clear guidelines might well have been helpful in the battle for Arab opinion. Arab media may not have had embeds but there were still unilaterals moving between units. However, the prevailing attitude of distrust meant that when key Coalition objectives were met they were only recorded by Western media, which had neither the authority nor the authenticity to impress an Arab audience. Some Iraqi civilians had welcomed Coalition forces, yet the imagery recorded by Western media such as Fox News and CBS carried little credibility with Arab audiences, and language difficulties presented obvious problems. The benefits of engaging with Arab media were seemingly offset by the perceived risks.

Wilkinson did recognise the importance of Arab media to the US campaign, but his description of US strategy seems to lack incisive thinking:

'It was a multi-level strategy. One part of it was making sure they had seats in the front row of the auditorium where they were able to ask questions. You know, Americans are still learning how to do international media; the British were just so much better at this than us. Not calling on seven US reporters in a row before an Arab reporter is an important thing to do. I met with the Arab press as often as possible. We tried to make special accommodations for them, prayer rooms, that kind of thing. My strategy was that the Arab press just wanted to be treated equally.'[44]

He acknowledges that this strategy achieved mixed results: 'The biggest lesson that I learnt about the Arab media was that we still have so far to go before we even understand how to communicate with the Arab world. We did a good job making our spokesmen available to them but we have a long way to go.' He considers the wider issue of the Arab media: 'The only time that we [the US] ever get serious with Arab media is in war or [when we're] about to do something that they probably won't like. I think our nation has got to get better at public diplomacy and in the times when things aren't bad.'[45]

The British contingent was also very conscious of the importance of the Arab media. Simon Wren remembered the important role played by the Islamic Media Monitoring Unit in the Foreign and Commonwealth Office, and the considerable contact that existed between the two organisations. In particular Wren wanted to know what the Arab media were saying and what the prevailing mood was: 'In a conflict as contentious as Telic you have a duty to inform people what it is you are doing and why.'[46] Wing Commander Ian Tolfts of the Royal Air Force was one of the senior British media operations officers in the Doha Press Information Centre. He believed that while the British tried hard with the Arab media they got little from his US colleagues: 'I certainly don't recall seeing any particular efforts by the US in trying to engage with the Arab media.'[47]

Wilkinson had no formal feedback on what the Arab press was saying, and was reliant on what he himself saw and what he was told: 'I did not see a lot of that [transcripts of Arab media reporting]. I had seven or eight TVs in my office and General John Abizaid, the deputy commander, spoke Arabic and he told me what they were saying and the bias.'[48] On the issue of Arab media bias Wilkinson's assessment is uncompromising: 'They are totally biased.'[49] He said of his meetings with the Arab media:

'There were a couple of our private media sit-downs where they stated their bias. One Arab reporter opened up with "I hate your country and I hate your policy towards Israel and Palestine, and now I would like to ask you a question." So I said OK! I did have one night of animosity, the night that the Arab reporters ran the images of the maintenance company, and after that I did not meet with Al-Jazeera again. I thought it was over the top and not consistent with the respect for the families.'[50]

There is an evident contrast here between the way in which the British and the Americans felt their relationship with the Arab media evolved. Wren is sceptical of suggestions of bias: 'They would give a fair wind to both sides of the argument. Because of their very nature they would have more people on who are anti-US than are pro-US, but that's basically because the US failed to engage with them.'[51] Wren noted that although they regularly attended the formal press briefings the Arab media were much more appreciative of private off-camera briefings (both attributable and non-attributable): 'We did this because the US did not....they did not care what they thought. They only really cared about the US media—they weren't bothered about international media one iota.'[52]

Many in the Arab media would agree with his observations. Yet it was not just the absence of information that caused problems: within the CPIC elements of the US media were openly hostile to the Arab media. 'A lot of US media were flying the flag, they did not act like the BBC, they were just trotting out the line. NBC, CBS, CNN and Fox—they all did it... [there was] huge hostility towards Al-Jazeera, in particular, when they broadcast pictures of the captured US troops—they had cables cut, equipment stolen.'[53] But can such accusations really be credible? Surely the media were there to report news, not to adopt a partisan approach to other media? Inspection of a recent Fox TV programme is sufficient to prove that such accusations are credible:

'Hi, I'm Bill O'Reilly. Thanks for watching us. Tonight, why Al-Jazeera is a terrorist outfit. And I am just furious about this. That is the subject of this evening's "Talking Points" memo.

'Once again the Arab TV network, which broadcasts out of Qatar, is helping the most vicious terrorists on earth. Al-Jazeera broadcasts images of kidnapped CARE director Margaret Hassan crying and pleading for her life today. You'll remember she was abducted in Iraq last Tuesday. Seeing this poor woman suffering is an atrocity in itself, but Al-Jazeera goes much further. The terrorists know their evil deeds will be broadcast worldwide on that network, thereby giving these killers more incentive to commit their crimes against humanity. By playing along with the terrorists Al-Jazeera has become a terror organization itself. Remember, that network actually broadcast the beheading of American Paul Johnson in Saudi Arabia.'[54]

'The US government should immediately brand Al-Jazeera a terrorist organization, expel their employees and ban the network in America. Currently it can be seen on some subscription TV channels. Canada actually allows Al-Jazeera to broadcast on its cable band. That's incredible, and other nations do it as well. The Bush Administration should also put pressure on the Qatar government to close down Al-Jazeera. Because that outfit reaches 30 million Muslims, the USA can't take direct action, like bombing it, as that would cause even more violence. But it can demand accountability from Qatar. This whole thing makes me sick. And every American should realize what's going on here. Imagine that poor woman suffering every second of every day, knowing these killers could cut her head off at any time. Instead of broadcasting the woman's anguish, Al-Jazeera should be turning in the terrorists with whom they are working.'[55]

Given the influence of Fox TV, it is no wonder that the United States had such a jaded view of the Al-Jazeera channel. The CENTCOM facility would be challenging for everyone. Its very existence suggested to the media that history might repeat itself. In the 1991 Gulf war General Norman Schwarzkopf had provided charismatic and straight-talking press conferences. However, the lavish briefing theatre built in CENTCOM headquarters for OIF signposted and advertised more than the US wanted or was able to deliver. The world's press eagerly anticipated the 'theatre' that was to come— this time in the figure of General Tommy Franks. They were hugely disappointed, and regardless of operational intent the Americans scored an early defeat in their media strategy.

## Kuwait Press Information Centre

Established at the Hilton Hotel in Kuwait City the Press Information Centre became a hub of massive press activity. By the end of the war more than 3,000 members of the media had been registered by the centre's small staff—fifty US officers (under the command of an Army colonel) and six British officers. The centre comprised an operations room where the course of the battle was mapped and which was always off limits to the press. There was a press centre where people rang in to book facilities and request interviews, and then there was a small media analysis cell which aimed to track reporting and if necessary offer rebuttal or clarification. However, the war moved much too fast for this to be successful. The centre's work was hampered by an absence of secure communications devices (the Americans had two secure telephones, the British had none—British staff resorted to using their British mobile telephones to remain in contact). While some bespoke media analysis was available, outlets such as Paperboy.com (an online resource of the world's newspapers) proved more useful. Although the centre had televisions, the absence of interpreters meant that they were invariably tuned to British and US stations.

The chief British spokesman was Colonel Chris Vernon, while his specialist adviser was, like Simon Wren, extracted from the Department of Transport to assist the operation. He became the media adviser to the commander of British Land Forces, General Robin Brimms, as well as overseeing many of the facilities that were run both before and during combat operations. Marcus De Ville, at the time of writing chief press officer at the Department of Transport, recalled the early days of the campaign:

'[W]hen operations started I moved forward to the FPIC [Forward Press Information Centre], which is where we had all the top [embedded] correspondents. This was the media hub, from where the correspondents would file their reports. On Day Three of the operation we moved forward—10 kilometres inside of Iraq.'[56]

It is clear that considerable thought had been given to the British infrastructure necessary to support the media campaign. As in Doha, there were differences between the US and the UK media strategy. De Ville considers the reaction of the US officers he encountered:

'The US were really jealous of our FPIC; they had embedded correspond-ents and they had the Coalition centre south of Kuwait city so there was a huge gap—there was no equivalent. They were really just reliant upon their embedded media. I think the US were less sophisticated in their media handling in general. The personnel involved, the influence they had over their top command, the way they structured it—it was very rigid… they did not have the flexibility to change things as they went on.'

The initial stages of the operation were, as in the other PICS around theatre, difficult times for the British media handling staff. The British emphasis on diplomacy contrasted with a considerable US 'force on mind' campaign, which sought to illustrate the capability of the Coalition in a cohesive manner. De Ville struggled to differ-entiate between the two lines: 'I found it difficult because they [the US] would speak on our behalf without asking us. It was meant to be a joint press centre but the questions were so specific about the UK or the US and there were some occasions when they answered questions about us.'[57]

Another common problem across theatre was the unfamiliarity of US personnel with international media. In the words of De Ville the Americans were 'shocked by the British media—they found them sensationalist, disrespectful and unbalanced—their media were very nationalistic and very supportive. They did not realise how difficult the British media could be.'[58] If this were the reaction to the media of the major Coalition partner, what would be the US reaction to the Arab media?

Lieutenant Commander Mark Hankey, one of the Centre's British staff officers, recalled that even here Arab media were in the minority, Al-Arabiya, Abu Dhabi TV and the Kuwait News Agency being stuck in his memory as the major players. There were no military Arabic-speakers on the PIC staff, either British or American, although the Kuwaiti Ministry of Information and Moral Guidance had provided a liaison officer, an Army colonel, to assist in host nation liaison. Inevitably this saw him being pulled into the role of translator.

Hankey encountered few difficulties with the Arab media; indeed in comparison to their Western colleagues he found them polite and unassuming. Hankey was tasked by the author with arranging the media facility on board the humanitarian aid ship, the Royal Fleet Auxiliary (RFA) *Sir Galahad* and later, a similar mission on the RFA *Sir Percival*. During this latter trip he was able to make direct comparisons between the Arab and Western media. During its passage to the Iraqi port of Umm Qasr the ship received notification that Iraqi insurgents had been detected in the marshy areas around the Khawr Abd Allah (KAA) river and its transit was to be delayed while they were dealt with. Hankey took the decision to inform the media of the reason for the delay, explaining that for operational security this information was not to be relayed to anyone else and in particular not used as the basis of reporting. The Arab media scrupulously complied with the request; however, Fox News chose to break the embargo and was caught by Hankey broadcasting live to America the reasons for the delay. Generally Hankey found the Arab media rather more pleasant to work with than their Western counterparts: 'Western media were very demanding— they often had tantrums. I never saw a tantrum from the Islamic media—they were well-behaved and very courteous and polite.'

Did he see or experience any anti-US or anti-Coalition rhetoric from Arab channels?

'No, not really. I look at it like this. They were the Fox News of the Middle East in sensationalising what was going on. The showing of the bodies turned a few people against them, but when we did the same thing with Saddam's sons there was hardly any outcry at all. Ultimately they were just another fish in a big pool of fish and they wanted to come on [military organised] media facilities—they did not step out of line.'[59]

As in other Centres, Hankey found the US staff conducted their relationship very differently to the British. While they happily mixed with the world's media in and around the CPIC, they were also much more ponderous in the way they did their business. Hankey recalls that the British conducted one media facility after another while for the Americans one facility was a big and slow undertaking. While British forces moved freely around the area, transiting between Iraq and Kuwait, the Americans were preoccupied with matters of force protection, which made them very slow.

## Bahrain: the Maritime Press Information Centre

The smallest of the Press Information Centres, that in Bahrain, was staffed predominantly by US Public Affairs Officers under the command of Captain Roxie Merritt of the US Navy. Situated in the Diplomat Hotel in the diplomatic district of Manama, the hotel seemed to many a long way from the action. However, Bahrain was the headquarters of the US Fifth Fleet and as such, if journalists wished to embark with US ships, the only feasible access point was via the Carrier Onboard Delivery (COD) flights from the secure military section of Manama international airport to the US aircraft carriers positioned around the Gulf. Bahrain was also the head-quarters of both the US maritime commander and his British col-league Rear Admiral David Snelson. With more than thirty British warships and auxiliaries in the Gulf region the command and control of the operation was a huge task, and Snelson had a staff of more than fifty officers working from a small operations room in the base. The four-man British media operations contingent comprised the author, Lorraine Coulton (like Wren and De Ville, a government information and communications officer), a non-commissioned officer expert in photography, and a reserve officer. Together with their US counterparts they provided daily briefings to the small number of journalists encamped in the hotel. They also provided the backstop to the thirty-one members of the British and US media embedded on board Royal Navy warships. The embedded media's arrival in Bahrain had been just in time for the start of the war and after a detailed briefing (where their obvious lack of knowledge about both the military in general and the navy in particular caused disquiet) they were moved forward to join their units. With the exception of one US reporter the navy embeds were exclusively British and they were to remain with their units for between three and five weeks, those on the aircraft carrier and command ship *Ark Royal* electing to stay longest.

In Bahrain too the link with the Arab media was never properly made. The only representatives were the *Bahrain Times* and the *Gulf Daily News*—both English-language newspapers and staffed by Westerners. Their corporate line was largely hostile to the invasion, but they occasionally availed themselves of the press facilities on offer; their Arabic-language counterparts were never seen by either US or British staff. However, this did not stop the PIC coming to the attention of the indigenous Arab media, who printed a story identifying both the location (by room number) and names of staff manning what was referred to as a 'hate-filled propaganda centre, waging war against the Muslim world'.[60] An active Al-Qaeda cell was known to exist within the small kingdom, and the press centre was forced to move, if only to another hotel room, in order to preserve an element of security. Despite the best endeavours of the media teams, the local Arab press never attended briefings at the Centre, and its coverage remained staunchly negative.

One of the most important moments for the maritime component was the arrival of the RFA *Sir Galahad* into the Iraqi port of Umm Qasr. Although it carried only 230 tonnes of aid, its arrival was hugely symbolic. It was designed to demonstrate that the Coalition was determined that Iraq would be rebuilt (here, after all, were the first deliveries of aid arriving even as combat operation still continued) and that it had been scrupulous in its targeting (the ship arrived in a container port the size of Southampton which had not been damaged). A careful press facility was planned, in which twenty members of the press would join the ship in Kuwait and a significant group would meet it on arrival at Umm Qasr.

For the media management teams this became a significant battle, not only with the Arab press for which the facility was primarily designed but also, disappointingly, with some senior British military figures who felt that the domestic market was the most important audience and which failed to understand the impact that the *Sir Galahad* story might have on Arab opinion. Nevertheless, a small group of Arab media was finally embarked—mainly from the press, as well as a camera team from Abu Dhabi TV. Attendance by the Al-Jazeera TV channel was precluded by its antagonistic relationship with the Kuwaiti government (Kuwait refusing it access to the country), so the story was largely lost to the wider Arab audience.

# ARAB MEDIA, BIAS AND THE COALITION

'When the US Government declares that Al-Jazeera is against it, its counterparts in Doha, Manama, Riyadh and Kuwait City would be likely to say
'"Join the club".'—Yousef Al-Shouly, senior producer at Al-Jazeera.[1]

Bias is difficult to quantify. Any channel broadcasting around the
clock for the duration of an armed conflict will make mistakes. Facts
are not always clear-cut and journalists inevitably have to make
decisions based on the sometimes scanty information available to
them at the time. Arab journalists, in particular, felt that they did
not have access to either enough information or to quality information from Coalition sources.

The senior British government information officer Marcus De
Ville, in consultation with the Army spokesman Colonel Chris
Vernon, decided that only certain members of their media pool
should be briefed on the forthcoming operational plan. That media
should be briefed was a common enough occurrence across theatre,
and within the confines of the *Green Guide* it allowed members of the
media to contextualise their reporting. However, the briefing was
not made available to everyone. 'Al-Jazeera were with us,' De Ville
recalled, 'but when we briefed the media on the plan, under
embargo, we took the decision that we could not risk briefing
them... we briefed all the other media but not Al-Jazeera; as a
result of that they got fed up and left.'[2]

The freelance media consultant Ashraf Fouad, who was working for Abu Dhabi TV during the conflict, reported serious arguments with both British and US media operations staff over the issue of access. He summed up the Coalition forces' attempts to engage with the Arab media: 'The relationship went very badly, more than very badly.... They depended on Sky, BBC, CNN as the only providers of the truth. They started from the pretext that these people do not like us and that we do not like them—you are guilty until you can prove yourselves innocent.'[3]

In the book *Embedded* the Al-Jazeera journalist Amr El-Kakhy considers his embed with US Forces. Journalists from Reuter, Associated Press and CNN had received briefings about the forthcoming operational plan, and when he inquired why he had not been included in that briefing he was told: 'You know, guys, you are a station with a reputation.'[4] He believed that US troops had pre-conceptions about Arab channels. He was asked: 'Why should we have Al-Jazeera? They are the enemy, it is the potential enemy's channel.'[5] Once when Ashraf Fouad was trying to get into the town of Nassiriya he was stopped by a US officer, who told him: 'Unless you are a British or US journalist, you are not passing.' Fouad was very angry; he had all the necessary permits from the Coalition to allow his passage, yet he was still prevented from working.

Some Western journalists saw a different side to the Coalition's media handling. SkyNews' Head of News, Nick Pollard, recounted the experience of one of his journalists embedded with the US 101st Airborne Regiment: 'There is one incident with the 101st when the commanding officer of a unit broke off a fire-fight to give a live interview, and then resumed the fire-fight, because he understood the importance of serving the media.'[6] In the words of the BBC journalist Adam Mynott, who was embedded with the US 15th Marine Expeditionary Unit, the 'commander of the unit had opted for a policy of total disclosure to the journalists embedded with his troops.... before the attack took place I had a clear idea of how the war plan should unfold.'[7]

Not only were the Arab media hugely under-represented in comparison with their Western colleagues but it is clear that there existed a predisposition to be hostile towards them in general and Al-Jazeera in particular. Whatever the reason for this, it appears the Arab journalists themselves did not drive it. Most British media operations staff interviewed commented on the politeness of the Arab journalists they encountered. The antagonism appears to have been based on a perceived reputation rather than on personal experience—perhaps an example of channels with 'reputations'.

A common theme in interviews with Coalition media staff is their frustration at the absence of Arabic-speakers, not just for day-to-day existence but for the important task of analysing the Arab media's coverage. Most military personnel had little or no access to television or newspapers (most news coming either from radio or from internal communications sources such as the British *Sandy Times* newspaper[8]) Therefore most people in-theatre had little idea what Arab media correspondents were actually saying in their reports.

The British failure to embed Arab media has already been discussed. However, when Arab journalists were actually encountered, the British appear to have done better in their relationships than their US counterparts. Ashraf Fouad again:

'I had a Palestinian journalist with me and he tried to explain to a British soldier that in the next war we hope there are 250,000 British soldiers and only 55,000 US soldiers—you are a nice man—you tell me to go away, but you tell me nice!'[9]

With the apparent paucity of both tactical and strategic information, compared to the continuous (albeit heavily censored) access to the Iraqi regime, questions of bias must be carefully considered.

When journalists are not provided access it is almost inevitable that the stories they produce will be deficient in facts and detail. The British forces saw this at first hand shortly before operations began in February and early March 2003. The overt focus on a diplomatic solution meant that the build-up and training of British military forces became 'presentationally difficult'. In the absence of dedicated press facilities, a media vacuum developed between the military and the huge numbers of media arriving in-theatre. This vacuum led to a series of largely spurious stories appearing in the press, many of them speculating over shortages of equipment or resources; unable to see troops for themselves the British media often ran wildly inaccurate stories, which proved very difficult for the military to rebut effectively. Yet odd stories do not themselves confirm allegations of bias. It is the evidence of institutionalised bias that is more important, and this is far harder to determine since it requires almost constant monitoring of a channel's output. However, there are specific programmes where anti-US and anti-Western sentiment has been openly discussed.

Al-Jazeera's political discussion programme 'The Opposite Direction' has achieved virtual cult status in the Middle East and its presenter Faisal Al-Qasim has become famous throughout the Arab world. When he first began his show, the provision of a platform for free discussion, and the shouting matches into which the programme often degenerated, were considered radical. The later adoption of telephone phone-ins to those discussions proved explosive and there have been many cases of regime spokesmen being harangued by callers from their own countries. This was inconceivable before Al-Jazeera. Another Al-Jazeera programme, 'Islamic Law and Life', has also courted controversy. Hosted by the scholar of Islam, Yusif Al-Qaradawi, the programme was quick to condemn the attack on the World Trade Center, yet later the same programme urged *jihad* in defence of Iraq. There are other events which observers say cast doubt on the objectivity of the channel's output. The 'Bin Laden' connection is a major source of grievance between the channel and the United States. The Syrian journalist Ahmed Zeidan produced a documentary entitled 'Bin Laden Unmasked', later attending the wedding feast of Bin Laden's son.[10] While the channel would no doubt argue that this was merely the action of an enterprising journalist cultivating his contacts, there are others to whom this would provide 'evidence' of a deeper sympathy within the channel and among its staff for Bin Laden and his ideals.

Another issue, considered in detail later, is the departure of Al-Jazeera's managing director in 2003 after a British Sunday paper levelled allegations of Iraqi influence. Al-Jazeera's strap-line for the Iraq conflict was 'War on Iraq' and not the favoured Coalition version, 'War on Saddam'.

How much responsibility should a channel take for the views of its invited guests? The provision of a public platform for known extremists, who may use it to make highly inflammatory remarks and perhaps even to incite violence, may be thought foolhardy. Yet an equally compelling argument suggests that providing such a platform is the purest form of press freedom. There are, however, examples of channels being deliberately controversial in the scheduling of their programmes. An Arab linguist employed by SkyNews to evaluate Arab reporting throughout the war recalls a particular incident just before the start of hostilities, which highlights this very issue: 'At the beginning of the war they [Al-Jazeera] ran a special for an hour about connections between the White House administration and the oil companies. It was a pretty loaded programme.'[11] Yet even this is debatable and in essence no different from some of the more controversial output of the BBC's 'Panorama' programme.

When asked about institutional bias Salah Nagm of Al-Arabiya believed that only a thorough academic study would determine the truth: 'The whole thing needs studying—there was no content

analysis to know if it was biased or not, and this will allow for flam-
boyant coverage on both sides.'[12]

In considering the issue the stance of the wider Arab media,
which are largely state-run, helps provide context. In Egypt, an
influential if slightly faded regional power and a key ally of the
United States, British embassy staff noted that while the country's
TV was largely factual and objective, its press was 'highly critical,
putting across strong anti-war messages, playing up Iraqi resistance
and civilian casualties'.[13] In Muscat the British embassy considered
the position of Oman, a country that has enjoyed a close relationship
with the West for many years. Embassy staff reported: 'Civilian
casualties and material damage receive dramatic highlighting in the
press.... Local press coverage is biased and unhelpful.'[14]

In Ba'athist Syria the TV coverage was described by the embassy
as 'outrageous', focusing on Iraqi successes, Coalition failures and
alleged Coalition atrocities. The British embassy in Damascus starkly
warned:

Some public diplomacy buttons simply do not work. For example, 'lib-
erating the Iraqi people'. The Syrians say that the Iraqis do not want to be
liberated, at least not by foreign soldiers. We must identify messages,
which do not strike a chord with this mostly hostile and incredulous
audience.[15]

Perhaps most telling is the considerable effort made by British
embassy staff in Damascus to place a letter from British Prime
Minister Tony Blair in the local press. Their efforts were wasted,
and the state-run media continued to devote significant airtime to
the pronouncements of the Iraqi Information Minister, who served
a regime with which, apart from sharing the Ba'athist ideal, the
Syrian government had fundamental disagreements. In Jordan, a
close friend of the West, the embassy believed that the press was
largely objective in its reporting, although editorials were consistently critical of the Coalition. However, Jordanian officials were

worried that emotion on the street would be stirred up by regular exposure to images of civilian casualties and dead bodies.

On 1 April 2003 the US State Department sent out a 'high priority tasking' e-mail to its embassies abroad. A forthcoming meeting of the US National Security Council would consider the global media coverage of the war so far, and the State Department was keen to know the extent of positive coverage, of which the e-mail highlighted examples: 'Positive photographs or television segments from the war in Iraq that have appeared in local media within the last week. An example of such images could be a US soldier assisting an Iraqi woman and child, Coalition members delivering humanitarian assistance, or local Iraqis welcoming Coalition members.'[16] In Turkey the US embassy reported 'overwhelmingly grim, negative, often front-page images of injured Iraqi civilians and dead women and children in coffins.... TV and print media in Turkey, increasingly focusing on civilian casualties, are tending to emphasize negative aspects of the war.'[17] In Pakistan the US embassy reported: 'The local press, both Urdu and English, has been focusing on civilian casualties. Injured children are a specialty.'[18]

In Bahrain, home to the US Navy's Fifth Fleet, the embassy reported that most of the images in Bahrain's Arabic-language newspapers had been very negative.[19] In Saudi Arabia the reports followed the same trend: 'We have not seen any positive pictures in the Saudi media. To the contrary, for the last two weeks, some pictures of a very graphic nature have been printed by most of the papers.... In today's *Arab News* front page, the top half is a picture of dead Iraqis and a full-page caption "Liberated by US bombs".'[20]

While Coalition diplomats made attempts to influence the Arab media in a more positive direction, those with experience of the region, and not the political appointees favoured by the Bush Administration, remained largely sanguine about the coverage. Most realised that the state press in Arab countries served as an outlet for pent-up anger and emotion; some regimes very publicly condemned Coalition operations, condemnation that they ensured was covered widely in their state media, while privately they offered advice and in some instances resources to the Coalition for the conduct of the war. But quiet and patient behind-the-scenes diplomacy did not fit the centrally-driven need for acceptance of the cause. The US-led Coalition needed positive images in the world's media to justify the war to its opponents.

Despite experience of recent operations in Afghanistan and two large-scale training exercises in the Middle East,[21] Coalition forces appeared ill-equipped to find themes that worked in the Arab media. Coalition troops were told to promote ideas such as 'a war not against Islam but against Saddam' and 'liberation, not occupation'. As has been noted, these failed to resonate. In an April 2004 interview Imam Husham Al-Huseini, director of the US Karbala Centre, said that much greater attention needed to be paid to Islam:

[The US] should rewind a year and start with some very gentle religious rhetoric, in a language the Shia understand. They should explain that they are the followers of Jesus Christ and they are the sons of Ibrahim, like all Muslims. They have come to the Holy Land from where Ibrahim came, because they want to rid the world of Lucifer—Saddam Hussein.[22]

This may not necessarily have proved effective strategy, but it highlights the absence of familiarity and understanding that so hindered the battle for Arab minds among Coalition planners. It was a battle that the US appeared less and less inclined to fight as the conflict progressed. With US media networks largely 'in the bag', the challenge of engaging and winning over Arab media was there to be met. It was an opportunity that was ultimately squandered.

## Depicting Coalition death

A defining moment of the war's coverage was the footage of dead and captured Coalition troops. Captured US servicemen were shown being 'interviewed' by their Iraqi captors. This was followed by footage of dead US and, subsequently, British servicemen. The coverage caused outrage in London and Washington—outrage that was quickly communicated to Al-Jazeera by the British civil servant Simon Wren:

'We had to show them, in a strong way, that we thought it unacceptable. Of course the Geneva Convention does not apply at all—they don't even sign it. However, you refer to it because the convention is a treaty that governments sign which sets out acceptable limits or rules of war. We referred to that as it was our baseline—a benchmark of acceptable behaviour. We knew that the Fadayeen [irregular Iraqi military personnel loyal to Saddam], who were using it as a propaganda tool, filmed the material but we were objecting to it on the grounds of taste and decency. There was a potential for the families of soldiers to see them.'[23]

It was not just the Arabic channels that showed the footage. In Britain SkyNews aired the images as well, and its correspondent in Doha received a similarly irate reaction from Wren:

'We had a huge shouting match with Sky when they showed it. I don't think I have ever sworn so much as I did at Geoff Mead [SkyNews correspondent]. I know they are good pictures but you should have more decency about them. Pixilation is irrelevant—the families know who they are.'[24]

The British spokesman Group Captain Lockwood immediately went on the record with the media, stating that the MoD condemned the decision to broadcast the footage of their bodies: 'We are shocked and appalled by this flagrant and disgraceful breach of the Geneva Conventions.... We deplore the decision by Al-Jazeera to broadcast such material and call on them to desist immediately.... We are also requesting all media outlets not to become tools for Iraqi propaganda by rebroadcasting such material.'[25] In Britain the tabloids went to town, *The Sun* calling Al-Jazeera's footage 'sickening' and suggesting that the soldiers had been executed. The commander of British forces, Air Vice Marshal Burridge, made similar comments: 'Quite apart from the obvious distress that such pictures could cause friends and families of the personnel concerned, such disgraceful behaviour is a flagrant breach of the Geneva Convention.'

The strength of the Coalition reaction came as a surprise to Al-Jazeera, as Jihad Ali-Ballout recalled:

'I think, with hindsight, we can look at it that, initially, we felt strongly that it is the media's prerogative to reflect what is happening on the ground as objectively as possible. Then we did some more thinking and realised an aspect that was perhaps a little bit hidden from us, in the heat of the battle so to speak—the impact of this footage on the ordinary person. Giving it some thought we realised that there was a cultural divide here. In the Middle East it is not shocking to see carnage—we have been living through it for decades.... be it in Lebanon, Yemen or Palestine, it has something to do with belief in fatalism. I began to understand the frustration on the public level. However, we felt that the outrage and condemnation, vociferous as it was, was due to this news running contrary to the strategy of the war as planned by some.'

'I was not in the newsroom every day. I was aware, however, of the flow of information from Western authorities ... no casualties, a smooth-running operation, a knife in soft butter and so forth. There was other important news coming from the other side—particularly from the Brits... Umm Qasr fell four times, I think, the uprising by Shi'ites in the south, the surrender *en masse* of the First Brigade had been announced by the Brits but it was not true (we interviewed the commander of that Brigade and he said that he had his forces intact). I think all of this was building up frustration with Al-Jazeera. We were not thinking of that—we were just doing our job as comprehensively and objectively as possible.'[26]

He too went on the record, telling the BBC: 'I'm not aware of any international law that prevents a journalist from doing his job. Al-Jazeera is not flavour of the month.'[27]

Nick Pollard of SkyNews expressed similar sentiments:

'I take the view that just because a government asks us not to show some-thing we should not automatically fall in line. You can't just show process without results.... The normal rules that we abide by in terms of taste and decency don't always apply in wartime. I believe that people at home ought to see what is going on and there is an obligation for viewers to watch it. I don't think war should be sanitised.'[28]

Pollard believes that Al-Jazeera was right to show the footage and considers it more holistically:

'I think it is a cultural difference. In Britain and in the US we are much more sanitised to these things. Lots of European countries will run footage uncut, and in other parts of the world. In war normal cultural differences get political overtones as well.'[29]

Professor George Joffé does not subscribe to the idea of cultural difference: acceptance of such images is indicative of the reality of day-to-day Arab life. He points out that most Arabs have had direct experience of conflict and which has often been very brutal. He concludes: 'There may be a higher tolerance but nothing innate in Arab culture that make them more acceptable to an Arab audience.'[30]

Cultural difference or not, there are wider implications here for war reporting. Ever since the Vietnam war there have been criticisms that war coverage has been 'dumbed down'. In particular the 1991 Gulf War will be remembered for images of Cruise missiles falling on road junctions but not for footage of the impact of those weapons. This is indicative of the apparent sanitisation of the effects of war—an accusation that can equally be made against governments and media outlets. There was certainly a widely-held belief in 1991 that a myth that real people—men, women and children—do not die in war but only enemy troops was being perpetuated.

Were the Arab media right to show these images? Certainly there was a reaction on the ground; many Coalition troops felt very angry that the imagery had been shown. Yet the reality is that the pictures were just too tempting for both Arab and Western networks. Was SkyNews disingenuous in the way it chose to air the imagery, reporting that Al-Jazeera was showing the pictures—a case of the media reporting the media as news. As with the Bin Laden tapes, the channels argue that this is news and that there is a higher public need to show 'reality'. This, of course, is not what the Coalition wanted portrayed: it is an intractable situation and there is no right answer. For the military it is simply unacceptable to show imagery that might distress the families. Both sides will remain firmly entrenched in their positions.

The decision to show the footage is believed to account for the decision of the New York Stock Exchange on 24 March to ban the channel from its Trading Floor, stating that it was offering access only to channels with 'responsible coverage of business news'.[31] Nihad Awad, executive director with the council on American-Islamic relations, told CNN he was disappointed by the move: 'The NYSE is behaving like the Iraqi regime The censorship of the press by the business community is unjustified. It sends a negative message that it's all right to shoot the messenger.'[32]

The incident also illustrates a fundamental absence of under-studying of the military by media organisations. The Pentagon, not unreasonably, requested that the images be removed from broadcast to allow US authorities time to inform the families. Al-Jazeera proudly stated that it complied with this request for nearly one hour, a space of time obviously insufficient for the immediate rel-atives of a US serviceman to be informed of his death—this process can sometimes take days, at the end of which the story is old news. In this instance the fact that Al-Jazeera was not widely available in the United States was beneficial and the families are unlikely to have seen the images before learning of their loved ones' demise. The issue of casualty notification is another intractable problem where, again, the media (from all backgrounds) and the military are unlikely to find common ground.

Of course Al-Jazeera was not the only Arab network to use the imagery. Abu Dhabi TV also showed the images, as well as focusing on civilian casualties. Much less protest followed their decision, which Nart Bouran, head of news at the channel, considered entirely acceptable:

'When your coverage is balanced all along, you tend to attract less negative criticism. Saying that, we were aware of the pictures we showed and there were occasions when we took out pictures that we thought were just "too much". We believe that we did not lose any human suffering story that others showed but we were a bit more sensitive and I stress that happened on a few occasions only. It also relates to the way you present it and the language you use to go along with it. Human suffering and pictures of dead bodies are part of the coverage and you cannot take them out and claim you have shown all sides of the story. They exist and they are a sad part of covering a war story.'

Bouran is philosophical about the issue of protest and believes that it all hinges upon perception:

'Arab broadcasters, unintentionally, have become a source of news for Western broadcasters that they would not normally carry if it was not reported by Arab stations. For example, I would be very interested to see how Western broadcasters would handle footage carried by Arab stations branded as "exclusive". Have Arab broadcasters become a licence for Western broadcasters to carry such material? I believe Arab broadcasters have to be careful as to what is reported in the West in their name. How they are perceived. Are they an observer or a player? What comes to mind of course is "exclusive" video of kidnapping and beheading.

We at Abu Dhabi TV have turned down offers in the past to buy such video or showing it as exclusive. It was an editorial decision that money should not be paid for it, and that no one should claim ownership.'

On 1 June the BBC aired a documentary about the Al-Jazeera network in which the controversial footage was aired, albeit with faces pixelated out. The programme caused a storm of controversy, above all with the biggest-selling British tabloid, *The Sun*. However, the more conservative *Daily Mail*, while attacking the BBC, also reminded its readers that this was probably a more realistic interpretation of the events of war than they had seen during the conflict itself.

One of the reasons for the Coalition being so upset by the coverage was that this very issue had been the subject of a meeting on 27 February 2003 between the US Department of Defense media team (headed by Victoria Clarke) and US-based media bureau chiefs. At the meeting the Pentagon emphasised the extreme sensitivity with which they would regard the issue of casualties:

[W]e're going to ask you to be extraordinarily sensitive. And this has to do with the identification of people who are injured and killed, military as well as media....

The issue has to do with the timing and identification of casualties. In the ground rules your reporters will see that reporting on casualties obviously is permitted but there are safeguards and conditions within the ground rules to try to prevent identification of battlefield casualties in real time. In other words, the sensitivity here is trying to allow the next of kin procedures to be able to get to family members and notify them of injured or killed family members before the first notification of it being in real time in the television coverage or a news story or a wire story that goes out there.

So we've tried to strike a balance that allows you to cover those varied realities of warfare and combat. But we've asked you to do it in a way that is sensitive to our needs to be able to communicate to our family members those tragic incidents that might occur on the battlefield.[33]

No one had thought of inviting the Arab media.

## The fall of Saddam's statue

Another controversial aspect of Al-Jazeera's coverage of the war was the commentary that accompanied the fall of the statue of Saddam Hussein in Baghdad's Firdous Square on 10 April. Before the statue was toppled it had been decorated first with a US flag and later with an Iraqi one. Lieutenant Casey Kuhlman of the US Marine Corps described the day's events to the *Guardian*: 'I heard a kind of collective gasp from the crowd and I turned around and saw an American flag go up. For about a split second I thought, that's cool, and then I thought, Oh my goodness, that's not cool at all.'[34]

The flag itself had been raised by US Marine Corporal Edward Chin, who had been handed it by his company commander, Captain Bryman Lewis: 'The Captain handed over the flag and directed us to fly it above the square.'[35] Although the flag was quickly removed and replaced by an Iraqi one, the damage had been done. In the eyes of the Arab world, Baghdad had been conquered and not liberated. The event formed the main item of news in bulletins across the world.

All three major Arab news networks covered the fall of the statue. The BBC Monitoring service in Caversham recorded Al-Jazeera's commentary:

A giant statue of the Iraqi President Saddam Hussein still reached into the sky with vigour, filling the square with the proud glory of a past which perhaps ended this morning. So the battle was not over and there was no better time for sending a message to the heart of Baghdad of the end of Saddam Hussein, represented in the toppling of his statue, live to millions of television sets across the world. But the act, in which a few young Iraqis participated alongside American troops, did not proceed without a few hiccups, or to be more precise, it did not proceed without unexpected symbolic turns, full of meaning. After the Iraqis failed to strangle the statue of leader General Saddam Hussein, after their rope broke and their tired arms stopped them, there was nothing for it but for the American troops to take up the difficult task. The scene was set and the dividing line between truth and reality disappeared to a great extent.

The American soldier who approached on the back of a tank did not have the presence of mind to remember that he was on non-American soil. [Soldier shown placing American flag on face of Saddam statue] Or maybe it was a deliberate insult, or maybe he acted out of ignorance. All the excuses are uglier than the sin itself. In any case, that was the scene which history will record. But then there was still the problem of interpreting the scene. Was it an American soldier strangling an American dictator, or a foreign invader chopping off another head? Does the world usually use this method to honour national martyrs? Are criminals usually hung with flags as masks? The problem had to be resolved in any way possible, especially as Iraq has its own flag. It appeared that the Iraqis taking part in the symbolic execution remembered that shortly. But then the [Iraqi] flag draped over Saddam Hussein carried the words Allahu Akbar [God is great] and had to be removed for that reason.[36] [Soldier shown placing Iraqi flag on face of statue] Nevertheless, the problem had still not been solved and confusion prevailed. The president had to be executed without any flag. He had to be denied that honour. A final moment brought another development which perhaps sent a slight fear into the hearts of the Marines. The statue toppled, but it did not fall fast. Even after it fell, he still had his feet left implanted in the reinforced Iraqi cement in the heart of Baghdad.

The power of the Arabic language has already been discussed. There is a series of words here that reinforced ideas of bias. The idea that Saddam was an 'American dictator' would be uncomfortable, but it reflects a broad theme in the Arab world of 'US hypocrisy'— Saddam had been fêted and supplied by the Americans during the Iran-Iraq war in the 1980s. The idea of 'invaders chopping off Saddam's head' is, even in English, a powerful one and conjures up images of the medieval crusades against the Islamic world. That Saddam should be described as a 'national martyr' and denied the honour of, metaphorically, being executed under an Iraqi flag cannot really be seen as anything other than biased.

Al-Jazeera's coverage must be assessed against other media outlets. With the possible exception of Kuwait, Arab media almost across the greeted the fall of the statue either with dismay or, in most region, cases ignored it completely. Jordan's *Al-Arab Al-Yourm* newspaper deplored the statue's rapid fall, believing it to be a plot to benefit Israel. The Egyptian paper *Al-Wafd* showed pictures of the tumbling of the statue, but failed to mention that Baghdad had fallen, and focused instead on continued resistance around one of the city's bridges. The state-run television channels of Algeria,

Libya, Morocco, Sudan, Syria and Tunisia all ignored the events completely. LBC focused its coverage around an Iraqi woman haranguing a US soldier: 'We have told him that these children are going to come to America and blow your civilians up.'[37] Al-Arabiya expressed amazement during its coverage: 'This is hard to understand. What happened to the Iraqi army? This is the scene that the US networks have been waiting for, now we will know if the US was really after freeing the Iraqi people, or after Iraqi territory.'[38] The reporters at Al-Arabiya were not the only ones to be surprised at the speed of victory. The CBS correspondent Lara Logan had been reporting from Baghdad for several days and covered the arrival of US troops live. She commented on the reaction of the city's inhabitants:

People are being increasingly emotional and upset. Many people have said it's a violation of Iraq's pride and dignity. This is something that the Coalition forces are going to have to work very hard to overcome, that even those people who do not support the regime of Saddam Hussein still feel that in some way this is an occupation. One man said to me 'I may not like Saddam Hussein but I don't like to see foreign invaders in my country.'[39]

Such reporting is not dissimilar to that of the Arab channels that were so heavily criticised. In countries across the world there was surprise at the defeat of the once defiant dictator's army.

Without a comprehensive media analysis it is possible to make only superficial observations about the day's coverage. It is apparent from these examples that, with the exception of Kuwait, Arab media were unanimously negative in their reporting of the 'liberation'. They fall into two camps. State-run television largely chose to ignore the scenes in the square—either through concern at the Coalition's progress (and by implication, therefore, dismay at the failure to defend Baghdad) or because Saddam's fate might be seen as a catalyst for potentially violent protest in their own capitals.

Both are equally likely, given the strength of emotion that this conflict engendered.

Pan-Arab satellite television also showed surprise at the speed of the US advance and the absence of Iraqi resistance. Certainly there had been considerable speculation over what would be the nature of the defence of Baghdad. Arab media had covered in detail the preparations being made for the city's defence, with vivid images of burning pits of oil, sand-bagged gun emplacements on street corners and heavily armed Iraqi citizens. All the Arab channels had reporters in Baghdad on that day and ultimately their coverage reflected the proclivities of the individual. Yet in raising a US flag, indeed in helping the very act of destruction, the Coalition may have done little to help its own cause. The apparent enthusiasm of the Americans to engage in the destruction of the statue has been considered by some Arab commentators as having given a green light to the looting and anarchy that followed; the destruction and desecration of the National Museum, and the apparent protection of the Oil Ministry. This is a particularly emotive subject.

One of the most insightful commentaries on the day the statue fell was that of Abu Dhabi TV. As the statue was pulled down, Saddam's feet remained stuck in the base of the statue. The Abu Dhabi TV anchor used the symbolism of the moment to explain that this typified Saddam and all that he stood for. 'Everyone was trying to pull him down and he just could not let go, his feet remained stuck to power. He has finally been pulled off by force.'

In his book *Blair's Wars* John Kampfner considers the British Prime Minister's reaction: 'In his office Blair stood, transfixed. This is the moment, he told his team. This is what it was all about.'[40] The toppling of the regime had been the explanation for the war? What about the weapons of mass destruction that had been the public reason for the campaign? Maybe their discovery would now follow.

## *Spies in Al-Jazeera?*

The chaos that followed the fall of Baghdad would spawn serious allegations against Al-Jazeera's journalistic objectivity. On 11 May 2003 the *Sunday Times* in London claimed that at least two members of Al-Jazeera staff had been agents of Saddam's regime, and critics of the channel used this to support their allegations of bias. The issue coincided with allegations made against the British parliamentarian, George Galloway, that he too had been employed by Saddam's regime. He subsequently won a high-profile libel case against those British and US newspapers that had published the story. Like the allegations made against the former weapons inspector Scott Ritter, they were proved to be utterly false. Indeed, as with Ritter, the foundation for the allegations was paperwork allegedly uncovered in various Iraqi government ministries and bunkers after the fall of Baghdad.

It was a difficult time for the Iraqi capital. Looting became a pastime among many of its residents, and government ministries became particular targets, not only for computers and furniture but also for their documents—ones that journalists and intelligence services were prepared to pay money for. But were the documents authentic? The *Sunday Times* allegations had their source in the Iraqi National Congress (the opposition group led by Ahmad Chalabi), but this is no guarantee of their provenance. According to Al-Jazeera's communications manager Jihad Ali-Ballout, it may be indicative of something else entirely. As he put it, '[Chalabi] has not been shy about his love, or rather lack of it, of Al-Jazeera.'[41] Their authenticity, or otherwise, has still not been confirmed, and Al-Jazeera's policy is not to comment on unfounded allegations. However, the channel did respond to the paper's questions at the time, emphatically denying the allegations. Ali-Ballout takes up the story:

There was reference in the so-called documents to senior people at Al-Jazeera holding meetings with Saddam Hussein. To me this reflects good journalism, as many a journalist would have given his right arm to talk with Saddam. There were also references to meetings that have taken place between Al-Jazeera and officials at the Ministry of Information in Iraq. Well, all journalists with experience in the Middle East acknowledge the fact that to be able to operate within any particular country, you have to be verified by the regime first. It is not the problem of the journalist that the higher echelons of the Ministry are also intelligence officers. One has to bear in mind that at the time [of the allegations] Saddam's regime was the legitimate government of Iraq, recognised by the UN, and with membership of the vast majority of members of the United Nations and international organisations and institutions. Similar to Al-Jazeera, the BBC, CNN and others had to deal with the existing government, whether they liked it or not. This, however, should not be translated into being 'agents', otherwise the list of 'collaborators' with Saddam's regime would stand at a mile long, and would contain some very notable names indeed.[42]

While this is not an unreasonable argument, suspicions remain because shortly afterwards the managing director of Al-Jazeera, Mohammad Jassem Al-Ali, left the network and returned to his former position with Qatar National Radio and Television. He had been seconded to Al-Jazeera in 1996 to help establish the channel, and Al-Jazeera maintains that his departure was entirely normal and certainly not a reaction to the newspaper feature. Indeed it points out that Al-Ali remained on the Al-Jazeera board of directors for some time after his departure.

Without verifying the authenticity of the supposed government papers it is difficult to make more than superficial comment on the allegations. Yet the issue raises more questions than it answers. If the papers were forged, as Al-Jazeera believe, then who attempted to orchestrate the smear campaign and for what objectives? Conspiracy theorists can point the finger at a number of different actors, state or otherwise, who may benefit from the ensuing negative publicity. Yet if the papers are accurate, then the whole ethos of the channel's journalistic integrity, objectivity and freedom are questioned.

Discussions with British Foreign Office and US State Department officials suggest that the controversy surrounding both the issue of bodies and the allegations of Iraqi collusion had a seminal effect upon the Qatari government. Publicly it remains an advocate of the channel's editorial independence, but privately, it was deeply concerned by the effect upon its own international relations. Sources have revealed that the Qatari government was worried enough by the allegations of bias to launch an official enquiry into the incident. The results of that inquiry are not in the public domain.

## Abu Dhabi TV

In the two months leading up to the war in Iraq Abu Dhabi TV began running twenty-four-hour news, and continued that uninterrupted schedule till late 2003, when it returned to its traditional eclectic mix of news, current affairs, films and entertainment. As in all media, the channel gave close consideration to terminology. Nart Bouran, its head of news:

'We decided to call it what it is: "war on Iraq". We stayed out of terminology battles until things were clear. War on Iraq, Coalition forces, Iraqi army. "Occupation" was used once it became an official description of the situation. We did not use "invasion", but "war on Iraq". The use of "resistance" was a bit more complicated. During the war we did use "resistance" in Umm Qasr and Basra, but after the end of the war that word was used sparingly, and never for occasions when an attack had taken place and innocent bystanders and civilians were involved. We are very careful in maintaining balance and neutrality in usage of terminology and that is obvious from our coverage.'[43]

The path to war was well signposted; as early as September 2002 the channel had begun planning its coverage of any future war. Perhaps drawing on its experience of Afghanistan, or perhaps just suspicious that the Arab media would not gain the access they needed, Nart

Bouran began considering how best they might affect their coverage. Uniquely the channel engaged in quiet discussions with staff at the British embassy, and a request was made through the FCO to a British private security company for an Arabic-speaking British reporter, preferably one with military experience, to join the Abu Dhabi team as a freelance with the declared intention of embedding with British troops. Discreet investigations around the ex-special forces community identified an ideal candidate, Alex Gardiner.

Gardiner had left the British Army's Special Forces (the 22nd Special Air Service Regiment) as a major in 1999, and immediately joined the Sultan of Oman's armed forces and took command of the 1st Regiment, Sultan's Special Force, based in Salalah. Uniquely he had actually joined the Omani armed forces rather than becoming attached to them as a loan appointment from the British army. Thus Gardiner appeared the ideal choice: he was fluent in Arabic, thoroughly immersed in Arab culture, and well known in the region. He was even able to offer some previous journalistic experience; during Operation Enduring Freedom he had worked in Afghanistan as a freelance cameraman, covering the action in the Tora Bora mountains with the Pashtun Mujahideen. Gardiner readily agreed to the plan, but before accepting Abu Dhabi TV insisted he undertake a screen test, in Arabic and English, at their Abu Dhabi headquarters. He passed it and in March 2003 arrived in Kuwait with a camera and a satellite transmission kit and orders to link up with the two-man Abu Dhabi TV team already installed at the British FPIC.

Gardiner recalls that his arrival was met with suspicion by the other embedded media, although he himself has nothing but praise for the Media Operations Officers who looked after him—British spokesman Colonel Chris Vernon in particular. Vernon made it clear to the other media representatives that he regarded the presence of Gardiner and the Abu Dhabi TV teams as important and ensured that they were included in all the facilities offered before the start of offensive operations. Yet it was not just the Western media that caused Gardiner difficulties; his two Abu Dhabi TV colleagues, a Moroccan correspondent and an Egyptian cameraman, became noticeably hostile as the operation grew in intensity, and Gardiner rang Abu Dhabi TV and complained about the difficulties he was experiencing.

The opportunity to shed the two presented itself on 25 March when the RFA *Sir Galahad* moved up-river into the port of Umm Qasr carrying 232 tonnes of humanitarian aid. The Bahrain Press Information Centre had been tasked with running the press facility and decided that primacy should be accorded to the regional, i.e. Arab, media. Lieutenant Commander Mark Hankey trawled the Kuwait CPIC and offered Abu Dhabi TV two spaces—which Gardiner quickly filled with the Moroccan and Egyptian staffers. After that Gardiner filed reports by himself from various facilities that were offered. Vernon arranged a trip into Umm Qasr as fighting in the city's outskirts continued; it was a second facility arranged at the Rumaylah oil fields that was to be of particular use to Gardiner. Here he came across the commanding officer of the Royal Irish Regiment—a former SAS officer, Colonel Tim Collins. Collins had already come to the public's attention before the start of the conflict with an address to his troops that captured the imagination of the press. He again attracted attention when he was accused by a US exchange officer of mistreating Iraqi civilians. Collins and Gardiner were old friends and Gardiner asked if he might become embedded with the Royal Irish, which at that time already had representatives from Sky TV and the *Mail on Sunday* newspaper from London. Gardiner's request was granted, no doubt assisted by both his friendship with Collins and his acquaintance with the commander of 16 Brigade, of which the Royal Irish were part.

Gardiner spent two weeks with the regiment and filed numerous reports via satellite not only to Abu Dhabi TV but to other international media such as ABC. He finally dis-embedded with the Royal Irish Regiment at Al-Qurna (confluence of the Tigris and Euphrates rivers and supposed site of the Garden of Eden) to return to the FPIC, and it was here that he came across representatives from the Al-Jazeera television network. Colonel Vernon had decided to brief the media on a forthcoming operation, but had refused to allow the Al-Jazeera team into the briefing tent, insisting it was for Western Coalition country media only. Yet Gardiner was allowed to attend and the Al-Jazeera team immediately pointed out that he was a member of Abu Dhabi TV. Vernon was unmoved by the ambiguity, even after one of the Al-Jazeera staff showed him his own British passport.

This exchange came after the airing of footage by the channel of captured and dead Coalition troops. The images had created uproar among servicemen and Western politicians alike (this is covered in detail in Chapter 5) and Vernon stuck by his decision that Gardiner could have access but not Al-Jazeera—regardless of who had a British passport. Al-Jazeera was angered by the perceived snub, and in Gardiner's words 'dramatically overreacted' to the incident.

Gardiner left Iraq on 18 April. He believed that interest in the military side of the conflict was on the wane, and the arrival of other Abu Dhabi TV crews from Kuwait, their focus very much on the civilian side of the story, convinced him that it was the right time to leave. He returned to Abu Dhabi via Kuwait, where he was met by Nart Bouran, who congratulated him on his work, before finally returning to England in late April.

What are we to make of Gardiner's experiences? There can be little doubt that in a personal perspective they were unique. Yet so too were they from a media perspective. Abu Dhabi TV, which regards itself as the voice of moderation in the Arab media world, achieved a spectacular coup—one unmatched by any of its regional competitors. Anticipating difficulties long in advance, the channel decided to employ an ex-British armed forces officer as one of its correspondents. This was a masterstroke, and the fact that they procured one as well connected as Gardiner was lucky. Unlike the other Arab media, Abu Dhabi TV had regular access to the inner command and decision-making process of the British forces. Gardiner was entirely trusted by the British media officers and attended numerous facilities. Clearly there was a symbiotic relationship here; although there was little formal guidance on engaging with the Arab media some officers recognised their importance without being specially instructed. Colonel Vernon welcomed Gardiner into the fold, despite his not having signed the *Green Guide*, not undertaken any of the required pre-deployment training and not being accredited through the London system.

However, Gardiner's reports were not always welcomed among the Arabs. He himself recalls that some of the duty editors at Abu Dhabi TV refused to air anything that he reported. Certainly he did not endear himself to his two Arab colleagues, who he felt were simply not up to the job of war reporting, and whom he detached from at the earliest opportunity. Neither was his footage always of the highest quality. He was operating, in field conditions, by himself and had little previous experience either as a journalist or as a news cameraman. Yet Nart Bouran was delighted with what he accomplished, and there is no doubt that the channel scored a significant success over its rivals as a result.

The issue also needs to be considered ethically. Were the British right to embed Gardiner on the strength of who he was when so many other journalists were left behind? This is an important point given the apparent absence of any controls placed over him (Gardiner did not even see the *Green Guide*, let alone sign up to it, and thus the MoD would have found it difficult if not impossible to exercise control over operationally sensitive material had it been necessary). A second point worthy of consideration is that Gardiner did not attend any of the MoD briefings or training courses, particularly those associated with protection from biological weapons. Once a journalist is embedded with a British unit, that unit inherits a duty of care over the individual; with Gardiner's extensive military experience this is a moot point, but nevertheless the principle remains. A perhaps more serious issue is that of the briefing provided for Western journalists from which Al-Jazeera was excluded. Was Colonel Vernon right to brief the Coalition media and include Gardiner in the pool while simultaneously excluding a British passport-holder from Al-Jazeera?

Both questions will stir strong reactions among the other Arab media, and inevitably Abu Dhabi TV's competitors considered Gardiner's background and questioned his objectivity in the reporting process. This study does not seek to castigate individuals, who at the time were operating in very difficult conditions and made decisions in good faith. However, on the wider plane, if the US and British governments are to comment on the objectivity and fairness of Arab TV channels, then they are morally obliged to be consistent and fair in their dealing with the same channels. Al-Jazeera's objections to the briefing do not seem unreasonable under these circumstances.

A final point to consider in relation to Gardiner's experiences is the level of cooperation that he was afforded. He himself says that the British media minders were '110 per cent on side and did an excellent job in fielding questions from egomaniacs in the press corps'.[44] He also came across US forces, and again he notes that they were happy to brief him on what was happening and were highly cooperative. Yet he is realistic in his assessment; when asked why this should be so, given the more general feeling of suspicion that permeated the theatre of operations, he replied simply: 'Because I was a Brit.'

The utopian ideal of media coverage—that all media should be regarded as objective and bipartisan and that coverage should be free and fair to all—is unlikely to be realised. Reporters should be provided with access regardless of background. In conflict this ideal is almost unattainable. Thus other Arab channels might note the experiences of Abu Dhabi TV and, if the occasion should arise again, consider if this might be a solution to their particular requirements.

## *Lebanese Broadcasting Corporation and the war*

Sultan Sleiman was the editor-in-chief of the LBC Baghdad bureau, heading a team of fourteen journalists and cameramen for the duration of the war. Sleiman is proud of his station's achievements during that period. He managed to secure for LBC the last interviews with the Saddam regime's officials Tariq Aziz and Naji Sabir, and he believes that he was the first journalist to announce both the arrival of US troops in the city and its subsequent fall. LBC had no Coalition embeds during the war; one of its correspondents did manage to join US troops in the first few hours of the push from Kuwait, but later detached and reported as a unilateral after becoming frustrated at the level of censorship he believed was being unfairly imposed on the Arab media. Throughout the conflict LBC coverage was devoted entirely to news of the war, and Sleiman believes that in terms of market-share LBC, together with Abu Dhabi TV, jostled for either second or third position, after Al-Jazeera and ahead of Al-Arabiya. LBC too was criticised for its coverage, particularly when footage of dead Japanese troops was shown. However, despite showing footage of dead British and US servicemen the coverage was not criticised by the Coalition authorities. Like the other Arab channels LBC aired interviews with US Administration officials Rice, Rumsfeld, Powell—and the British Foreign Secretary Jack Straw.

Like the other Arab channels, LBC referred to the conflict as 'War *on* Iraq' and to US and British troops as 'invading forces' and, after the end of hostilities, as 'occupiers'. His policy for subsequent coverage is equally precise: 'If an attack is against civilians we say "suicidal attack" or "armed attack"; if it is against US or UK troops we use the term "resistance".'

Sleiman is particularly proud of the station's coverage of the toppling of the statue, which he placed in the same context as the destruction of the Berlin Wall. He described the events as a rather badly-directed American play, in which no one quite seemed to know what to do: 'Once they put an Iraqi flag on the face of the statue, then they replaced it with a US flag, then they put up the two flags, and finally they took away both flags. As for the base of the statue, some people tried to break it with hammers, but when they didn't succeed an American tank did the job.'

Like many of his colleagues in both the Arab and Western media, Sleiman questioned the utility of the Press Information Centres: 'We think that the US and UK press centres were not important to us and not credible.' He considered the interaction between the Coalition and the Arab media on two planes:

'The problem of the Coalition forces in its relation with Arab media had two phases: the first one is the reality itself which is the justification of the attack on Iraq. It was not convincing and was proved later to be false. The second phase is that the Coalition forces considered all the Arab media as an enemy and dealt with them on this basis.'[45]

He was also critical of the personalities at the Coalition Press Information Centres, and his observations might explain the coverage afforded the Iraqi Information Minister, Mohammad Said Assahaf: 'The press centres used to express the policy of one side of the conflict the same as the Iraqi press centre but without a character like Mohammad Said Assahaf.'[46]

## Al-Arabiya

Al-Arabiya has achieved rapid growth since its birth. As already noted, launching a new satellite news channel is extremely expensive, and to launch one before a major regional conflict and enjoy the level of coverage and success that Al-Arabiya appears to have done, those costs must have risen especially high. To consider the economic impact of the war, a comparison can be drawn with the British satellite news provider SkyNews, which by its own admission enjoyed considerable success during the war but saw its overheads rise by £5–10 million. Nick Pollard, its head, believed that if the war had continued for three months rather than three weeks, those costs might have become unsustainable, particularly at a time when the channel's continuous news coverage meant that the usual advertising breaks were either dropped or spread much farther apart.

The costs to Al-Arabiya must have been significant and one can only speculate how much influence over its output Sheikh Walid has extracted for his money. Sam Barnett is more sanguine over the idea of influence than some of his Arab colleagues: 'It is his [Sheikh Walid's] company so he has a considerable influence.' Salah Nagm, however, is robust in his defence of the editorial freedom of his channel: '[MBC and Al-Arabiya] have their own editorial teams and are commercially driven. They try to provide speedy and accurate news to the Arab world.'[47] Privately senior staff at the channel confided that the Sheikh's influence is felt, but not in news or editorial policy; his interest is in the business aspects. Like any good businessman, they claim, he wishes to see a return on his investment.

Like Al-Jazeera, Al-Arabiya has received its share of criticism. Pro-Saddam supporters threatened Al-Arabiya staff in Baghdad with death after the channel criticised the excesses of Saddam's sons and showed footage of beatings supervised by his half-brother Watban during its 'Inside Iraq' programme. The Americans have called the channel highly irresponsible after it broadcast images of masked men threatening to kill their fellow citizens.

The channel has scored notable scoops over its main rival, Al-Jazeera, including interviews with Saddam's family and, after the war, with the former Iraqi Information Minister. Sheikh Walid is candid about the first few months of the new channel. 'We paid too much attention to what Iraq was saying and people were not getting enough of the other side.... We called the Coalition side "invaders" although we soon changed this.' However, he believes that giving more coverage to Iraq was largely due to the US failure to respond to requests for interviews.

The issue of editorial control or influence is complex but extremely important when considering bias. Again, parallels may be drawn with SkyNews, which is owned by Rupert Murdoch's News Corporation. Nick Pollard is adamant that he has complete editorial freedom, and cites particular examples such as Murdoch's attempt to take over the Manchester United football club and the development of digital TV services in Britain, where SkyNews covered the story objectively without influence or pressure being bought to bear.

While Pollard believed that he had editorial freedom (and Britain's tight broadcasting regulatory system makes this much more believable than other News International outlets such as Fox News) he acknowledges that Murdoch has a healthy interest in the business success of Sky. This is in effect the argument advanced by Al-Jazeera, Al-Arabiya and Abu Dhabi TV stations. The cynicism that might greet the Arab networks' proclamations of independence is due to the region's inglorious history of censorship and tendency towards the hidden hand of influence. Certainly, the level of complaints that has been raised against Al-Jazeera and the Qatari government cannot have been comfortable for either party, yet it is credible that a symbiotic and co-dependent relationship can exist without sacrificing of editorial control to influence.

# CROSSING THE RUBICON: THE OTHER FACE
# OF THE INFORMATION CAMPAIGN

'The West won the world not by the superiority of its ideas or values or religion but rather by its superiority in applying organised violence. Westerners often forget this fact, non-westerners never do.'—Samuel P. Huntington[1]

The media campaign was just one element of the Coalition's information strategy, a strategy that in Britain spanned various government departments and organisations, from the Department for International Development (DFID) through to the Ministry of Defence, the FCO and the intelligence services. Collectively they participated in what is known by an often misunderstood term, 'Information Operations'. In its examination of the conduct of the Iraq war the House of Commons Defence Select Committee asked for a full definition of the term during its witness hearing of 16 December 2003. In a full answer the MoD's Director of Targeting and Information Operations (DTIO), Air Vice Marshal Heath, stated:

'The concept of Information Operations for the military is to garner cross-government activity, not just military activity, to contribute towards influence and persuasion. I like to think of it as a continuum, that if you get it right it starts during pre-war fighting where you are looking towards dissuasion and coercion; it continues into military operations; and, of course, it then wraps up and it is just as essential that you carry it through into post-conflict restoration and reconstruction.'[2]

Within this definition there are a number of associated activities. Some are militarily classified and therefore remain largely unknown outside the small community of IO practitioners. However, there are areas of work that are now in the public domain and these are in the fields of electronic warfare (broadly defined as the interception of the enemy's communications), computer network operations (a crude analogy to 'hacking'—a term familiar in the civilian environment), and information insurance (the protection of sensitive data from the enemy). Perhaps the most visible and interesting discipline is Psychological Operations (often abbreviated to Psyops). During the Iraq conflict this became more evident than ever.

Psychological warfare is a sinister name for what in many instances is merely a commonsense approach to disheartening the enemy and winning over public opinion. Its now attracts considerable media attention, both in analysing its morality (some journalists see it as a 'dirty' or 'underhand' technique, perhaps entwined with shadowy personalities from the security services) and in measuring its success. There is also a relationship to the media campaign, albeit at a deliberately remote level. For example, the author was asked to look for unusual activity in the Sierra Leone media during the civil war crisis in that country in May 2000. Within hours of a covert leaflet-dropping campaign, Sierra Leone Radio was reporting the effect of the leaflets on upcountry village communities, information that was used to great effect by the British military commanders. However, that relationship must always be tenuous at best, since the first suggestion that a Media Operations Officer is somehow engaged in Psychological Operations will work against the effectiveness of that officer's job and result in a loss of credibility and trust by the media itself, whose natural suspicion will be intensified.

Without the resources of its larger Coalition partner Britain nevertheless played a full, if small, part in the wider US-led information campaign. This campaign had in many instances been going on for some time in before the start of hostilities. Since 1991 the Iraqi regime had been the object of increasingly well-policed sanctions, designed to halt the build-up of military weaponry and in particular of WMD. The principle was that under these sanctions, more properly known as the oil-for-food programme, Iraq would be allowed to export its oil production but only in exchange for certified goods such as food products and medicines. Over the years a substantial maritime interdiction force had been operating in the Northern Arabian Gulf, which by early 2003 comprised representatives from twenty-one countries. The fleet of vessels patrolled the northern end of the Gulf—enforcing a plethora of UN Security Council Resolutions including 661 (implementation of an Iraq embargo) and 986 (the oil-for-food programme). The success of the UN maritime operation had attracted significant media attention, becoming the focus of numerous media facilities, the most recent British one held on board the *Chatham* only days before the start of the invasion.

They appeared to have a good story to tell. The Coalition blockade (which interestingly comprised maritime components from four Arab Gulf states) had reduced the amount of oil smuggled illegally from 1.3 million tons in 2001 to half a million in 2002.[3] Given that the price of smuggled Iraqi oil was worth around ten times the legal barrel price, this was a significant amount of money that was not now finding its way into Saddam's coffers. But it was also money that, despite the best intentions of the UN, was not available for the benefit of the Iraqi people. In support of these operations the United States had regularly, if intermittently, targeted the northern and southern no-fly zones, frequently dropping leaflets and broadcasting radio signals to the civilian population.

As the countdown to conflict began, so the tempo of the Coalition's information campaign intensified and some early indicators of its existence became public.

The much-reported 'defection' of the Iraqi Deputy Prime Minister Tariq Aziz on the eve of the war was perhaps the first occasion that the wider public saw the effect of information operations. Initially rumours began to circulate around the media community that he might have defected; these rumours quickly gathered momentum after the British Foreign Office minister Mike O'Brien told Parliament of unconfirmed reports that Tariq Aziz had defected and re-located to northern Iraq.[4] On the face of it the rumour seemed plausible. Aziz was the only Christian member of the higher ruling élite, was known to be a man of considerable education, and had a wide range of contacts from his years as Foreign Minister. The rumours were tempting although O'Brien's validation for the news—a Bulgarian 'source'—was somewhat sketchy. Tariq Aziz himself moved quickly to suppress the rumour. He appeared at a hastily-arranged press conference in Baghdad wearing military uniform and carrying a pistol, and told the assembled press corps: 'The rumours are part of the psychological war being waged by the United States.' However, much more sophisticated and covert systems were already in play.

## Commando Solo aircraft

One of the most interesting units deployed during the war was the 193rd US Special Operations wing of the Air National Guard, based at Harrisburg, Pennsylvania. Flying specially converted C-130 aircraft, the unit has two particular capabilities. The EC-130E(CL), colloquially referred to as the Comfort Levi, is used for electronic intelligence-gathering and intercepting enemy signal traffic via a series of antennae fitted right across the aircraft. Much more intriguing in the context of the battle for hearts and minds is the EC-130(RR), referred to as the Commando Solo aircraft. Each aircraft costs around $70 million and is equipped with highly advanced radio and TV transmission equipment as well as sophisticated jammers. This equipment allows the aircraft's eleven-man crew to provide an airborne broadcast platform for deployment anywhere in the world. Capable of broadcasting on AM/FM and HF frequencies, the aircraft had begun their most recent work in the region in December 2001, broadcasting messages and Western-style music[5] directly into Iraq from a radio station called Information Radio. Most of the material was produced in the United States by the army's 4th Psychological Operations group based at Fort Bragg, North Carolina. By its own admission the group has a prestigious work output. In the purpose-built $8.1 million centre specially trained servicemen, including linguists and analysts, are able to produce more than one million leaflets in an hour,[6] the material directly targeted in consultation with the operational commander (in the case of the Iraq war this was CENTCOM).

The Commando Solo broadcast radio messages targeted both Saddam's military infrastructure and the civilian population. The following transcript is indicative of that output:

People of Iraq. Throughout the history of the world, mankind has shown a desire to progress and expand. Great leaders have built vast civilizations and empires that spanned continents. These leaders have sponsored education programs, paved vast roads, and built housing for the less fortunate. The leaders of the past have turned deserts into arable land, and created innovations which made life easier for their people. The great leaders of the past are known for their generosity and charity towards their own people, as well as their neighbouring lands. In Afghanistan, once the Taliban was removed from power, the standard of living drastically improved. Relief aid is pouring into Afghanistan and is appropriately distributed. Schools are open and people all across Afghanistan are better off.[7]

However, it was not merely radio; much of the material distributed was in leaflet form. US Air Force B52 aircraft based at Fairford RAF station in England flew long-range missions to the region,

Commando Solo being far too valuable an asset to place anywhere too close to the front line. The B52s were able to carry a huge payload; on 17 March 2003 (just days before the war began) the CENTCOM PIC announced that 1,440,000 leaflets had been dropped by Coalition aircraft that day, spread across western and southern Iraq and targeting both civilian and military sites.

The leaflets had many purposes. In his autobiography *American Soldier* the CENTCOM commander General Tommy Franks highlighted two overriding imperatives. One was to dissuade Iraqi troops from using WMD as ordered by Saddam, and the second was to ensure the integrity of the oil fields. Many of the leaflets provide the frequencies for the Commando Solo radio broadcasts, while others encouraged civilians to disassociate themselves from the regime. Those dropped over military targets gave precise details of how to surrender, including the way in which military vehicles should be arranged and the distance that troops should move back from their units.

There was a final useful offshoot of the leaflet campaign. Regardless of what was written on them, the leaflets themselves demonstrated to the recipients that the Coalition could evidently drop leaflets at any place and at any time; Saddam's air defences were virtually non-existent and, as Franks recalls, 'Where there are leaflets today there might just be bombs tomorrow.'[8]

Until recently the activities of the squadron have been surrounded in secrecy. Indeed its participation in the 1991 Gulf war was never officially acknowledged. In his memoirs of the war the former CENTCOM commander General Norman Schwarzkopf includes no references at all to the psychological warfare campaign. In *Storm Command* his British counterpart General Sir Peter de la Billière made more reference to the success of leaflet drops, but only in passing and with only an obscure reference to the Commando Solo aircraft.[9] De la Billière did however point out the rather amateurish and half-hearted approach that the British brought to the idea, compared to the very substantial effort by the Americans.

For all the secrecy, details slowly leaked out. The 4th Psychological Operations group dropped more than 29 million leaflets during the 1991 Gulf war, as well as establishing a US radio programme entitled 'Voice of the Gulf'. This featured excerpts from the Quran, interviews with Iraqi prisoners and, in an interesting take on operational security, the next day's bombing targets. Among Iraqi defectors 75% said they had been influenced in their decision by the leaflets and/or radio.[10] However, in the 2003 Gulf war details emerged far more quickly. The Americans were quite open about the missions, making press statements and placing copies of the leaflets on the CENTCOM website. Their view was 'the wider the media coverage the better'. Jarol Manheim, a professor at George Washington University, considered how the growth of international media has made the objectives of the Psyops campaign easier to achieve. Paradoxically, the growth of Arab media has been especially useful in this regard. Manheim was succinct: 'You didn't have Al-Jazeera before!'[11]

The airborne campaign was not the only radio system established by the Coalition. Radio Tikrit, which uses a transmitter in Kuwait, started out by pretending to be a pro-Saddam station but suddenly switched sides to carry a message very similar to Information Radio. The Voice of the Liberation of Iraq, believed to have been based in Iraqi Kurdistan, also began appealing to the Iraqi military not to put up a fight against the Americans.

Another technique used by the Coalition was the targeting of e-mails and text messages. This is still a hugely sensitive area for the Coalition and one which official sources are absolutely unwilling to discuss. However, other sources reveal not only its existence but also its apparent success. One of the most celebrated underground commentators on the progress of the war was known by the pseudonym Salam Pax, an Iraqi who for the duration of the conflict was able to maintain an internet diary (or blog) of his experiences. Here he recalled that on 12 January 2003 an e-mail was sent to all users of his internet service provider (ISP) telling it to offer no resistance to Coalition troops and to provide information about weapon storage. The ISP was shut down by the regime authorities very soon after. The story was repeated in the *Independent on Sunday* (London) on 11 January 2003:

US officials also disclosed that the Pentagon has been sending e-mail messages to Iraqi generals to warn them against carrying out any order from President Saddam Hussein to use chemical or biological weapons against US or allied forces. The e-mails are 'consistent with all of the messages we have been trying to send to Saddam Hussein', one official said. 'It's just another means.'

Without more substantial information we must beware of attaching too much importance to what might be no more than hearsay information. However, the proliferation of computer viruses on the internet and the civilian targeting of text messages for advertising purposes suggests that such measures were well within the capability of the Coalition and that in whatever medium the regime chose to communicate (be it text, e-mail, phone or fax) the Coalition would have been able to make its message heard.

As Coalition forces advanced through the country similar, less sophisticated psychological messages were enacted. Some of these were of questionable effectiveness and even bizarre. Around Saddam's hometown, Tikrit, US forces planned to put up posters of Saddam with his face superimposed on the bodies of Hollywood heroines and other stars. This was instigated in an attempt to enrage his followers and supporters and draw them out of their enclaves and hiding places. Thus Saddam appeared in a number of guises, from actresses Zsa Zsa Gabor and Rita Hayworth through to Elvis

Presley. One of the posters showed Saddam's head on Elvis's dancing body with a gold crucifix hanging on his hairy chest. This may not have been thought through quite as carefully as it should have been. Many Arabs already had fears that this operation was nothing but a Christian crusade—gold crucifixes would have resonated badly with the bulk of Iraqis despite the secular nature of the country under Saddam's regime. Associated Press (AP) repeated the observations of one young Iraqi translator working with the Americans around Tikrit: 'Maybe it is funny for the US soldiers, but I think most locals will find it very insulting.'

## Chatham *radio broadcast*

From the very outset the Americans had been particularly proactive in their information operations. Britain's engagement began relatively late in the operation. This was due to the Rules of Engagement (ROE) profile within which the British armed forces were required to operate. ROE are issued in order that action taken by them is lawful and within the parameters of political acceptability. In essence ROE govern the use of force in its widest sense, be it the physical firing of weaponry to any posturing conduct by the forces that could be interpreted as hostile. It was this latter clause that prevented their earlier engagement in the wider Coalition information operation (the United States having very different ROE). Immediately before the start of the military campaign Britain was still strongly pursuing a diplomatic solution—we have seen already how the military media operations campaign was put on hold, despite there being a massive appetite for news from British domestic media. Such news stories were considered by the government to be inconsistent in presentation with the public diplomacy phase; active engagement in Information Operations would have been equally inconsistent with that view. However, when the ROE were finally changed and allowed to become militarily more permissive, it was the Royal Navy that fired the first salvos in those operations.

The frigate *Chatham*, like the other ships in its class, is equipped with formidable communication interception equipment, allowing it to play a full part in the electronic war that was being played out. Its embarked Arabic-speaking Communications Technicians could tune into Iraqi broadcasts, both civil and military, and feed their analysis to the overall build-up of Coalition intelligence. However, the ship was able to play much more than just a passive, listening role in the operation. On 21 March the *Chatham*'s captain Michael Cochrane was ordered to begin a daily nineteen-hour radio broadcast, beginning each evening at 8 p.m., relaying into southern Iraq specially prepared tapes of pop music (both Western and regional) as well as messages instructing the Iraqi military how to surrender to Coalition forces. This was the first time that a Royal Navy warship had ever been so tasked and it proved so successful that on 31 March the ship was directed to extend its radio broadcasts to cover twenty-four hours, a result of difficulties with other Coalition broadcast units. This round-the-clock operation continued till 2 April when *Chatham* handed over the broadcasts to the US warship *Tarawa*. *Chatham* had by then broadcast twenty-five different radio programmes totalling 296 hours. In an interview with its embarked war correspondent Captain Cochrane was convinced that his ship's broadcasts had been useful, citing examples of Iraqi soldiers surrendering in the manner prescribed by the leaflets and broadcasts; however, he confessed to having little idea of the actual content of the broadcasts made from his ship.[12]

The content of those messages was almost certainly assembled by the British 15th Psychological Operations group based in the Defence School of Intelligence at Chicksands, Bedfordshire. This tri-service unit was established in the aftermath of the 1991 Gulf conflict and defines its role on its own website as 'influencing attitudes in order to affect behaviour in support of a military commander's mission. This is done with planned, culturally sensitive, truthful and attributable activities directed and disseminated by various means.' The group is composed of both regular and reserve personnel, and draws heavily on the media and communications industry for its expertise and to man its Analysis and Plans section and the radio, print and TV equipment. In consultation with its larger US counterparts 15 Psyops Regiment made a significant contribution to the British Information Operation. Sources within the service have suggested that while the United States may have possessed better equipment, the sophistication and nuance of the British-produced material was significantly superior to that produced by the Americans, particularly for the Arab audience. The *Chatham* was not the only success of 15 Psyops Regiment, which later drew heavily on its civilian media experts to establish Radio Nahrain (Two Rivers Radio) which broadcast a daily and eclectic mix of news, public service messages and music from northern Kuwait, Shaiba and, finally, its offices in Basra. The British forces' in-theatre newspaper *Sandy Times* even printed a small feature about the station's work in its thirty-second edition.[13] The unit also became involved in the various wider Iraqi media initiatives that developed subsequently. Overseeing the entire British military Information Operation was the MoD's Department of Targeting and Information Operations, a London-based civilian and military organisation of ninety-eight people including psychiatrists, anthropologists and other specialist analysts. Britain also paid a US civilian organisation, Rendon, for specialist consultative advice.

As has already been discussed, the whole Information Operation came in for particular media scrutiny. The left-leaning *Guardian* newspaper in London ran an article in January 2004 which considered the whole process:

Information dominance came of age during the conflict in Iraq. It is a little discussed but highly significant part of the US government strategy for full spectrum dominance, integrating propaganda and news media into the military command structure more fundamentally than ever before.... The 2003 attack on Iraq will be remembered as a conflict in which information fully took its place as a weapon of war.[14]

Yet for all the public scrutiny the effectiveness of the whole information campaign is very difficult to quantify. As the *Chatham*'s captain observed, there were instances of Iraqi soldiers surrendering to Coalition troops waving IO leaflets, and the commander of the 15(UK) Psyops Regiment is convinced that the duration of fighting around Basra was reduced as a result of an effective Psyops campaign. However, with so many different influences it is not always possible to attribute enemy action (or inaction) to a particular stimulus. Indeed it is this very absence of clarity, and the constraints imposed by the ROE discussed earlier, that led to such late deployment of the British Psyops effort. It is clear that some senior commanders have still to be convinced that Psyops can 'shape the battle space' in the same way as high explosives can; by its very nature it requires time and space in which to evaluate the target audience and identify themes that will have some effect. Yet once the decision had been made to begin the fighting phase of the operation, time was at a premium. The 15(UK) Psyops commander recalls his frustration while gaining approval for Psyops to begin: 'We were trying to get basic surrender messages and the like approved at the same time as HQ was trying to get the ground war going.'[15]

The objectives of the information campaign evolved quite rapidly after the invasion. At first considerable work had been done to reduce the likelihood of the use of WMD and to prevent the destruction of the oil supply infrastructure, as happened in 1991. Thus the focus of the operation was almost exclusively on an Iraqi (and military) audience. Senior staff at DTIO freely acknowledged the effect and influences of the pan-Arab satellite TV media such as Al-Jazeera in the wider Arab world, but in the closed environment of Iraq these were not big drivers and few people had access to anything other than state-provided news. Little consideration was therefore given to working with, and influencing, the pan-Arab media. However, as the conflict evolved and the strength of feeling in the wider Arab world came to be better understood, the Coalition made efforts to engage with the pan-Arab press. Soon after the fall of Baghdad Lt Cdr Paula Rowe, the media operations officer at the Joint Force Headquarters in Northwood, England, escorted out a carefully selected group of Arab press for a comprehensive briefing tour of British units in southern Iraq. This group had been selected in consultations between the British military and the FCO Islamic Media Monitoring Unit.

Despite the changing objectives of the information campaign, it is apparent that a disconnect existed between those running the Information Operation and those engaged with the media operation over the wider Arab media. Guidance was not formally produced for commanders in the field on the benefits of engaging with the Arab media, and its importance was never endorsed with conviction by the MoD press office. DTIO exerted no influence over the embedding process run by the MoD press office, nor was it asked for advice, and senior staff have privately reflected that this was a mistake. Although the level of engagement is now much better, cultural unfamiliarity still causes problems. However, the most serious failing was perhaps expectation management. Across the Information Campaign the Coalition had told the Iraqis and later the population of the region that after the end of the fighting the Coalition would rebuild the country. This was a message beamed out from Commando Solo's transmitters, spelt out in leaflet drops and articulated in the media by military spokesmen. The reality was different, however, and the chaos and violence that followed the 'liberation' did not meet the expectation built by the Coalition. Of course, these statements had been reported widely by the regional media and never more so than by the pan-Arab satellite TV stations. In the words of one senior officer, 'The lack of Phase 4 [post-conflict] planning wasted the grace period and we will pay for it for a long time to come.'

## US public diplomacy

A common question in the United States after 9/11 was 'Why do they hate us?' It became the agenda for news and discussion programmes across the nation, and spawned numerous books. There are of course any number of disparate ideas, but perhaps it was the perception that America was becoming a pervasive society, through globalisation slowly empire-building in the Arab world, that best encapsulates many of the emotions that led to that dreadful day. The Spanish-American philosopher George Santayana (1863–1952) theorised what such an empire might constitute:

The authority that controlled universal economy, if it were in American hands, would irresistibly tend to control education and training also. It might set up, as was done in the American zone in Germany, a cultural department with ideological and political propaganda. The philanthropic passion for service would prompt social, if not legal intervention in the traditional life of all other nations, not only by selling their innumerable American products but by recommending, if not imposing, American ways of living and thinking.[16]

The issue became the subject of a study undertaken by the former US ambassador to Israel and Syria, Edward Djerejian, in 2003. Together with experts in public diplomacy, the media and the Arab and Muslim regions of the world Djerejian was charged to 'study the efficacy of the Department's public diplomacy efforts aimed at this region and recommend new ideas and policy initiatives'.[17] In his report to the Committee of Appropriations in February 2004, Djerejian began by emphasising the importance of public diplomacy in the Arab world given that in his view 'the bottom has indeed fallen out of support for the United States'. He concluded:

Americans, on the one hand, and Arabs and Muslims, on the other, are trapped in a dangerously reinforcing cycle of animosity. Arabs and Muslims respond in anger to what they perceive as US denigration of their societies and cultures, and to this Arab and Muslim response Americans react with bewilderment and resentment, provoking a further negative response from Arabs and Muslims.

The need to communicate American values is not new, although the scale of the task is now self-evidently greater than ever. The United States has engaged before in proactive policies to alter perceptions in the Arab world. Djerejian's study was preceded by a project conducted by internationally renowned marketing executive, Charlotte Beers, who had been hired by the US State Department to address the same problem. A commercial marketer for many years, she instigated a $15 million marketing campaign entitled 'Shared Values', which produced a series of TV advertisements depicting the daily lives of US Muslims. The programme was launched in Indonesia, the world's most populous Muslim country, but failed to find outlets in the Middle East; many in the Arab world belittled the campaign as simple-minded and condescending. Media reports both abroad and in the United States were generally negative and the project was widely viewed as propaganda. Both CNN and the *Wall Street Journal* reported that the channel had totally failed to register with Muslim audiences. Charlotte Beers was more upbeat, claiming that it had been successful because it had started a dialogue. No formal quantitative evaluation was ever made public, which suggests that this was an over-optimistic interpretation of the campaign's achievements. In March 2003 Charlotte Beers resigned from the State Department and the project collapsed.

However, her work formed the basis of a new project focused on commercial radio. In spite of the affluence of the Gulf states, many

Arab populations continue to live near or below the poverty line, particularly in the populous states of North Africa and in Gaza and the West Bank. Outside the big cities few speak English, and the TV set, a common-enough feature in cafés and community centres, has yet to enter everyone's home. For many the primary source of information is radio, and it was through this medium that the United States sought to spread its message through the instigation of Radio Sawa ('Radio Together' in Arabic). A mix of traditional and Western music, with news and views thrown in, it has proved remarkably successful with Arab youth, although cynics suggest this is mainly due to the quality and mix of the music. Even so, the network is widely listened to, although it is difficult to measure its success in influencing its audience's views towards the United States.

Encouraged by this success and puzzled by the 'Why do they hate us?' idea, the US Congress voted for, and funded, the establishment of a pan-Arab TV network, Al-Hurra (the free one). Costing $62 million, the channel broadcasts live to twenty-two Arab countries on Nilesat and Arabsat satellites, the same satellites as are used by the major regional Arabic channels. It is administered by a presidentially-appointed Federal Agency called the Broadcasting Board of Governors (BBG), an agency that sponsors all non-military US international broadcasting. Its sister-organisations include the long-established Voice of America, Radio Free Europe and Radio and TV Marti (aimed at Cuba). The channel's spokesmen believe that Al-Hurra offers a more balanced alternative view to that currently presented in the region (an objective remarkably similar to the reasons given for the establishment of Al-Arabiya TV). The channel believes that Arab views of US foreign policy are conditioned not only by US policies but by the way the existing Arab networks present them and the continuing emphasis on coverage of the Palestinian situation. Enter Al-Hurra. Described by the *New York Times* as 'the most ambitious United States government-sponsored international media project since the Voice of America began broadcasting in 1942', the channel airs news, views and dubbed documentary programmes twenty-four hours a day. Ironically many of its Arab correspondents are themselves former Al-Jazeera staff. For its inaugural broadcast the channel interviewed President Bush, who publicly stated that Al-Hurra will 'cut through the hateful propaganda that fills the airwaves of the Muslim world'. The decision to show the President may have been an inauspicious start for the channel, as initial reactions were sceptical: 'It is just like everything that America does; they say that every other Arab station is wrong and that they are right.'[18] However, Al-Hurra staff were undaunted by the criticism. They believe that with their mixture of US media executives and long-time Arab journalists, they can draw together the best values of American and Arab journalism, while presenting the best chance to date of deepening understanding of America and Americans throughout the region. Mouafac Harb, a former Washington bureau chief for the London-based Arabic daily *Al-Hayat*, is Al-Hurra's news director. He told the *New York Times*: 'Al-Hurra's goal would be to disseminate objective, balanced news.' The Middle East media consultant Ashraf Fouad tried to be objective about the channel:

'If you look at it from the positive side it is much needed and it is long overdue. They should get involved in the debate. But if you look at it from the negative side then it is unacceptable. How dare you come and air a channel like this to try and brainwash my people, when your law in the US bans you from airing something like this in the US? It is against the constitution to broadcast a government channel in the States.[19] How dare you say that we are sheep, and that you can show us this, but you can't show it to the American people? The intelligentsia of the Arab world took great exception to this—it is an insult. They are broadcasting from Virginia. The guy in the morning is reading in the newspaper about a game of baseball while I am reading that a bomb went off in the house next to me. We are in different worlds for the urgency [*sic*]. The journalists are OK—some are quite good—but the argument that "I came to Al-Hurra because I want to say the truth for the first time..." So for the last fifty years you have been lying to us?... you made your name on lies for LBC or Abu Dhabi? They were beating you and you could not say what you wanted? On the opening day the editor of *Al-Hayat* was interviewed. He said: "What can the beautician [Al-Hurra] do to the ugly face [American foreign policy]?"'[20]

Abd Al-Sattar Qasim, Professor of Political Science at Nablus University, takes a tangential view: 'Al-Hurra will encourage licentious Western lifestyles...promiscuity and other forms of immorality.... This would vindicate the views of those who are saying that the station's *raison d'être* is to undermine Islamic culture and values.'[21] General John Abizaid, an Arabic-speaker and deputy commander of US forces during the war, told the *New York Times*: 'It is a battle of ideas as much as it is a military battle.'[22] Al-Hurra is one weapon in the US armoury for that battle, and it is one that the US Administration is convinced is working. The channel now has a specialised Iraq offshoot, and President Bush continues to authorise large budget increases.

In a regular series of e-mail updates the channel claims consistent gains in market share. In its 23 August 2005 e-mail it stated: 'Al-Hurra TV and Radio Sawa are now reaching a total unduplicated audience of 35 million adults (15 and over) per week according to the latest ACNielsen survey released today. This represents the fourth consecutive audience increase since the inception of the ACNielsen surveys of the stations. The latest survey also shows that in spite of high levels of anti-American sentiment throughout the region, both Al-Hurra and Radio Sawa are regarded as credible sources of news and information by their audiences.' Yet such figures may not tell the whole story. Simply asking how many people have watched the transmissions rather obscures the central issue, which is: have people actually listened to the presentation of more US-favourable views and news, and if they have, have they changed their perceptions of the United States? Only time will tell and Ambassador Djerejian, for one, is unconvinced. In his report to the Appropriations Committee he noted: 'Our interviews with people in the region... reveal a high level of scepticism about state-owned television of any sort. Whether Al-Hurra will be effective is uncertain.' However, he is resolute in his belief that 'something' needs to be done: 'We cannot let the extremists define us. We must define ourselves. The challenge is clear. Our commitment to wage this struggle for ideas should be equally clear.'

The US Congressional Research Service produced a report for Congress in July 2003, which considered the specific challenges posed to US foreign policy in the Middle East by the Al-Jazeera network. Its analysis of the channel's Iraq war coverage examined both sides of the debate but concluded with a quote from Professor Samer Shehata of Georgetown University: 'The war coverage on Al-Jazeera compares favourably with the war coverage on American networks. It is from a perspective of what the war is like for the Iraqi people.... I have never seen anything favourable to the Iraqi regime on Al-Jazeera.'[23] The document provided a series of policy options for Congress including the purchase of airtime on Arab networks (a derivative of Charlotte Beers' campaign), the active involvement of US officials, particularly Arabic-speakers, and for proactive engagement with moderate Arab TV networks. The document also suggested reform of Arab media through the US Middle East Partnership Initiative,[24] as well as the establishment of an alternative Arab television channel (this was to be Al-Hurra). The variety of policy initiatives, with their various arguments for and against, is indicative not only of recognition of the problem but also of a lack of clarity over how to address that problem. US officials have made themselves available on Arab networks, yet they still feel the experience has been counter-productive; money is being spent on training, yet the effect of Al-Hurra is unsatisfactory. The report concludes with an argument that it claims is widely circulated in Arab intellectual circles: 'The best way to combat the coverage of channels such as Al-Jazeera would be to focus on US foreign policy regarding the Arab-Israeli conflict.'[25]

A statement of the obvious? Some believe that the United States is now so unpopular that even this would fail to change perceptions. It is encouraging that the importance of channels such as Al-Jazeera is now recognised; unfortunately such recognition was not widespread during the planning phase for Operation Iraqi Freedom.

## 8

## THE VIEW FROM BAGHDAD

In both the 1991 Gulf war and throughout Operation Iraqi Freedom members of the world's media were encouraged to operate from the Iraqi capital, Baghdad, albeit under often tight restrictions imposed by the Iraqi Information Ministry. A key effect of those restrictions was that it became very difficult to assess the true feelings of the Iraqi people. Because of the presence of Iraqi regime 'minders' it was often impossible for correspondents to penetrate beyond the rather false air of support for Saddam and his regime; even when Western journalists were able to escape their minders, Iraqis were reluctant to be interviewed for fear of what might befall them if their participation became known.

Saddam had successfully created one of the world's most totalitarian regimes. His image permeated every aspect of society; people would see his photograph every morning in the newspapers, travelling to work they would see his imagery on roadside advertising hoardings, and in their places of work, and in cafés and municipal buildings his image was everywhere—often accompanied by slogans extolling his greatness. Even young children were required to start their school day by chanting praise for Saddam Hussein and the Ba'ath Party. Forbidden to watch anything but state TV, Iraqis would watch either this or the Shabab (youth) channel— its programme output was the responsibility of Saddam's son Uday. Occasionally some might pick up the Iranian Al-Alam channel which could be received with a conventional antenna and did not require a dish.[1]

This is not to say that other outlets did not exist—even in a society as tightly controlled as Iraq, some people were able to acquire satellite receivers or use the internet, but for the average person the significance of these was dwarfed by the overpowering nature of the state broadcast system—a system that placed Saddam on such a pedestal that when his regime finally collapsed the population could scarcely believe it. The BBC correspondent Paul Wood described the problem as the 'prison of the mind that every single Iraqi citizen lived in'. It seemed as if everyone was prepared to fight to the death for Saddam; of course the reality was very different.

Since the 1991 Gulf war the world's media had been travelling to the ancient capital and staying in either the Al-Rashid Hotel, famous for its floor mosaic of President George H.W. Bush and its supposed underground regime command bunkers, or the less comfortable but allegedly safer Palestine Hotel, which overlooked the presidential palace but was considered to be far enough from it not to be a target. Regardless of where they stayed the sheer obstinacy of the Iraqi regime, with its multi-level bureaucracy and decision-making paralysis, made the experience frustrating and time-consuming. Nevertheless Baghdad was an important story and the world's media flocked to the pariah state's capital.

As the pace towards war gathered momentum, the Iraqi regime appeared to change its tactics in dealing with the media. Uday Hussein publicly criticised the Information Ministry in early October 2002 for its treatment of the US cable channel CNN. The channel had covered in some detail a series of protests that had erupted in the city following Saddam's decision to release many of the detainees at the Abu Ghraib prison. As people flocked into the prison in search of their loved ones, an unusual and uncharacteristic wave of public discontent swept the city; surprisingly the protests were not met with the usual bullets and secret police but with pleas from the ruling élite for restraint. CNN covered the event live, including sounds of gunfire from the street, and as a direct result were ordered by the Information Ministry to leave the country. The story ran in newspapers around the world. The *New York Times* noted:

Any hint of protest against Mr Hussein's government is a matter of alarm to Iraqi officials, because it conflicts with the official line that all Iraqis love their government. But coming as they did immediately after the prison amnesty and a presidential referendum on Oct. 15 that Mr Hussein won with a claimed 100 per cent of the vote, the protests threatened to undermine Iraq's bid to counter American pressures by presenting him in a new guise—that of a magnanimous, forgiving father figure with the unquestioning support of his people.[2]

The decision to oust the American news organisation backfired; the international condemnation that followed clearly rankled with the dictator, who was keen for his regime to appear in as favourable a light as possible. Direct criticism came from Uday's paper *Babil*, which said: 'We find it useful to remind people that the news media of the 1970s are not at all the same as the fact-searching media of the 21st century.' The Ministry then appeared to backtrack. The *New York Times* observed the change of heart:

A flurry of enhanced amiability at the official media centre in Baghdad, headquarters for visiting reporters, appeared to be part of a wider effort by President Hussein to present a more moderate image to the world in the face of American war threats.[3]

That amiability, of course, had limits—limits that appeared to be applied equally to both Western and Arab media. Ayman Gaballah, the Baghdad correspondent for the Al-Arabiya network, based himself in the city for the duration of the conflict. Very tight controls were exerted by the regime:

'You had to do what the regime said—otherwise you went to prison or were shot. I could not say that US tanks were here in Baghdad over the bridge. You could not pan the camera across. They were everywhere. They take you and let you see children—they say: "Take your footage from here and there." The correspondent in the field has to tell of the effects regardless for the viewers, but in a place like Baghdad I myself had to make a compromise. I go to Baghdad because I think it will fall therefore we have to keep our presence there in the days before the fall. I can sacrifice saying that US tanks are here today but tomorrow... tomorrow is a different day.'[4]

The May 2003 edition of *World Press Review* carried an interview with a Scandinavian reporter who for safety wished to remain anonymous. He told the magazine that he had never worked under such difficult conditions as those in Iraq: 'The level of censorship and control exerted by the regime was such that people were absolutely unwilling to deviate from the prepared party line (defending the President and proclaiming death to the invaders). Therefore understanding exactly what the Iraqi people thought was next to impossible. Even if you were able to escape your minder the people regarded you with suspicion regardless.'

Aside from the minders' presence the physical business of reporting was expensive. The Press Centre at the Iraqi Ministry of Information imposed numerous fees for its services. In *Embedded* the *New York Times* photographer Tyler Hicks enumerated the various costs associated with day-to-day business: '[The Information Ministry] extort as much money from you as they can ....Sat phone fee $100 per day; press centre fee additional $100 per day.'[5] Ali Achmed, director of Abu Dhabi TV, recalled the chaos of working in the city and the risks that correspondents occasionally needed to take:

'In Iraq the situation was that two months before the war there was no real centralised government—there was a lot of chaos. Yes there was more control over Baghdad but other cities less so. In some cases if you want to film you need government escorts to take you there but that was not always the case. You can't be the best journalist and always go by the book—sometimes you have to cross the line.'[6]

For most of the media working in the country the route to Baghdad had begun in the Jordanian capital Amman at an iron-grilled window that came to be called the 'window of shame'. Here journalists would sometimes spend days applying for their visas, the 'shame' referring to the amount of bribery and grovelling needed to secure the all-important stamp in the passport. Paul Wood, one of the BBC correspondents in the city, recalls that British broadcasters were in a better position than most because the Iraqi regime wanted them in the country and therefore the process was shorter. Wood recalled that after arriving in Baghdad he was allocated his secret police minder who, some days before the bombing began, quietly revealed his fears of what would happen when the Coalition troops took the city. Wood paid the minder $1,000 to keep him and his cameraman safe, which allowed the man to evacuate his family from the city. The agreement was that Wood would then keep the minder safe once the city fell. Despite all the backhanders and private deals correspondents were still subject to the random whims of the regime. If they failed to attend a press facility at the Iraqi Information Ministry they would be summoned by the chief minder to explain their disrespect. Rageh Omar, one of the other BBC staff based in the city, recalled the official Iraqi government statements and the uncertainty over their validity. Certainly some of the more outlandish claims by the Iraqi Information Minister Mohammed Saeed Al-Sahhaf were easy to disregard, yet many others were considered plausible; when the regime claimed that cluster bombs had been dropped on the town of Hilla this was proved to be correct. When the Defence Minister General Sultan Hashim Achmed told the press corps that he expected Iraq to be surrounded within five to ten days, he too was proved correct. Other statements were less credible, such as Al-Sahhaf's announcement that the Iraqi armed forces had actually allowed the Americans to enter the Baghdad airport complex as part of a strategic plan.

Despite all the restrictions, the Al-Arabiya correspondent Gaballah believed that access actually deteriorated after the city fell to US troops:

'With Saddam's regime there were few people who had the say, a few giants, but the Americans have many different directions. You may get permission and go to a location to film and then it is refused.'[7]

Indeed he claimed that the only time he came under direct physical threat was after the city had fallen and he was attempting to film Iraqi prisoners: 'They [soldiers] were arresting some Iraqis, putting them on the ground, and we filmed it. One of the soldiers allowed me to take pictures and then the other one hit me. They were American.'[8]

### Shooting the messenger?

The press's preferred home, the Palestine Hotel on Street 47 in Baghdad, was a location well known to Coalition commanders, both from previous notification and representation and from the on-screen reporting during the bombardment of the city. It had been one of the regime's 'preferred locations' for the media ever since the 1991 Gulf war.

On the morning of 8 April a battalion of US troops entered the area around the hotel and encountered considerable armed resistance. The nature of the resistance was such that the US troops believed that an Iraqi 'spotter' must be located somewhere, probably quite high up to afford him a view over the entire area. US commanders directed troops to hunt for the spotter, a search that culminated in a tank attack on the Palestine Hotel from where a US army officer believed he had sighted someone with a pair of binoculars.

Two journalists were killed in the attack: Taras Protsyuk, a Ukrainian cameraman working for Reuters, and Jose Couso, a cameraman with the Spanish network Telecinco. Three other members of the press corps were injured. This was a hugely unfortunate occurrence for the Coalition, and one which many observers feel that the Pentagon has still to explain fully and convincingly. Yet the media death toll would continue to rise. That very same day an Al-Jazeera journalist, Tarek Ayoub, was fatally wounded when the network's office on the banks of the Tigris was struck by a US bomb. For Al-Jazeera it was a repeat of events in Afghanistan: on 13 November 2001 the Al-Jazeera bureau in Kabul was hit by US aircraft, which the Americans stated was a mistake—cynical Al-Jazeera staff called it calculated retribution. Fortunately no one was killed in that attack.

Predictably events at the Palestine Hotel caused outrage among the world's media community. The New York-based Committee to Protect Journalists wrote an open letter to US Defense Secretary Donald Rumsfeld accusing the United States of violating the Geneva Convention. The entire incident was filmed by the French TV station France 3, the footage adding to accusations that the US attack had been deliberate. The French correspondent Caroline Sines said: 'I was at the Palestine Hotel at the moment of the attack.... Our film shows that the US tank took its time targeting the fourteenth floor of the hotel, where many of the journalists are staying, at a moment of complete calm.'[9] The journalist Richard Engel was less circumspect. In response to the US statement that there had been hostile intent from the hotel, he wrote: 'That's nothing less than total bullshit. There was no fire.'[10] Conflicting explanations from different US commanders and spokesmen did little to improve the already tense relationship. General Buford Blount (commander of the Third Infantry Division) told the media: 'The tank was receiving fire from the hotel, RPG [rocket propelled grenades], and small arms fire, and engaged with one round. The firing stopped.'[11] Other officers gave conflicting opinions. Some stated that an Iraqi bunker existed next to the hotel. These explanations were contested at the time by the statements of resident journalists interviewed immediately after the event. The death of the Al-Jazeera reporter was of particular interest to a largely sceptical media. Was this a deliberate act and a repeat of the bombing of Al-Jazeera's Kabul bureau, perhaps because of its perceived 'military significance'? Had US pilots been ordered to target Al-Jazeera's offices, perhaps as punishment for the channel's reporting of the dead US soldiers some days before? Conspiracy theories abounded, and assumptions, many based on incomplete or inaccurate information, quickly solidified into 'fact'.

The probability is that human error almost certainly accounted for both events, as it did in the targeting of a British Household Cavalry armoured vehicle by an A-10 Thunderbolt and when a Royal Air Force jet aircraft was shot down on the third night of the war. The reality is that in conflict mistakes are made by tired, nervous and often scared young men and women—mistakes that may prove fatal. In the case of the attack on Al-Jazeera the issues were complex. The Al-Jazeera bureau was next to a villa often used by the Iraqi Information Minister Mohammed Saeed Al Sahaf. Between the villa and the network offices was an electrical generator which US forces almost certainly targeted. The Commission to Protect Journalists concluded in its own inquiry into the incident that the attack was 'not deliberate but was avoidable'. The Committee believed it had uncovered a communications breakdown within the US army chain of command and questioned whether targeting information held by senior officers was largely disseminated to troops on the ground. The Committee stated: 'Pentagon officials and commanders in Baghdad had been widely aware that the Palestine Hotel was full of international journalists.... About 100 were lodged there.'[12] Indeed, after the experiences of Kabul the Al-Jazeera network had publicly provided Rumsfeld with the Global Positioning System (GPS) position of their Baghdad offices.

Regardless of the circumstances of the attack the fact remains that the 2003 Iraq conflict has, statistically, been the most dangerous conflict in history for journalists. From the start of the war up to the time of writing, thirty-six journalists had been killed and at least nine of them were as a result of 'friendly fire' incidents. This was the second-highest ranking for cause of death after insurgent actions accounting for nineteen lives.

Given the location and rhetoric of the war it would be natural to presume that the Iraqi regime gave primacy to the pan-Arab media. Yet this was apparently not the case, and it was as difficult for the Arab media to work in the country as it was for their Western colleagues. Saddam Hussein may well have made a similar gamble to that of 1991, believing that allowing Western news organisations in and encouraging them to film the destruction and death of war would, through the channel's audiences, encourage dissent and condemnation. Given the strength of the world's opposition to the conflict this was a reasonable assumption, yet in reality, and like the 1991 conflict, it was a failed strategy. On 3 April Al-Jazeera announced that it would be suspending its television coverage from Baghdad in response to the Iraqi Information Ministry banning two of its reporters, Diyar al-Omair and Tayseer Alouni. As we saw in previous chapters, the channel is not unaccustomed to such bans around the region but to be barred from covering the most important story in the Arab world at that time could not have been a pleasant prospect. Al-Jazeera's editor-in-chief Ibrahim Helal told the BBC: 'They cannot dictate to us who can and cannot work.' The channel's announcement came as a shock to the regime and the ban on the two journalists was rescinded the following day. This was a foretaste of what was to come; at the time of writing the channel remains banned from Iraq—a direct order from the Iraqi government.

The view from Baghdad was never clear, and given the difficulties experienced by journalists of all nationalities one might even question if it was worth the effort. The Iraqi Information Ministry used the media shamelessly, and at times comically, to project its own view of the world. Yet the view was irresistible to editors and channel controllers, and the bombardment during the first few hours of the war made compelling viewing. What is apparent, however, is that the Iraqi regime, as in the 1991 conflict, attached equal importance to the presence of Western media such as the BBC and CNN and to the Arab regional media. For all his outlandish and at times ridiculous statements, it would be easy to forget that the opening salvos in the Iraq war's battle for hearts and minds were fired not by the Coalition but by the rather comical figure of Mohammed Saeed Al Sahaf. Most, however, will remember the incredible 'firework' displays of the Coalition's 'shock and awe' bombardment, which were captured for the world to see by a small group of journalists in the beleaguered capital.

# THE RECKONING

'I dogmatise and am contradicted, and in this conflict of opinion and sentiments I find delight.'—from Sir John Hawkins, Life of Samuel Johnson, 1787

9/11 was a horrific, disgusting and unprecedented act that forced the world's last remaining superpower to confront how it was perceived in the wider world. What it found caused it a profound shock, but how did the United States use this newly-found knowledge? This book is not intended to assess the rights or wrongs of the 2003 war in Iraq, although the publicly-claimed connection between Saddam's regime and the 9/11 Al-Qaeda hijackers now appears tenuous. So too does the existence of weapons of mass destruction on which the case for war was so robustly constructed. What is apparent is that in the aftermath of the 9/11 attacks the United States found itself in a very difficult position. Over and above its sentiments of anger and fear, it was profoundly shocked at the idea that an unprovoked attack of this magnitude should be launched on its shores. And in its fear and confusion its President, who in the wake of 9/11 had increasingly defined the world in terms of good or evil, appeared to fall under the spell of a highly-organised group of intellectually superior individuals who appeared to have been waiting for just such an internationally calamitous event to translate their beliefs from mere conjecture and debate into hard US foreign policy.[1]

On the day the Iraq war began the eighty-five-year-old West Virginian Democratic Senator, Robert Byrd, said on the floor of the Senate:

'I weep for my country...what is happening to this country? When did we become a nation that ignores and berates our friends? When did we decide to risk undermining international order by adopting a radical and doctrinaire approach to using our awesome military might? How can we abandon diplomatic efforts when the turmoil in the world cries out for diplomacy?'[2]

While Byrd's comments ostensibly fell on deaf ears in the Senate chamber, his comments had resonance across the wider world; many people did indeed question America's self-appointed role as world policeman, a role that at worst usurped the authority of the UN and at best paid it lip-service. The United States was clearly in a difficult position. It had, after all, been the main supporter of the long-established UN-brokered sanctions operations against Saddam's regime. Since 1991 these had increased in complexity and expense, ultimately involving military forces from a large number of mainly Western states. It was evident that these sanctions were harming the Iraqi people, and in the already angry Arab media their suffering was often compared with that of Arab children in the occupied Palestinian territories. Comments by previous US Administration officials had done little to assuage feelings. The former US Secretary of State Madeleine Albright was famously asked if the death of half a million Iraqi children was a price worth paying for the sanctions operations. Understandbly her reply—'We think the price is worth it'[3]—was badly received in the Arab world. So what did the value of the sanctions operations amount to? It has been subsequently shown that the sanctions were ultimately successful, though at a substantial cost. The Iraqi Survey Group finally concluded that the regime possessed none of the stocks of deadly weapons on which certainly Britain built its case for war. Of course this does not mean that

Saddam Hussein did not have aspirations for such capabilities—nor, as Halabja so clearly illustrates, would he have had any scruples about using them had he been so equipped. Saddam had for years tried to subvert the UN sanctions operations. He regularly attempted to export oil stocks out of the country illegally, and the sophisticated UN operation that grew in the northern Arabian Gulf is a testimony to the efforts his regime expended.

The question which the United States asked itself was essentially a simple one: diplomatically, how long could such (mis)conduct be allowed to continue? Saddam had been flouting UN sanctions since the end of the 1991 Gulf war; the UN may be an imperfect organisation and subject to the same whims and fallibilities as individual governments, but it is the agreed arbiter for international conduct. At some stage its decisions would inevitably need to be enforced. However, the issue was the justness of that enforcement and whether it should have been conducted unilaterally and without the Security Council's blessing.

While many in the Arab street would have been delighted to see the US armed forces receive a bloody nose from Saddam's forces (for the same reason as some sections of Palestinian society cheered when the hijacked planes crashed into the twin towers of the World Trade Center), there was never any doubt that a US-led Coalition would prevail militarily over Saddam's forces. But there was much more at stake than a mere demonstration of military might. The United States had publicly stated its goals and objectives for the war, which—after defending the American people and eliminating Saddam's stocks of WMD—was to 'liberate' the Iraqi population.[4] This had to be publicly proved. When Victoria Clarke issued her Public Affairs guidance to the US military in February 2003, it is inconceivable that the battle for hearts and minds would not have been at the forefront of her thinking. For an operation that had been planned since January 2002,[5] the importance of harnessing regional support should and was factored into the planning process from the outset. In October 2002 the US Defense Secretary Donald Rumsfeld had drawn up a list of twenty-nine issues which he felt were of paramount importance to the success of the operation. He wrote: 'Iraq could successfully best the US in public relations and persuade the world that it was a war against Muslims.'[6] Yet for all these apparent good intentions, a solid relationship with the Arab media never materialised—Arab embeds were seemingly sacrificed for an 'in-bed' relationship with US and British media, to which almost without exception the Coalition gave primacy. For those Arab media that did make it on to the field of battle, higher-level Pentagon clearances and assurances now appeared hollow and subsidiary to the prevailing opinion of troops on the ground where matters of access were concerned.

Despite the arrival of a senior White House press manager, the US arrangements for the Arab media were not rated highly when compared to those of other Coalition countries. James Wilkinson himself said: 'The news has got to come from the front lines.'[7] But which side of the lines? With so few Arab media embedded with Coalition forces, events behind Iraqi lines would inevitably form the core of Arab coverage. The effect of the war on civilians would become a mainstay for all Arab media coverage. CENTCOM had issued little or no guidance to deployed units on the importance of engaging with the regional media, so when Coalition forces did meet Arab media they appeared ill-prepared and uneasy about the experience. This absence of understanding lay at the root of the disagreements that would follow. Simply put, the Coalition saw the satellite news services of the Arab channels packaged, boxed and presented in the same way as CNN or the BBC. And why wouldn't they be, since most of the staff had been trained by the BBC? Yet Western media do not generally allow their presenters to inject emotion, feeling, exaggeration or—when the occasion might arise—sensationalism into their reports. Organisations such as the BBC tend towards a more distant and detached appraisal of events. In all but certain programmes (such as BBC Radio 4's 'From Our Own Correspondent'[8]) the presenter takes an impartial viewpoint and allows viewers to form their own opinions. Yet these are features of the Arab world's media and the Americans did not anticipate, the demagoguery of these new stations, nor were they prepared to deal with it. It is disquieting that the US media manager Jim Wilkinson should have actually agreed in his candid admission that the United States had 'no idea' how to communicate with the Arab world. The strands of his Arab media policy were immature at best; the provision for Doha-based correspondents of a prayer room and seats at the front of the CENTCOM auditorium was a useful courtesy but can hardly be described as 'policy'. And what importance was attached to the reports that followed? Wilkinson also admitted that he learned of Arab reporting only from one of his generals, and while higher-level media analysis may have been undertaken in the United States he evidently saw no sign of it. Yet this clear absence of understanding did not stop Wilkinson declaring that Al-Jazeera was 'absolutely biased' and severing all contact with the channel after it had screened images of dead and captured US troops.

Wilkinson's assertion that Arab media 'just wanted to be treated equally' may in essence have been correct. However, it can now be seen that in view of their importance they should have been given priority. He would have done well to read *To Prevail: an American Strategy for the Campaign against Terrorism*, a 2001 publication of the Washington-based Center for Strategic and International Studies. In this paper the Center considered the best way of targeting foreign media: 'Simply including the foreign media in press conferences or in press room briefings does not suffice; exclusive or limited pool interviews garner significantly more airtime for the interviewee.'[9]

Wilkinson acknowledged that when it came to dealing with Arab media the British operation in the Doha headquarters was much more sophisticated. The twice-daily provision of the senior military spokesman Group Captain Lockwood to Arab media saw a positive relationship develop; British representatives were much better informed of Arab media coverage than their US counterparts, and a close liaison was established between Doha and the Arab media experts in the FCO who were able to monitor trends and opinions.

The lack of finesse and nuance on the part of the Americans can partly be attributed to their largely unconditional domestic support. What debate may have existed in US civil society before the war had been pre-defined either by the enormity of the events of 9/11 or by the overwhelming supportive stance taken by US media networks. Professor Mark Crispin Miller describes US media coverage of the war as 'dazzling heroic spectacle. Nothing goes wrong, everything goes right. No one gets hurt. You don't see any bloodshed.... If you question that, you are not a patriot.'[10] Professor Nancy Snow quoted the American talk-show host Bill Mayer when she considered those in the media who were not 'on message': 'When you ride alone you ride with Bin Laden.'[11]

US troops went to war in Iraq with a righteous determination and a resolve that reflected the views and sentiments then prevailing in US society. As the historian Richard Crockatt observed. 'In the wake of September 11, America's global agenda could carry only enhanced moral and political force, given the scale of the harm done to America.'[12] Survey after survey, speech after speech established a connection between Bin Laden and the regime of Saddam Hussein. Like the US public, still traumatised by the World Trade Center and anthrax attacks, the TV networks believed in their President at America's time of need. As eminent Cambridge University academic Stefan Halper observed: 'Significant parts of the [US] media seemed frozen in the White House headlights.'[13] Even Fox News, the channel that seemed to fuel US public sentiment so vehemently, admitted that it might have got it wrong. The director of newsgathering at Fox, David Rhodes, told a conference in Qatar: 'We were widely laughed at for our colour-coded security threat warnings.... All media in the US share a certain amount of guilt for taking these images and passing them on.'[14]

For the other key media actors in the conflict the story was very different. The British media appeared split down the middle—some of the biggest-selling tabloids and broadsheets printed daily condemnation of the war policy, and in-theatre their correspondents were asking difficult and contentious questions—impertinence that was at times anathema to the US military. In the Arab world public opinion was the opposite of that in the United States. In Arab eyes the war was morally wrong, a huge number of civilians would die, and the Americans were once again demonstrating a duality and a contempt for Arab society and opinion.

As the conflict developed the United States finally seemed to become interested in what the Arab world was seeing, and government officials began questioning Arab coverage of the conflict. This interest was largely represented as criticism. Where once Republicans and neo-conservatives had praised channels such as Al-Jazeera for their free speech, as the war progressed senior officials such as Rumsfeld and Wolfowitz questioned the Arab station's objectivity, seemingly concluding that it was inherently biased against the West. In London, however, minds were more open and the channel's importance was mentioned on a number of occasions in both Houses of Parliament. In the Upper Chamber on 23 May 2002 Baroness Symons of Vernham Dean expressed approval of 'the positive contribution of Al-Jazeera to encouraging free debate on political and social issues in the Middle East.'[15] On 3 April 2003 Ann Clywd, commenting on the difficulties Al-Jazeera was having in Baghdad, asked the House of Commons: 'I have several times over the past week made representations to the House authorities asking that at least one Arabic channel should be placed alongside the twenty-four channels at our disposal in the House. It is important to see the images that the Arabs are seeing, so that we can better judge the progress of the war and assess why certain people react in certain ways.'[16]

Perhaps most illuminating were the questions put to the Prime Minister on 24 March 2003. Mrs Alice Mahon, Member of Parliament for Halifax, asked: 'Has the Prime Minister studied the footage from Al-Jazeera, which went in to report on the fifty or so civilians who were killed in Basra after the bombing or shelling? There were terrible pictures of women and children—one child with half its head blown out. Just before I came into the Chamber, I heard a report on the radio that we are shelling Basra yet again. How does the Prime Minister think that we can protect civilians when that kind of thing is happening?'[17]

It is paradoxical that it was the United States which from the outset had led the effort to engage with the Arab press, yet it appeared to give up just as the conflict began. However, in Britain engagement with the Arab media had been poor, but as the war progressed many corners of the British government seemed to recognise that Al-Jazeera and the other pan-Arab channels needed to be listened to. Even the channel's arch-nemesis, the Labour Party's communications supremo Alistair Campbell, has publicly stated that his initial views of the channel's output may have been incorrect. On 24 November 2004 he was interviewed by the channel, on air, and contrary to many of the assertions he made before and during the conflict he told the Al-Jazeera interviewer Al-Badri:

'I found out that contrary to the view of the Americans, who consider Al-Jazeera to be a negative tool, you look at yourselves as a factor of change and reform and modernisation in the Arab world. This is what we want and what we are endeavouring to realise. The visit opened my eyes to new things.'[18]

There was one sense in which the US analysis may have been correct. Arab media *were* almost uniformly biased in their reporting of the conflict. Arab journalists had to report a deeply unpopular war to a sceptical and angry public. As Al-Jazeera's Cairo correspondent Hussain Abdul Ghari explained, 'The Iraq war has a different significance to us, as we are an Arab satellite channel with a country in our region that has been attacked.' The very personal nature of the war for Arab journalists was demonstrated when Shakir Hamid, *paterfamilias* to the Abu Dhabi TV team in Baghdad, broke down on TV on learning that his older brother and his two children had been killed during Coalition bombing of Nassiriya.[19] The news presenter Hisham Diwani recalled: 'As an Arab journalist, once you have discovered the truth and given an accurate account of events, you cannot stay aloof and not condemn the actions of this occupation. This is your role as a journalist: it gives the occupying Coalition forces no hope of winning the Iraqis' hearts and minds.'[20] Yet at the same time, as the British parliamentarians noted, Arab media provided a very important, perhaps unique perspective on the war—an indicator of wider Arab sentiment.

Clearly the Arab media reflected the wider public opinion on the Arab street. But to what extent did it lead it? Arguably the Arab media could not have reported a war in an Arab country, to which the entire Arab world objected, in anything other than a pro-Arab manner; to do so would have been commercial suicide. Arab audiences live in Amman, Riyadh, Cairo and Tangier—apart from tiny minorities, they do not live in Washington or London. Yet it is more complex than this; Arab journalists shared '*asabiya*' with Iraqis, indeed some of them were themselves expatriate Iraqis who had no particular reason to love Saddam's regime but who could not support the assault on their country. For many Arabs the wider war against terrorism had become a war against Islam and therefore a war of national and cultural survival. As the distinguished reporter Max Hastings observed during the Falklands war in 1982, 'No British reporter could be neutral when his own country was fighting: objectivity was a peacetime luxury, and reporting an extension of the war effort.'[21] Accepting that Arab media had a greater level of personal familiarity with the conflict than their Western counterparts is important when considering allegations of bias.

Were, then, the pan-Arab satellite news channels institutionally biased against the United States and Britain in their news reporting? The absence of detailed and objective academic analysis of the coverage makes this difficult to assess; however, that which has been undertaken suggests that the station's news output was *not* institutionally biased against Coalition forces. Against Israel perhaps but not against the Coalition. A very senior FCO official was unequivocal on the issue: 'Al-Jazeera news is not institutionally biased.'[22] However, there is a corollary to this, namely the question of bias in other aspects of pan-Arab satellite programmes. As has already been noted, there is clear evidence that many of the discussion programmes, notably 'The Opposite Direction' on Al-Jazeera, were inflammatory in their coverage of events and intentionally so. Jihad Ali-Ballout makes no apologies for the programme's content:

'People arrive at the impression that our programming leaves something to be desired, but they have to look at it in the context of what the programme is and what our editorial policy is. We do not want to be the censor; this is another price that America has to pay for democracy.'[23]

Debate in the Arab world, while equally vociferous, remains inconclusive. Fouad Ajami, Professor of Middle East Studies at Johns Hopkins University, wrote: 'They [pan-Arab TV networks] mimic Western norms of journalistic fairness while pandering to pan-Arab sentiments.'[24] The Saudi journalist Jamal Khashoggi looks at their effect on the Arab masses: 'They are being led by the masses, they don't lead the masses. They know the taste of the Arab street and the Arab street is anti-US… they are just like the *NY Post!*'[25] And, it might be argued, not dissimilar to the British *Daily Mirror*, which deliberately took an anti-war stance to boost its circulation.[26] Dana Suyyagh, a Canadian-educated Arab journalist, formerly of Al-Jazeera and now a producer at Al-Arabiya, considers one of the most contentious issues—Arab channels providing a mouthpiece for Bin Laden: 'Maybe. But that would make us Bush's mouthpiece as well. He gets more airtime actually.' Hatiz al-Mirazi, Washington bureau chief for Al-Jazeera in 2001–5, believes that in the Arab world 'we have been accused of making Al-Jazeera a mouthpiece for the US government. Almost daily we bring on spokesmen for the Administration.'[27] And this is more than can be said of other Arab media—the refusal of the Syrian press even to print a letter from the British Prime Minister Tony Blair is arguably indicative of a more sinister attempt to muzzle debate than Al-Jazeera has ever attempted.

Some Arab media analysts point out what they believe were three obvious shortcomings in pan-Arab TV reporting. The first was the inability of Arab channels to communicate the attitude of the Iraqi people toward their regime. Iraqis were not seen criticising the regime, and the writer Abdel Karim Samara wondered why: 'Was this state censorship or self-censorship due to fear of the regime and its oppression?'[28] The second fault was the absence of knowledge of the Iraqi opposition, its capabilities and internal relations. This was shown in the common assumption that the future of Iraq was played out only by forces in the field, i.e. the Iraqi and Coalition armies. The third dimension was the lack of credibility of some reports, with battles described by correspondents as fierce, while the same station later reported that they had been no more than short exchanges of fire. The apparent failure to balance coverage of Saddam's regime has been noted before. Sheikh Abdullah Bin Zayed

Al-Nahayan, the UAE Culture Minister, delivered a scathing address to Arab media for failing to oppose Saddam before the war.[29]

While these may be valid criticisms, the channels believe that their work was deliberately impeded by the Coalition—a view that resonates with many Western observers. Arab media were comprehensively, though not invariably, treated very differently from their Western counterparts. From the outset Arab media were not embedded with Coalition forces due to concerns over operational security. Almost by accident one or two teams did meet up with British units, but even so the degree of exposure they were afforded was less than that of their Western colleagues. Their embeds with US forces were equally problematical.

The issue of operational security deserves further consideration. As has been shown, the military have a deep-seated distrust of journalists, although increasingly their utility is discussed and planned for as often as their potential as a liability. During the Iraq conflict the media were taken into the confidence of the military commanders: from the British viewpoint this was largely due to confidence in the *Green Guide* and to the relationship that had slowly been nurtured between known defence correspondents and senior officers over a series of operational deployments. Thus the BBC's Paul Adams was given almost complete access to the highly classified plan of attack in advance and trusted to retain the secret. The Americans had more difficulty. The former talk show host Geraldo Rivera drew a map in the sand during a live broadcast on Fox News, which military commanders believed revealed highly sensitive strategic information. He was quickly removed. We have also seen how Fox TV broke the embargo on board RFA *Sir Galahad* during the transit to Umm Qasr. One might therefore argue convincingly that military commanders were right to fear the media; also that their obvious distrust of the Arab media over security issues was not entirely well-founded—the Western press could be equally fickle if the story demanded.

The only Arab team that appeared to get anywhere close to the same level of access was from Abu Dhabi TV—fronted by the Arabic-speaking ex-British Army major, Alex Gardiner. In retrospect, this was an extremely clever move on the part of the station, which clearly had the foresight to realise that it might have more difficulty gaining access than Western channels. Some commentators have observed that Abu Dhabi TV performed surprisingly well during the Iraq war, adopting a generally unsensationalist approach.[30] Certainly military personnel were much happier dealing with a journalist who had experience or understanding of service life. This is indicative of a wider problem throughout the military-media interface. The loss of dedicated defence correspondents, resulting in an absence of knowledge of even basic facts about the military, has led to both misunderstanding and resentment.

Given the absence of Arab media one must question if there was a concerted campaign to exclude them. There is ample evidence that the Americans regarded them with suspicion, yet US PAG had been quite clear: international media would have access, including organisations from the Arab world. Implementation of that PAG on the ground was not always smooth. Certainly the nature of the relationship between the US military and the Arab media appeared to be conditioned by experience of their own domestic media. The largely pro-war US media pool presented the military with few challenges. Their focus was positive and, like the soldiers they filmed, many had an absolute belief in the justice of the war. The Arab media did not share these sentiments. Their reports could not be predicted and their agenda was governed not just by the current conflict but also by grievances over Palestine and Afghanistan, and over Iraqi civilians to whom US media briefings often dispassionately referred as 'collateral damage'.

In advance of military operations the Pentagon has required all embed media, including Al-Jazeera, to provide detailed information on their electronic equipment. In particular it wanted the serial numbers of satellite telephone equipment, including the INMARSAT terminals used for sending video files, and the live 'videophone' pictures which represented the prime means of video communication from the embedded reporters. The request caused unease in several Western news organisations—there was suspicion that the information might be used for jamming transmissions. Certainly the Americans exercised the capability to suppress similar Iraqi communications devices. Whether such suppression was *deliberately* extended to the media can only be guessed at, a number of media organisations observed unusual call failure codes from their systems. In the field these were simply attributed to network congestion, but later examination of the subtle differences in the error codes led at least one telecommunications expert to suggest that they may have been the result of deliberate intent.[31] An extension, perhaps, of the information operation?

Recurring incidents intensify the debate. The Al-Jazeera.net website was hacked early in the campaign, users being directed to a site entitled 'Let Freedom Ring' and displaying a large Stars and Stripes. Conspiracy theories quickly spread and many at the channel wondered if the US government had been responsible. After investigation it became apparent that a 'patriotic' zealot and computer expert, John Racine, had been to blame. He stated that he 'acted after learning in March [2003] that Al-Jazeera's website had posted photos of American prisoners of war and soldiers killed during the US invasion of Iraq'. Racine was finally caught by US Federal authorities, sentenced to community service and fined $2,000. Al-Jazeera was forced to rely on a mobile phone text messaging service for its news. The service, which operated in both English and Arabic, was made available to subscribers in more than 130 countries, and has subsequently proved profitable for the channel.[32] The hacking incident proved damaging to the wider debate over the war, and Al-

Jazeera was rightly aggrieved. So successful has its internet site been that, according to the internet search engine Lycos, the word 'Al-Jazeera' beat both 'sex' and 'war' as the top internet search term.

The hacking of the website was an irritant to the channel, but at worst it was no more than an inconvenience. The loss of the journalist Tarek Ayoub in a mistaken US bombing attack on the channel's Baghdad offices was a huge blow and was regarded with deep suspicion, especially as this was the second occasion on which the channel's offices had been targeted inadvertently (as was claimed) by US forces in two consecutive conflicts. Regardless of the circumstances of the hacking and of the tragic death of Tarek Ayoub, the Arab TV networks surely presented the technologically superior Americans with an ethical and operational dilemma—the choice between interfering with the much articulated right of free speech on the one hand and, on the other, struggling to defend their actions in an increasingly uphill battle for Arab hearts and minds.

If Arab news networks were excluded by the Coalition did this mean that they were affording the Iraqi regime undue prominence? The extensive coverage of the Iraqi Information Minister—with his long and rambling press conferences often broadcast in full—suggests that this may have been the case. But if a network is not provided with access, then it will have difficulty filling its airtime. Twenty-four-hour news coverage is precisely what its name implies, and in the absence of embedded reports the on-duty editor will fill the schedule with whatever information is currently available. This is one of the enduring complaints of continuous satellite TV news. Often news has to be recycled, and sometimes weak stories may gain undue prominence in the absence of other, more newsworthy material. Western networks are no different, yet they were able to fill their programming schedules with continuous imagery and reports from the huge number of embedded reporters. Indeed some minor fire-fights were covered for hours by news

networks in the absence of other substantive footage. Arab channels, with no direct access to Coalition troops, focused on areas
about which they could report—notably civilian casualties.

Arab news reporting was neither perfect nor consistent, but
neither was that of their Western counterparts and critics. When
Arab networks caused uproar by showing dead bodies, so did British
and American networks. The US Secretary of Defense Donald
Rumsfeld led the attack on Al-Jazeera's use of footage of dead and
captured US troops, saying that according to the Geneva Convention it was not permitted to photograph and embarrass or humiliate
prisoners of war. Yet US authorities failed to criticise CBS, which
broadcast the faces of the dead on its 'Face the Nation' programme
or SkyNews, which also broadcast the images, and in a case of
double standards subsequently chose to release unpalatable photographs of the bodies of Saddam's sons Uday and Qusay. Rumsfeld
told a Pentagon press conference that the photographs 'would help
convince frightened Iraqis that Saddam's rule was over, a consideration that far outweighed any sensitivities over showing the
corpses'.[33] Why then should Arab networks show any sensitivity?

When Arab networks were accused of unrestrained support for
the Iraqi regime or for using inflammatory words and terminology,
similar accusations were levelled at US networks. The US Administration accused Arab networks of using the term 'occupiers' pejora-
tively; Arabs questioned the use of the strapline 'Operation Iraqi
Freedom' by FoxNews, arguing that 'freedom' is a loaded term.
One observer summed up the dilemma: 'Arabs are disinclined to
take advice on objectivity from US journalists wearing a US flag on
their lapel.'[34]

A key element of the Coalition media campaign was the belief
that Arab opinion could be won over by a quick victory. The military ordered its combat camera teams[35] to focus on scenes of jubi-
lation and welcome by Iraqi civilians, yet there proved to be few of

these. The Arab media certainly focused on civilians, but their interpretation was of the human cost of war. Casualties were a considerable source of interest, and realistically there was little that the Coalition forces could do to mitigate this. However, guidance from CENTCOM might have prevented other self-defeating errors by the US media.

The subsequent occupation of Iraq placed Coalition troops under the magnifying-glass of the world's media, above all the Arab channels, which have given extensive coverage to the undignified manhandling of tribal elders and intrusive searches of women by US forces. The placing of a US flag on the statue of Saddam, allegedly on the orders of a US Marine Corps captain, was such a crass and inappropriate act that it immediately confirmed the worst fears of an already hugely sceptical wider Arab audience.

It might be suggested that the Arab press would be naturally critical of the Coalition and would choose to focus on failures and setbacks rather than positive achievements. (The shock the Arab world felt when US forces were seen in Baghdad is attributable to the style of Arab media coverage which tended to play down the military successes of the Coalition.) Of course negative reporting was not the prerogative of the Arab media—many of their Western colleagues filed similar reports. The Australian journalist Paul McGeough of *The Age* newspaper noted the lack of sensitivity of US troops after the end of hostilities:

I have just returned to my Baghdad hotel on Abu Nuwas Street, which runs along the east bank of the Tigris, when a US Humvee roars past. Blaring from a block of six big speakers strapped to its rooftop is John Mellencamp's 1980s American anthem 'Pink Houses: Ain't that America? You and me! Ain't that America? Something to seeeee!' This may be a huge joke for someone whose global horizon ends at his extended fingertips, but such vulgar and contemptuous performances announce to the Iraqi people. 'The hell with you and your culture. We own your country and we'll do what we damn well please. And if you're praying as we blast by in our Humvee, then too bad.'[36]

In Tikrit one US Army colonel told Associated Press: 'The enemy is a coward. He continues to hide behind women, children and his own population.' Yet Arab TV channels regularly aired coverage of Iraqi men being forced to lie face-down in the dirt with their hands tied behind their backs while their families looked on at what was clearly a humiliating scene. The paradox was acute, and the inability of senior officers to recognise the effect on Arab opinion of images and statements such as these was disastrous. The absence of sophistication among US troops was probably based on understandable but remediable ignorance. British forces in the southern part of the country were praised for their handling of sensitive situations, many commentators referring to the experience gained in Northern Ireland. This may be the case although British troops generally have a less 'gung-ho' attitude than their US counterparts.

It is clear that as the leader of Coalition forces in Operation Iraqi Freedom the United States failed to rise to the challenge of the Arab media. Far from the campaign being waged *in* the Arab media, it appears that it was waged *against* it. The Administration's rhetoric, particularly against Al-Jazeera, was often repeated by Western news organisations and as a consequence was picked up by Coalition troops in the front line. Had Iraqi TV been able or even willing to embed with British forces, and had Nick Pollard's wish for SkyNews to be embedded with Iraqi forces been realisable, then suspicion would have been justified. To a certain extent it was understandable. Yet, as the House of Commons Defence Select Committee observed, there exists in the military an inherent distrust of all media: 'We believe that the importance of the media campaign in the modern world remains under-appreciated by sections of the Armed Forces.'[37] The media often do themselves no favours, as with the tabloid fascination for sensationalist stories of equipment and leadership failings, which have certainly reinforced suspicion in senior sections of the British military. Even the embedding of known British correspondents caused consternation among certain British commanders, and thus reactions to Arab correspondents were like fear of the unknown.

The House of Commons Defence Select Committee considered the impact of the UK Information Campaign when it interviewed the MoD's director of Targeting and Information Operations in December 2003. He was asked to measure the success of the operations, and replied:

'We were unable to counter the high level of cynicism and hostility that we were meeting in open forum, predominantly in the media. We had no eloquent answer to most of that.... I suspect we were slightly naïve in thinking we would be more persuasive with some of those regional neighbours than we were.'[38]

Similar thoughts have been echoed privately around the Pentagon and some Washington think-tanks. It is apparent that the United States needs to approach regional public diplomacy in a fundamentally new way, opening direct dialogue with the Arab and Islamic world through its already existing and increasingly influential transnational media. Yet this requires a fundamental change in mindset. While the United States seeks to portray what it regards as 'truth', it has to overcome its institutionalised intolerance of any 'truth' that hints of anti-Americanism; it believes that existing transnational media are inherently biased. Evidence suggests that from a cultural viewpoint alone this may be the case, yet a more fundamental question needs to be asked: does it even matter if Arab media are biased? The fact remains that channels such as Al-Jazeera, Al-Arabiya and Abu Dhabi TV enjoy a legitimacy and credibility throughout the Arab world that Al-Hurra can only aspire to. Can the US risk *not* engaging with them?

In *The Clash of Civilisations* Samuel Huntington expresses the belief that inherent differences in culture will be the seeds of future conflict. Undeniably huge cultural differences exist between Western Christian and Arab Muslim cultures. Events such as 9/11 have caused people to focus on these differences rather than on similarities. Arab media networks have massive public support throughout the Muslim world,[39] and undoubtedly reflect a strong vein of Muslim and Arab opinion. It is not surprising that they largely play to the predispositions of their audiences. If the West wishes to enhance its dialogue with the Middle East, if it wishes to explain its policies, then it has to do so through a credible forum. That forum must consist of organic pan-Arab TV channels and not networks like Al-Hurra. Jihad Ali-Ballout believes that the time has now arrived for Arab media to be viewed as professional organisations:

'You must deal with us in the same way as you treat CNN and the BBC. If you want to reflect your point of view, to an audience that already harbours cynicism, then your only medium is Al-Jazeera. But don't expect Al-Jazeera to be bowled over by reputation. Al-Jazeera will provide you with a platform for your views but this will not guarantee acceptance of your stance—we go back to Al-Hurra. By merely disseminating a point of view the battle is not finished. It takes more than information to convince public opinion of your good will towards the Arab world.'[40]

Al-Jazeera is not perfect; its programmes can be lurid, sensational and over-heated. It may not always report events perfectly, inaccuracies may creep in as the channel battles against its competitors to bring the news to Arab screens first. It experiences almost identical problems to every other twenty-four-hour news broadcasting organisation throughout the world. Yet unlike the BBC and even the heavily-slanted Fox TV, Al-Jazeera is stalked by its critics who seize upon its occasional mistakes as clear evidence—if not proof—of its bias and anti-Western stance. But even if you accept a small percentage of the nonsense that is written about it, there is one undeniable truth that cannot be distorted: it is the nearest the Arab world has to an independent media organisation. And given the importance placed by the United States on free speech and the enthusiasm for it that US supporters for emerging democracy in the Middle East once expressed, the criticisms are unsustainable. In the words of Kenton Keith, a former US ambassador to Doha, 'For the long-range importance of press freedom in the Middle East and the advantages that will ultimately have for the West, you have to be a supporter of Al-Jazeera, even if you have to hold your nose sometimes.'

However, it is apparent that the Americans have chosen to hold their noses all the time. The US Administration and its international Coalition partners missed numerous opportunities to win Arab hearts and minds, at every level, throughout the immediate post-9/11 period. The pain and distress of that event and the unifying sympathy it elicited throughout most of the world was squandered—not through the invasion of Afghanistan (which most sensible people could see directly related consequence to cause), although this had its detractors in the Arab world, but through the subsequent war in Iraq which many of the closest friends of the United States could not bring themselves to support. Having largely lost international support, the United States, in particular, then failed completely to get its justification and messages across to sceptical international opinion, particularly in the Arab world, through an arrogance and duality of attitude that at times defied belief. The massive efforts of the Coalition's covert information operation, the leaflets and radio broadcasts, the text messages and e-mails, were only partly effective in the absence of honest and transparent engagement with the region's organic media. Yet there was little engagement of any kind during the conflict and very little in the post-conflict reconstruction phase. Repeatedly those media outlets so praised by neocons in the late 1990s for their free expression and democratic principles became the object of vitriolic attacks—attacks veiled in any number of guises but all ultimately resulting from the Arab media's refusal to 'toe a US party line'.

The former CENTCOM commander General Anthony Zinni is forthright in his opinion: 'Our whole public relations effort out there has been a disaster.'[41] For those who have a genuine affinity with the ideals of American society, the continuing inability of the current US administration to address the problem of public diplomacy in the Middle East is deeply worrying. New ideas are urgently needed, ideas outside the often idealistic and ingenuous thought-processes of neocons, who argue that US-inspired democracy is the answer to all of the region's problems.

## EPILOGUE

On 1 May 2003 US President George W. Bush flew out to join the US Navy aircraft carrier *Abraham Lincoln*, cruising just off the coast of California. In a carefully choreographed media facility he piloted the aircraft and posed, in flying overalls, with members of the ship's company before changing into a more statesman-like suit and, standing beneath a banner proclaiming 'Mission Accomplished', declared that major combat operations were over. Once again choosing to link the tragedy of 9/11 with Saddam's regime he told the world: 'The battle for Iraq is one victory in a war on terror that began on September 11 2001 and it still goes on.'

Yet even his own Defense Secretary Donald Rumsfeld had publicly cast doubt on the validity of links between Saddam's regime and Al-Qaeda: '...I have not seen any strong, hard evidence that links the two.'[1] These comments contrasted with previous public assertions that the two were inextricably linked. In September 2003 Rumsfeld had stated that the United States had 'credible' information that Al-Qaeda had sought contacts in Iraq to help them acquire WMD. Further, he asserted that the presence of senior al-Qaeda leaders in Baghdad was backed by 'solid evidence'.

At the time of going to press, in late 2005 more than 2,000 US servicemen and women have been killed in Iraq and several times that number wounded. Of the dead more than half were killed after the President's 'Mission Accomplished' declaration. Clearly peace has not descended over the country and significant military operations continue to be run against the large number of insurgents who target military and civilian staff alike. The taking of hostages has increased, and their brutal execution, dressed in orange boiler suits and beneath banners espousing Al-Qaeda, suggests that whether or not a terrorist problem existed in Iraq before the war, one certainly exists now. Iraq has joined Afghanistan as the front line in that battle.

Despite the replacement of the US-run Coalition's provisional authority by an Iraqi interim government, it was by no means certain whether conditions would be sufficiently stable to guarantee that the first Iraqi elections could be held safely. Donald Rumsfeld publicly declared in September 2004 that this might not be possible in all areas of the country, and although they were subsequently held in a largely peaceful environment large segments of Iraqi society, notably the Sunnis, did not participate with elections. While the UN has now re-engaged in the process (the murder of its envoy Sergio Vieria de Mello led to a pull-out from the country), it struggles against a tide of lawlessness, and with only thirty-five staff in the country (as at September 2004) this seems an almost impossible task.

Those Coalition countries that provided military assistance for the operation have seen mixed fortunes over the intervening eighteen months. In Spain the ruling party of José Aznar was defeated in elections, and the new government quickly removed Spanish troops from the region. In Britain Tony Blair's premiership has been consistently dogged by criticism of his handling of the Iraq matter, and accusations that he knew that weapons of mass destruction no longer existed in Iraq before the invasion. The inquiry, chaired by Lord Butler, into the perceived intelligence failings appeared to exonerate the government, yet many critics believe that there was a cover-up and refused to accept the report's findings. Calls from the Scottish Nationalist Party to impeach the Prime Minister fell on stony ground. However it is quite clear that the issue of the war dogged the Labour Party throughout the 2005 General Election campaign and led to the leak and then subsequent embarrassing release of the previously secret legal advice from the Attorney General on the validity of the conflict. Although Blair retained power, his majority dropped in the House and if further evidence were needed of the effect of the war on British public opinion, it was the rise in popularity of the Liberal Democrat party—the only mainstream party to have consistently opposed the conflict.

In the United States the presidential opinion polls suggested a close call, yet in the event the electorate voted on issues of national security. Tellingly, 23% of the electorate were estimated to be 'born again' or Evangelical Christians,[2] and overwhelmingly they voted for Bush and the Republican Party. Despite the bloody conflict in Iraq, and the rising toll of US casualties, the so-called Bush Doctrine still appears to be in the ascendant and firmly under neo-conservative influence. Bush continues to reserve the right to pre-emptive unilateral action—a policy that contradicts the UN Charter's Article 51 and its conditions for the use of force—and to see his actions as a natural progression in a war on terrorism. He assiduously believes that the establishment of a Western-style democracy in this most strategic part of the world will set an example that the entire region will follow.

And through it all Arab television channels have relayed imagery and news to their ever-expanding audiences. It is sadly apparent that the relationship between the Coalition and the Arab media is as fragile as ever, and that fragility has been extended to include the Iraqi administration. Al-Jazeera has moved from a one-month ban on operations in Iraq to an extended period of absence. Paradoxically, and in spite of the current ban, the Iraq war has actually been good for Al-Jazeera, and the channel itself appears progressively to strengthen its position. In July 2004 it scored a major public relations success when it announced at its first-ever world forum the inauguration of a new code of ethics—the first in the Arab media world. Before a specially invited audience largely composed of media professionals the channel invited criticism and debate of its conduct and reporting. Nearly 200 representatives of the world's media attended, including senior representatives from both the BBC, Sky TV and, surprisingly perhaps, Fox TV. As a specially invited observer, the author anticipated seeing a predictable division in opinion between representatives from West and East, and true to expectations journalists from the Arab world, Africa and Asia all spoke strongly of the positive effects of the channel, praising its ability to counterbalance the Western media. The latter were especially criticised, and many used the forum to denigrate US policy in the region. Yet when representatives from the West spoke, although they did not share the ingrained distaste of the Arabs for US Middle East policy, their comments on the channel and Arab media in general were quite similar. Even the attendance of the head of news output from the channel's nemesis, Fox TV, did nothing to dilute the obvious affection and trust felt by the majority of the audience for Al-Jazeera. Indeed, during the conference the South African public broadcast network signed an agreement to use Al-Jazeera footage, a move already made by other world networks.

What the conference showed was that for a significant proportion of the world's media, the channel that Donald Rumsfeld accused of having 'a pattern of playing propaganda over and over and over again' is seen as an honest conduit of Arab feeling and as such is regarded as vital to balancing the debate. The South African television representative, who appeared with the author on the channel's flagship discussion programme 'The Opposite Direction', berated the treatment of Arab media with considerable ferocity. The intensity of his rhetoric and the comments of many of the other delegates, particularly those from the Indian subcontinent and east Asia, highlighted a more worrying development. While the popularity of Arab media has grown, the trust and credibility inspired by the West's flagship news providers have diminished. It is apparent that the BBC and CNN, on which many relied for all their news, have lost power in the region. One might argue that this is only to be expected; that people will tune to stations in a foreign language only for as long as no stations in their own language exist. This is certainly true of the early incarnation of Al-Jazeera, which grew out of the embers of the BBC Arabic service. Yet there is a deeper issue. That the BBC and CNN, in particular, have lost appeal and credibility as a result of the Iraq war is beyond doubt. Although the inquiry into the death of the government scientist Dr David Kelly did much to boost the BBC's reputation, many delegates at the conference spoke of the perception that the Western media had been universally 'sucked in' by the issue of weapons of mass destruction and not been as questioning as they should have been. In many eyes only Arab channels had questioned the validity of the claims; hence only Arab channels could now be trusted to be objective.

However, in recognition of some of the criticisms levelled against it, the channel chose the conference to detail its new code of ethics. In a ten-point document it set itself a series of journalistic goals and standards, ranging from adherence to the journalistic values of honesty, impartiality and fairness through to the differentiation of news material, opinion and analysis. The code highlights the particular importance the channel attaches to this latter statement and the consequent resolution 'to avoid the snares of speculation and propaganda'.[3] A further, important standard concerns mistakes. The codes state that the channel will 'acknowledge a mistake when it occurs, promptly correct it and ensure that it does not recur'.[4] Although modest in comparison to the codes of ethics employed by organisations such as the BBC, many Western critics of the channel will welcome them. The US State Department's Arab spokesman Nabil Houray has been particularly critical of the channel's perceived inability to rectify mistakes in reporting. So too has the former head of the British government's strategic information unit, Alistair Campbell, who recalls his anger when the channel's Baghdad reporter asked live on air if the British House of Commons was debating the reports of British soldiers executing Iraqi prisoners of war. 'There had been no reports ... no executions.'[5]

While these are commendable objectives and will be welcomed, the channel had a much more startling revelation: its intention to begin broadcasting a new English-language service—Al-Jazeera International, a progression from its highly successful English-language website aljazeera.net. In 2002 the channel's English website received more than 161 million visits, with some 811 million page impressions. It is evident that there is a clear market for an English-language interpretation of news events from the Arab viewpoint. There is a number of reasons for this decision. First, the channel remains short of advertising revenue, and the expansion of its services to embrace children's TV, sport and the English-language market opens up the potential for its generation, free perhaps from the influence of the Saudi royal family who have put off potential advertisers in the Arab world. Secondly, the channel recognises that there is a substantial Arab diaspora, particularly in Europe and North America. While many of them have access to existing Al-Jazeera services, there are a large number who either have only rudimentary command of Arabic or have not kept up the language at all. But how will such a channel look? The channel's managing director, Nigel Parsons, has already declared that Al-Jazeera International will not directly mirror its bigger Arabic brother, and in deference to more conservative Western viewing preferences (and certain Western government guidelines on taste and decency) it will in particular adopt a very different editorial policy regarding imagery. It is therefore unlikely that shots of dead US and British servicemen, or of some of the more gruesome and intimate injuries of Iraqi civilians, will feature in the English-language channel's future programming schedule. In one sense that is regrettable: Al-Jazeera has made its name by showing the 'other' side of the debate, airing imagery shunned by other networks. A change in this policy may dilute its strong brand image and cause it to go the way of its English-language website, aljazeera.net, which is regarded by some as a much watered-down version of the Arabic site, providing little sense of the channel's more controversial output.

Sadly the channel is almost certain to face a struggle in gaining distribution across the United States and finding a foothold in the closed and complex circle of US broadcasting, tightly controlled as it is by media tycoons and multinational corporations, many with connections to the Bush Administration. These may well refuse outright to carry the new broadcaster. Media observers and academics are already lining up to predict its failure. Trevor Partiff, British associate professor of political science at the American University in Cairo, has told the press that he fully expects to see the 'Zionist lobby' mobilise against the new channel, and there is evidence to suggest that this may well prove to be the case. When Al-Jazeera (Arabic) applied for a Canadian broadcast licence, the president of the Canadian Jewish Congress submitted a strongly-worded objection to the Canadian broadcasting regulator, citing what he described as the programme's agenda of 'hate propaganda'. Although the licence was subsequently granted, a series of pre-conditions were placed on the distributor requiring its censorship of potentially offensive material.

Mohammed Dourrachad, deputy director of Abu Dhabi TV, told TBS On-line Arab media magazine: 'There is a constant call for Arab viewers to have a channel in English to carry our side of the story to the West—particularly the USA.' The enthusiasm for the world's networks to use Arab satellite stations' footage, the evident confidence that many place in it, and the urge for the Arab world to be heard are compelling.

Thankfully the percentage of Muslims who are attracted to Osama Bin Laden and his policies is small, but their strength is that they are impervious to any counter-persuasion. It is among the vast majority of moderate Muslims that the West must seek to make its mark. In the words of the 9/11 Commission report,

The setting is difficult. The combined gross domestic product of the 22 countries in the Arab league is less than the GDP of Spain. 40 per cent of adult Arabs are illiterate, two thirds of them women. One third of the broader Middle East lives on less than two US dollars per day. Less than 2 per cent of the population has access to the internet. The majority of older Arab youths have expressed a desire to emigrate to other countries, particularly those in Europe. In short, the US has to help defeat an ideology, not just a group of people, and we must do so under difficult circumstances.... how can the United States...help moderate Muslims combat the extremist ideas?[26]

There are many answers to this but surely one of the most obvious is to engage with the Arab media and not demonise them or try to clone them in one's own mould. And to engage it is necessary to listen and understand what drives them. And when the West has learnt this it will learn the answer to Richard Holbrook's often repeated question: 'How can a man in a cave out-communicate the world's leading communications society?'

On 1 October 2004 the author was awarded his Iraq Campaign medal by the British maritime commander, Admiral David Snelson. Quiet, gentle and obviously of great intelligence, the Admiral had briefed the men and women of his ships before the start of the war that the campaign was right and just and that there was a real threat of WMD.

After the medal presentation the Admiral invited the fifty or so recipients to gather round informally. As if understanding our own thoughts, he told us that in the current political climate receiving an Iraq medal was probably not a very popular thing to do, and that when we put on our best dress uniforms, people might ask us what the medal ribbon signified. On finding out that it is for service in the war in Iraq they might perhaps scorn its worth and its wearer. He said it might be as long as ten years before the validity and worth of the invasion of Iraq could be properly assessed. But we should take pride in the medal since it signified that we had done all that our country had asked of us in exceptionally trying circumstances.

Despite the Admiral's good words, acceptance of the medal presented a moral dilemma to the author, who has become more and more opposed to the events of March and April 2003. Yet it took the wise counsel of the British Military Assistant to Ladakr Brahimi, the UN Special Representative in Iraq, to place the matter in perspective. Colonel Simon Diggins, with the benefit of much experience, observed: 'I know how you feel about the medal but ... "you did your duty" and there is nothing dishonourable in that. A serviceman's honour lies in dutiful obedience to a lawful command. In the end, we did receive a lawful command, validated by Parliament.'

When politicians make decisions for war it is the ordinary people—in this case British, Iraqi and American—who suffer the consequences. The most they can hope for is that their conduct will be honourable and humane, and that their part in often horrific events will be accurately and fairly portrayed for the world to see.

# NOTES

## Introduction

1. This doctrine has become the source of much debate in the international legal community since it appears to run counter to the United Nations founding Charter. Article 2 (4) of the Charter stipulates that states should refrain from the 'threat of the use of force'. Article 51 allows for self-defence by a state but only 'if an armed attack occurs' against that state. Thus the extent of anticipatory self-defence, which is in essence the Bush doctrine, is an area of considerable doubt.

2. In 1996 Samuel Huntington wrote that future wars would be caused by differences of culture and civilisation. This has become known as the 'Clash of Civilisations'. See Samuel P. Huntington, *The Clash of Civilisations: And The Remaking of World Order*, London, Simon and Shuster, 1996.

3. A broadcasting strategy to win media wars. *Washington Quarterly*, vol. 25, Issue 2, spring 2003.

4. R. Clarke, *Against All Enemies: Inside America's War on Terror*, Washington, DC: Free Press, 2004, p. 246.

5. In her book *Information War* Nancy Snow considers the use of the term 'Arab Street' as a catch-all phrase in the media for Arab citizens. The term seemed to position the Middle East as an area particularly prone to mob rule, people who could not possibly have a healthy attitude towards the United States. Nevertheless, it is a term now in common use to describe Arab public (and not regime) opinion and is used here in this context. See Nancy Snow, *Information War: American Propaganda, Free Speech and Opinion Control since 9/11*, New York, Seven Stories Press, 2004.

6. B. Simms, *Unfinest Hour: Britain and the Destruction of Bosnia*, London, Penguin Books, 2001, p. 54.

7. Ibid, p. 58.

8. President Mubarak told students in Alexandria: 'Not one Arab leader above will be able to control the angry masses.' *The Independent*, 28 August 2002.

9. International Institute for Strategic Studies, *The Military Balance*, London: Taylor and Francis, 2003, p. 95.

10. F. Halliday, *Islam and the Myth of Confrontation*, London, I.B. Tauris, 2003, p. xi.

11. US Government, *The 9/11 Commission Report*, New York: W.W. Norton, 2004, p. xv.

12. Ibid, p. 375.

13. Author's private diary.

14. 'Planned operations to convey selected information and indicators to foreign audiences to influence their emotions, reasoning, and ultimately the behaviour of foreign governments, organizations, groups, and individuals. The purpose of psychological operations is to induce or reinforce foreign attitudes and behaviour favourable to the originator's objectives.' US Department of Defense definition.

15. S. Carruthers, *The Media at War*, London: Palgrave Macmillan, 2000, p. 5.

16. Ibid.

17. Ibid.

18. UK Ministry of Defence, *Operations in Iraq: Lessons for the Future*, paragraph 10.4.

19. Military signal from US Secretary of Defense dated 10 February 2003 to US military forces.

20. *Washington Post*, 19 April 2002.

21. Pew Survey, *What the World Thinks in 2002*. Online at <http://people-press.org/reports/display.php3?ReportID=165>.

22. A. Lennon, *The Battle for Hearts and Minds*, Cambridge, MA: MIT Press, 2003, p. 279.

## Chapter 2  *Attitudes to Conflict*

1. T. Franks, *American Soldier*, New York: Regan Books, 2004, p. 315.

2. Clarke, op. cit., p. 32.

3. BBC News, *The Day that Shook the World: Understanding 9/11*, London: BBC Books, 2003, p. 128.

4. US Government, *The 9/11 Commission Report*, New York: W.W. Norton, 2004, p. 335.

5. B. Woodward, *Plan of Attack: The Road to War*, New York: Simon and Schuster, 2004, p. 27.

6. S. Halper and J. Clarke, *America Alone: The Neo-conservatives and the Global Order*, Cambridge University Press, 2004, p. 266.

7. R. Kagan, *Paradise and Power: America and Europe in the New World Order*, New York: Atlantic Books, 2003, p. 4.

8. *Daily Mirror*, 29 January 2003.

9. Online at <http://news.bbc.co.uk/1/hi/uk_politics/2158574.stm> (accessed March 2004).

10. Online at <http://www.channel4.com/news/2003/05/week_4/28_wmd.html> (accessed May 2004).

11. Online at <http://observer.guardian.co.uk/iraq/story/0,12239,1164078,00.html> (accessed May 2005).

12. 'British Military Chief reveals new legal fears over Iraq War', *The Observer*, 1 May 2005.

13. Online at <http://news.bbc.co.uk/1/hi/uk/2765041.stm> (accessed July 2003).

14. Online at <http://news.bbc.co.uk/2/hi/europe/2765215. stm> (accessed July 2003).

15. N. Chomsky and E.S. Herman, *Manufacturing Consent: The Political Economy of the Mass Media*, New York: Vintage, 1995.

16. Online at <http://www.mcb.org.uk/tragedy133.php> (accessed January 2005).

17. Muslim Council of Britain, press release, 'A Black Day in our History', 20 March 2003.

18. Joint press release by Church of England and Roman Catholic Church, 20 February 2003.

19. Online at <http://www.cofe.anglican.org/cgi-bin/news/item_frame.pl?id236> (accessed January 2005).

20. BBC News, 27 February 2004.

21. *Iraq's Weapons of Mass Destruction: The Assessment of the British Government*. Online at <http://www.number-10.gov.uk/output/Page271.asp> (accessed March 2004).

22. S. Mackey, *The Saudis: Inside the Desert Kingdom*, New York: W.W. Norton, 2003, p. 180.

23. BBC News, *The Day that Shook the World: Understanding 9/11*, London: BBC Books, 2003, p. 132.

24. H. Amin, *Watching the War in the Arab World*. Online at <http://www.tbs.com> Winter Edition 2003 (accessed January 2004).

25. Author's interview with Ashraf Fouad, Abu Dhabi, 10 March 2004.

26. President Bush learned something of the sensitivities of Arab culture on 16 September 2001, when he described his war against terrorism as a crusade. This word provoked a hail of criticism in the Arab press. The Al-

Qaeda leader, Osama Bin Laden, later used the same term in a statement calling for Pakistanis to rise up and resist 'the US crusade'.

27. The UNSC unanimously adopted UNSCR1441 which stated that 'Iraq has been and remains in material breach of its obligations under relevant resolutions', and that 'not later than 30 days from the date of this resolution, a currently accurate, full and complete declaration of all aspects of its programmes to develop chemical, biological and nuclear weapons, ballistic missiles and other delivery systems' had to be made.

28. *The Times*, 6 March 2003.

29. Richard Perle (chairman of the Defence Policy Board and adviser to the Israeli delegation at the Camp David Peace talks), Douglas Feith (Under Secretary for Defense and author of a series of publications asserting the moral superiority of Israelis over Arabs) and John Bolton (Under Secretary of State).

30. W. Shawcross, *Allies: The United States, Britain, Europe and the War in Iraq*, New York: Atlantic Books, 2003, p. 55.

31. Author's interview with Professor George Joffé, London, 26 February 2004.

32. *Washington Post*, 30 August 1999.

33. Author's interview with Professor George Joffé, London, 26 February 2004.

34. F. Gardner, 'Middle East Values', e-mail (24 October 2003).

35. Online at <http://abc.net.au/pm/content/s809017.htm> (accessed May 2003).

36. President Ronald Reagan delivered a speech to the National Association of Evangelicals in Orlando, Florida, in which he referred to Communism as 'the focus of evil in the modern world'. As a result it became known as the 'evil empire speech'.

37. A speech made by President Reagan during a visit to West Berlin in 1987 and a reference to the Wall that separated East and West Berlin.

38. International Institute for Strategic Studies, *The Military Balance*, London: Taylor and Francis, 2003, p. 333.

39. Online at <http://www.newamericancentury.org/> (accessed March 2004).

40. J. Gray, *Al Qaeda and What it Means to be Modern*, London: Faber and Faber, 2001, p. 95.

41. G. Kepel, *Bad Moon Rising: A Chronicle of the Middle East Today*, London: Al-Saqi, 2003, p. 128.

42. Shawcross, op. cit., p. 55.

43. Woodward, op. cit., p. 17.

44. Halper and Clarke, op. cit., pp. 182–200, 299–301.

45. Ibid., p. 186.

46. *Baltimore Sun*, 2 April 2003.
47. *Los Angeles Times*, 11 April 2003.
48. *Extra* (the magazine of Fairness and Accuracy in Reporting), May/June 2003, p. 24.
49. Pew Research Center, 'January 2002 News Interest Index'.
50. *New York Review of Books*, 26 February 2003.
51. *Wall Street Journal*, 17 Aug 2002.
52. Ibid., 14 September 2001.
53. D. Frum, *The Right Man*, London: Weidenfeld and Nicolson, 2003, p. 177.
54. R. Clarke, *Against All Enemies*, Washington, DC: Free Press, 2004, p. ix.
55. *New York Times*, 8 October 2002, Washington, DC: Free Press, 2004.
56. Online at <www.pollingreport.com> (accessed August 2004).
57. CNN, Fox, NBC, CBS and ABC. FAIR Survey.
58. *New York Times*, 10 October 2003.
59. Online at <www.commondreasm.org/views04/0429-11.htm> (accessed October 2004).
60. Gallup Poll, 'News Media Get Good Marks for Terrorism Coverage', 26 February 2003.
61. Online at <http://207.44.245.159/audio1001.htm> (accessed April 2005).
62. Online at <http://www.ncccusa.org/news/03news4.html> (accessed June 2004).
63. P.J. Boyer, 'The New War Machine', *The New Yorker*, 30 June 2003.
64. W. Clarke, 'Winning Modern Wars', *Public Affairs*, 2003, p. xii.
65. CBS News, '60 minutes', TV programme, 21 May 2004.
66. US Government, *The 9/11 Commission Report*, New York: W.W. Norton, 2004, p. 34.
67. J. Kampfner, *Blair's Wars*, New York: Simon and Schuster, 2003, p. 311.
68. *Sydney Morning Herald*, 24 September 2003.
69. The expression proved of particular interest to the German press; one German newspaper declared that the decision to send troops was insolent while another declared that the Poles were not a Trojan horse but a Trojan donkey.
70. *Los Angeles Times*, 8 March 2003.
71. R. Crockatt, *America Embattled: September 11, Anti-Americanism and the Global Order*, London: Routledge, 2003, p. 68.
72. Lt Gen. William Boykin, quoted in *New York Times*, 17 October 2003.
73. Franks, op. cit., p. 19.
74. In 1996 only 7 per cent of US citizens held a passport.

75. R. Denton, *The Media and the Persian Gulf War*, New York: Praeger, 1993, p. 247.

76. Z. Sardar and M. Davies, *Why do people hate America?*, London: Icon Books, 2002, p. 41.

77. Ibid. p. 43.

78. *Washington Post*, 14 February 2002.

## Chapter 3 *Towards Free Arab Media*

1. K.D. Karlekar, *Freedom of the Press 2003: a Global Survey of Media Independence*, Freedom House, 2004, p. 4. Online at <http://www.freedomhouse.org/research/pressurvey.htm> (accessed November 2003).

2. Author's interview with Professor George Joffé, London, 26 February 2004.

3. B. Lewis, *The Multiple Identities of the Middle East*, New York: Schocken Books, 1998, p. 96.

4. Author's interview with Jihad Ali-Ballout, Qatar, 15 March 2004.

5. K.D. Karlekar, op. cit. p. 25.

6. Author's interview with Ashraf Fouda, Abu Dhabi, 10 March 2004.

7. Online at <www.cpj.org/Briefings/2001/aljazeera_oct01/aljazeera_oct01.html>.

8. John L. Esposito, *Unholy War: Terror in the Name of Islam*, New York: Oxford University Press, 2002, p. 41.

9. Authors interview with Jihad Ali-Ballout, Qatar, 15 March 2004.

10. From a cartoon by Ahmed Toughan used by Al-Jazeera. Mohamed El-Nawawy and Adel Iskander, Al-Jazeera: the Story of the Network that is Rattling Governments and Redefining Modern Journalism, Cambridge MA: Westview Press, 2003.

11. *The Middle East*, issue 343, March 2004, p. 52.

12. L. Graz, *The Turbulent Gulf: People, Politics and Power*, New York: St Martin's Press, p. 167.

13. Al-Jazeera, op. cit. p. 31.

14. Author's interview with Jihad Ali-Ballout, Qatar, 15 March 2004.

15. Ibid.

16. Ibid.

17. Quote from Nabil Al-Hamir, Bahrain Information Minister, BBC, 10 May 2002. Online at <http://news.bbc.co.uk/1/hi/world/middle_east/1980191.stm> (accessed November 2003).

18. *Financial Times*, 1 October 2002.

19. K.D. Karlekar, op. cit. p. 4.

20. *TBS Journal*, interview with Mohammed Dourrachad. Online at <http://www.tbljournal.com/dourrachad>

21. Author's interview with Sam Barnett, Dubai, 15 March 2004.

22. Online at <http://news.bbc.co.uk/1/hi/world/middle_east/3236654.stm>

23. E-mail correspondence with author.

24. *Washington Post*, Foreign Service, 13 October 2001, p. A22.

25. Al-Jazeera's decision to launch an English-language channel is partly driven by recognition that many second- and third-generation Arabs resident abroad are often unable to speak Arabic, but wish to keep track of events in the Arab homelands.

## Chapter 4  *The 1991 Gulf War: Who Learned the Lessons?*

1. Bruce Watson, *Military Lessons of the Gulf*, London: Greenhill Books, 1991, p. 208.

 2. For a complete account of the media coverage of the war see Robert Harris's seminal study, *Gotcha: The Media, the Government and the Falklands Crisis*, London: Faber & Faber, 1982.

 3. G. McLaughlin, *The War Correspondent*, London: Pluto, 2002, p. 91.

 4. P. de la Billière, General Sir, *Storm Command*, London: HarperCollins, 1992, p. 219.

 5. G. McLaughlin, *The War Correspondent*, London: Pluto Press, 2002, p. 95.

 6. Carruthers, op. cit., p. 242.

 7. McLaughlin, op. cit., p. 89.

 8. Khaled Bin Sultan, General, *Desert Warrior*, London: HarperCollins, 1995, p. 452.

 9. Huntington, op. cit., p. 59.

10. A. Abukhalil, *The Battle for Saudi Arabia*, New York: Seven Stories Press, 2004, p. 35.

## Chapter 5  *War in Iraq: Managing the Media Battle Space*

1. *New York Times Co.* v. *United States Court of Appeals for the Second Circuit* no. 1873. Argued 26 June 1971, decided 30 June 1971.

 2. *New York Times*, 20 March 2003.

 3. Online at <http://www.tbsjournal.com/Archives/Spring03/rushing.html> (accessed June 2003).

 4. US Government, *The 9/11 Commission Report*, New York: W.W. Norton, 2004, p. 337.

 5. President George W. Bush's address to Congress, 20 September 2001.

 6. Meeting with the author, 18 October 2004.

 7. White House Press Office news release, 14 March 2003.

 8. Literally 'a generous month'.

 9. Online at <http://www.state.gov/secretary/rm/2003/19064pf.htm> (accessed June 2004).

10. Reuters, 16 July 2004.

11. Online at <http://www.state.gov/secretay/rm/2003/21938pf.html> (accessed June 2003).

12. US Department of Defense news transcript, 25 February 2003.

13. Online at <http://www.inthesetimes.com/site/main/print/790> (accessed June 2003).

14. A fact verified by the author's visit to Al-Jazeera HQ in Doha, March 2004.

15. Online at <http://www.defenselink.mil/transcripts/2002/t12042002_t204cent.html>

16. Signal from SECDEF WASHINGTON 101900Z February 2003 to US Forces recorded in author's private diary.

17. Britain referred to embedded media as 'war correspondents'; the US used the term 'embeds'.

18. E-mail correspondence between the author and Squadron Leader Tom Rounds, RAF, 2 June 2003.

19. Author's interview with Simon Wren, March 2004.

20. UK MoD, *Working Arrangements with the Media in Times of Emergency, Tension and Conflict or War.*

21. Author's interview with Nick Pollard, London, 25 March 2004.

22. BBC, op.cit., p. 111.

23. Author's discussion with Colonel Paul Brook, deputy director Media Operations, Ministry of Defence, London.

24. E-mail correspondence between the author and Lt Col. Sean Tully, 8 March 2004.

25. Questionnaire completed by Colonel Chris Vernon.

26. Author's private e-mail dated 11 March 2003.

27. Author's interview with Jihad Ali-Ballout, Doha, 15 March 2004.

28. *Al-Wafd*, 22 April 2003.

29. Franks, op. cit., p. 411.

30. Author's telephone interview with James Wilkinson, Washington, DC, 31 March 2004.

31. Author's discussion with Colonel Paul Brook, Ministry of Defence, London.

32. Author's interview with Simon Wren, London, 26 February 2004.

33. Ibid.

34. Ibid.

35. BBC, op.cit., p. 110.

36. Ibid., p. 111.

37. B. Katovsky and T. Carlson, *Embedded: The Media at War in Iraq*, Guildford CT: Lyon's Press, 2003, p. 39.

38. Author's telephone interview with James Wilkinson, Washington, DC, 31 March 2004.

39. Ibid.

40. Ibid.

41. Ibid.

42. Ibid.

43. Online at <http://www.truthout.org/docs_04/033004d. shtml> (accessed July 2004).

44. Author's telephone interview with James Wilkinson, Washington, DC, 31 March 2004.

45. Ibid.

46. Author's interview with Simon Wren, London, 26 February 2004.

47. Questionnaire completed by Wing Commander Ian Tofts, RAF.

48. Author's telephone interview with James Wilkinson, Washington, DC, 31 March 2004.

49. Ibid.

50. Ibid.

51. Author's interview with Simon Wren, London, 26 February 2004.

52. Ibid.

53. Ibid.

54. This is factually incorrect. Al-Jazeera has never broadcast a beheading on TV.

55. Fox TV show, *The O'Reilly Factor*, broadcast 8.00 p.m., 22 October 2004.

56. Author's interview with Marcus DeVille, London, 2 March 2004.

57. Ibid.

58. Ibid.

59. Author's interview with Lt Cdr Mark Hankey, Ministry of Defence, May 2004.

60. Author's private diary.

## Chapter 6  *Arab Media, Bias and the Coalition*

1. Online at <http//www.allied-media.com/arAbu Dhabi TV/aljazeera/ inside_al_ta.htm> (accessed February 2004).

2. Author's interview with Marcus DeVille, London, 2 March 2004.

3. Author's interview with Ashraf Fouad, Abu Dhabi, 10 March 2004.

4. Katovsky and Carlson, op.cit., p. 182.

5. Ibid., p. 181.

6. Author's interview with Nick Pollard, London, 24 March 2004.

7. BBC, op.cit., p. 23.

8. A newspaper written in Qatar by Coalition forces and disseminated around theatre for British Forces to read.

9. Author's interview with Ashraf Fouad, Abu Dhabi, 10 March 2004.

10. Online at <http www.robert-fisk.com/articles136.htm> (accessed August 2004).

11. Interview with SkyNews media logger, London, 5 April 2004.

12. Author's interview with Salah Nagm, Dubai, 15 March 2004.

13. British Embassy assessments recorded in contemporary author's private diary.

14. Ibid.

15. Ibid.

16. E-mail from CMS Task Force PDPA-A to US embassies and consulates, 1 April 2003.

17. E-mail from Martin R. Quinn, Public Affairs Officer, US Embassy, Ankara, 2 April 2003.

18. E-mail from Terry J. White, Press and Information Officer, US Embassy, Islamabad, 4 April 2003.

19. E-mail from Aleta Wenger, Public Affairs Officer, US Embassy, Bahrain, 2 April 2003.

20. E-mail from Robert Keith, Public Affairs Officer, US Consulate, Jeddah, 2 April 2003.

21. Exercise Bright Star was held by CENTCOM in 1998 in Egypt. Exercise Saif Sarea II was conducted by the British military in Oman in 2001.

22. Middle East Consultancy International (private circulation e-mail).

23. Author's interview with Simon Wren, London, 26 February 2004.

24. Ibid.

25. Online at <http://news.bbc.co.uk/2/hi/middle_east/2889255.stm>

26. Author's interview with Jihad Ali-Ballout, Doha, 15 March 2004.

27. BBC World News, 24 May 2003.

28. Author's interview with Nick Pollard, London, 25 March 2004.

29. Ibid.

30. Author's interview with Professor George Joffé, London, 26 February 2004.

31. Online at <http://www.cnnmoney.com> 25 March 2003 (accessed October 2003).

32. Ibid.

33. Online at <http://www.defenselink.mil/transcripts/2003/t02282003_t0227bc.html> (accessed April 2004).

34. *The Guardian*, special edition, 'One Year On', 19 March 2004.

35. Ibid.

36. The Iraqi flag flown by the US was an old version, missing the line *Allahu Akbhar*—God is Great—in Arabic. This had been added by Saddam after the 1991 Gulf War to ingratiate his regime with religious leaders. The return of this, an older flag, was redolent with feeling to Arabs—a fact seemingly unknown to the US troops.

37. Courtesy of BBC Monitoring Service, Caversham.

38. Ibid.

39. Online at <http://www.cbsnews.com/stories/2002/08/06/iraq/scence/printable517611.shtml> (accessed January 2005).

40. J. Kampfner, *Blair's Wars*, New York: Simon and Schuster, 2003, p. 328.

41. E-mail correspondence with Jihad Ali-Ballout, 31 March 2004.

42. Ibid.

43. Author's interview with Nart Bouran, Head of News, Abu Dhabi TV.

44. Author's telephone interview with Alex Gardiner.

45. Author's interview with Sultan Sleiman, LBC.

46. Ibid.

47. Author's interview with Salah Nagm, Dubai, 15 March 2004.

## Chapter 7  *Crossing the Rubicon: the Other Face of the Information Campaign*

1. S. Huntington, op. cit., p. 51.

2. Examination of Witnesses (Questions 1571).

3. US Navy official figures.

4. Online at <http://www.publications.parliament.uk/pa/cm200203/cmhansrd/vo030319/debtext/30319-17.htm> (accessed February 2005).

5. Work conducted by the US military suggested that music by the popular music performers Celine Dion and Sheryl Crow was particularly favoured by Iraqi audiences.

6. David Miller, *Tell Me Lies: Propaganda and Media Distortion in the Attack on Iraq*, London: Pluto Press, 2004, p. 92

7. CENTCOM Website.

8. Franks, op. cit., p. 449.

9. De la Billière, op. cit., p. 271.

10. Jowett, O'Donnel and O'Donnel, *Propaganda and Persuasion*, New York: Sage, p. 9.

11. 'A Battle Waged on Iraq's Airwaves', *Baltimore Sun*, 22 March 2003.

12. Robert Fox, Iraq Campaign 2003 Royal Navy and Royal Marines, p. 113.

13. Online at <www.operations.mod.uk/telic/sandy7.pdf>

14. *The Guardian*, 8 January 2004.
15. Author's interview with Commanding Officer 15 (UK) Psyops Regiment.
16. Quoted in J. Gray, *Al Qaeda and what it means to be modern*, London: Faber and Faber, 2004, p. 99.
17. US State Department Press Release, 5 June 2003.
18. *Christian Science Monitor*, 20 March 2004.
19. Reference to a 1948 statute, the Smith-Mundt Act, which prevents the US Federal government from disseminating political information within the United States.
20. Interview with Asraf Fouad, Abu Dhabi, 10 March 2004.
21. Online at <www.english.aljazeera.net> 5 April 2004 (accessed July 2004).
22. R. Clarke, *Against All Enemies*, Washington, DC: Free Press, 2004, p. 263.
23. Jeremy Sharp, '*The Al-Jazeera News Network: Opportunity or Challenge for US Policy in the Middle East*', online at <http://fpc.state.gov/documents/organi-sation> p. 6.
24. A presidential initiative founded to support economic, political and educational reform efforts in the Middle East.
25. Jeremy Sharp, op. cit., p. 14.

## Chapter 8 *The View from Baghdad*

1. Salam Pax, *The Bagdhad Blog*, London: Atlantic Books, 2003, p. 148.
2. *New York Times*, 'Threats and Responses: Foreign Correspondents; Iraq Offers West's Reporters a Kinder, Gentler Face', 28 October 2002.
3. Ibid.
4. Interview with author.
5. Katovsky and Carlson, op. cit. p. 247.
6. Interview with author, Abu Dhabi, March 2004.
7. Interview with author, Dubai, March 2004.
8. Ibid.
9. Inter Press Service, 10 April 2003, 'US Government Accused of War Crimes against Journalists'.
10. Richard Engle, *A Fist in a Hornet's Nest*, London: Hyperion, 2005.
11. 'US Kills Journalists', *Saudi Gazette*, 8 April 2003.
12. CPJ news release, New York, 5 November 2004.

## Chapter 9 *The Reckoning*

1. For a particularly interesting debate on the moralistic standpoint of the President and on the moral and philosophical debate for war in Iraq the reader

is directed to Chapter 8 of Peter Singer's study *The President of Good and Evil: Taking George W. Bush Seriously*, London: Granta, 2004.

2. Martin Bell, *Through Gates of Fire: a Journey into World Disorder*, London: Phoenix Press, 2003, p. 225.

3. CBS '60 minutes' TV programme broadcast 12 May 1996. Interview between Madeleine Albright (US ambassador to the United Nations) and Lesley Stahl.

4. *Goals and Objectives of War*, issued, 21 March 2003 and online at <www.defense-link.mil/news/mar2003/t03212003_t0321sd1.html> and publicly stated by President George W. Bush at the United Nations, September 2002, when he told the General Assembly that 'Liberty for the Iraqi people is a great moral cause and a great strategic goal'.

5. The United States has contingency plans for a wide range of possible military operations. OIF was one such contingency plan referred to by its CENTCOM designator, 1003V.

6. Bob Woodward, *Plan of Attack*, London: Simon and Schuster, 2004, p. 206.

7. Author's telephone interview with James Wilkinson, Washington, DC, 31 March 2004.

8. Even this format has been criticised. This particular programme, which encourages correspondents to add their own views, was criticised by the Israeli government when the BBC Middle East correspondent said on air: 'I cried when Yassar Arafat left his compound' shortly before his removal to a French hospital in November 2004.

9. A. Lennon, op. cit. p. 289.

10. *The Bush Dyslexicon*, Department for Media Studies, University of Ulster.

11. Nancy Snow, op. cit. p. 77.

12. Bill Katovsky and Timothy Calcon, Embedded, p. 164.

13. S. Halper and J. Clarke, op. cit. p. 316.

14. Online at <mediaguardian.co.uk> 13 July 2004.

15. House of Lords *Hansard*, 23 May 2003, column 875.

16. House of Commons *Hansard*, 3 Apr 2003, column 1095.

17. House of Commons *Hansard*, 24 March 2003, column 29.

18. Interview Al-Jazeera, 24 November 2004. FCO briefing document.

19. *Gulf Times*, 8 April 2003.

20. Online at <www.opendemocracy.net/> loosing the battle for Arab hearts and minds.

21. Carruthers, op. cit. p. 6.

22. Interview with senior FCO diplomat, March 2004.

23. Interview with Jihad Ali-Ballout, Doha, 15 March 2004.

24. *New York Times*, 18 November 2003.

25. *Washington Post*, November 2000.

26. Author's discussions with *Daily Mirror* defence correspondent.

27. Online at <www.insightmag.com>

28. Abdel Samarra, 'Arab Media and the Iraq War', *Palestine-Israel Journal*, vol. 10, no. 3 (2003).

29. Online at <www.arabmediawatch.com> 20 October 2003

30. Author's discussion with senior FCO diplomats.

31. An independent expert, who wishes to remain anonymous, has studied these error messages. He believes they were almost certainly the result of a sophisticated jamming campaign.

32. Subsequently this has evolved into a further mobile telephone service, entitled 'Al-Jazeera Assawtiyyah'. This is an Arabic news service that allows people to listen to Al-Jazeera news by dialling a local telephone number on their mobile phones.

33. Online <www.cnn.com/2003/world/mideast/07/24/sprj.irq.sons/>

34. *International Herald Tribune*, 23 August 2003.

35. Military personnel trained as cameramen who deploy to theatres of operations to record imagery for civilian media.

36. 'Why the US is Failing in Iraq', *The Age*, 16 August 2003.

37. House of Commons Defence Select Committee, Report on Iraq, Summary Document, para. 124.

38. Evidence from Air Vice Marshal Heath, RAF, House of Commons Defence Select Committee, 16 December 2003.

39. Al-Jazeera was carried by Indonesian TV throughout the war.

40. Author's interview with Jihad Ali-Ballout, Doha, 15 March 2004.

41. Remarks at Central Defence Intelligence Board of Directors dinner, 12 May 2004.

## Epilogue

1. Agence France-Presse, 5 October 2004.

2. *Middle East International Magazine*, 19 November 2004, p. 12.

3. Point 9. Al Jazeera code of ethics, issued 12 July 2004.

4. Point 7, ibid.

5. *The Guardian*, Inside Story, 15 September 2004.

6. US Government, *The 9/11 Commission Report*, New York: W.W. Norton, 2004, p. 376.

# BIBLIOGRAPHY

*Author's interviews*

Simon Wren, Senior British Media Advisor to Commander British Forces for Operation Telic, London, 26 February 2004.

Jihad Ali Ballout, *Al-Jazeera* Communications Manager, Qatar, 31 March 2004.

Mr Wilkinson, Media Advisor to General Tommy Franks, Washington DC, 31 March 2004 (phone).

Professor George Joffé, London, 26 February 2004.

Mr Nart Bouran, Head of News, Abu Dhabi TV, July 2004.

Sultan Sleiman, Head of News, LBC, July 2004.

Nick Pollard, Head of News, SKY TV, London, 25 March 2004.

Salah Nagm, Head of News, Al-Arabiya TV, Dubai, 15 March 2004.

Ashraf Fouad, media analyst, Abu Dhabi, 10 March 2004

Marcus DeVille, Media advisor to Commander British Land Forces Iraq, London, 2 March 2004

Colonel Paul Brook, Deputy Director Media Operations, Ministry of Defence, London, 15 May 2004.

Lieut Cdr Mark Hankey, RNR, London, 15 May 2004.

*Books and magazines*

Abukhalil Asíad, *The Battle for Saudi Arabia*, New York, Seven Stories Press, 2004.

*Arabies Trends: The International Magazine on Arab Affairs*, Paris, March 2004.

Baylis, John, *Strategy in the Contemporary World: An Introduction to Strategic Studies*, Oxford University Press, 2003.

Bell, Martin, *Through Gates of Fire: A Journey into World Disorder*, London, Phoenix Press, 2003.

Bergen, Peter L., *Holy War Inc. Inside the Secret World of Osama Bin Laden*, London, Phoenix, 2001.

BBC News, *The Battle for Iraq*, London, BBC Publishing, 2003.

BBC News, *The Day That Shook the World: Understanding September 11th*, London, ABC Books, 2001.

Carruthers, Susan, *The Media at War*, London, Palgrave Macmillan, 2000.

Clarke, Richard, *Against All Enemies: Inside America's War on Terror*, New York, Free Press, 2004.

Council on Foreign Relations, *Foreign Affairs*, Washington, DC, Sept./Oct. 2003.

Crockatt, Richard, *America Embattled: September 11, Anti-Americanism and the Global Order*, London, Routledge, 2003.

De La Billiere, General Sir Peter, *Storm Command*, London, Harper Collins, 1993.

Denton, Robert, *The Media and the Persian Gulf War*, New York, Praeger, 1993.

El-Nawawy, Mohammed, and Iskander, Adel, *Al-Jazeera: The Story of the Network that is Rattling Governments and Redefining Modern Journalism*, Boulder, CO, Westview Press 2003.

Esposito, John, *Unholy War: Terror in the Name of Islam*, New York, Oxford University Press, 2002.

———, *What Everyone Needs to Know About Islam*, New York, Oxford University Press, 2002.

Franks, General Tommy, *American Soldier*, Washington, Regan Books, 2004.

Frum, David, *The Right Man*, London, Weidenfeld and Nicolson, 2003.

Gray, John, *Al Qaeda and What it Means to be Modern*, London, Faber, 2004.

Graz, Liesl, *The Turbulent Gulf—People, Politics and Power*, London, I.B. Tauris, 1992.

Halliday, Fred, *Islam and the Myth of Confrontation*, London, I.B. Tauris, 2003.

Halper, Stefan, and Clarke, Jonathan, *America Alone: The Neo-conservatives and the Global Order*, Cambridge University Press, 2004.

Herman, E., and Chomsky, N., *Manufacturing Consent: The Political Economy of the Mass Media*, New York, Pantheon, 1988.

Hudson, Miles, and Stanier, John, *War and the Media*, Stroud, Sutton, 1999.

Huntington, Samuel P., *The Clash of Civilisations: And The Remaking of World Order*, London, Simon and Shuster, 1996.

International Institute for Strategic Studies, *The Military Balance 2002/3*, London, Oxford University Press for IISS.

Karlekar, Karin Deutsch, *Freedom of the Press 2003: A Global Survey of Media Independence*, Freedom House, 2004.

Kampfner, John, *Blair's Wars*, London, Simon and Schuster, 2003.

Katovsky, Bill, and Carlson, Timothy, *Embedded: The Media at War in Iraq*, The Lyons Press, 2003.

Kepel, Gilles, *Bad Moon Rising: A Chronicle of the Middle East Today*, London, Saqi Books, 2003.

Lennon, Alexander, *The Battle for Hearts and Minds: Using Soft power to Undermine Terrorist Networks*, Cambridge, MA: The MIT Press, 2003.

Lewis, Bernard, *The Multiple Identities of the Middle East*, New York, Schocken Books 1998.

Mackey, Sandra, *The Saudis Inside the Desert Kingdom*, New York, Norton, 2002.

McLaughlin, Greg, *The War Correspondent*, London, Pluto Press, 2002.

Miller, David, *Tell Me Lies: Propaganda and Media Distortion in the Attack on Iraq.* London, Pluto Press, 2004.

Pintak, Lawrence, *Seeds of Hate and How America's Flawed Middle East Policy Ignited the Jihad*, London, Pluto Press, 2003.

Pax, Salam, *The Baghdad Blog*, London, Atlantic Books, 2003.

Sardar, Ziauddin, and Davies, Merryl Wyn, *Why Do People Hate America?* London, Icon Books, 2002.

Sharp, Jeremy, *The Middle East Partnership Initiative: An Overview 23 July 2003*, US Congressional Research Service: http://fpc.state.gov/documents

Shawcross, William, *Allies: The Unites States, Britain, Europe and the War in Iraq.* London, Atlantic Books, 2003.

Singer, Peter, *The President of Good and Evil: Taking George W. Bush Seriously*, London, Granta, 2004.

Simms, Brendan, *Unfinest Hour: Britain and the Destruction of Bosnia*, London, Penguin Books, 2001.

Simpson, John, *The Wars Against Saddam: Taking the Hard Road to Baghdad.* London, Macmillan, 2003.

Snow, Nancy, *Information War: American Propaganda, Free Speech and Opinion Control since 9/11*, New York, Seven Stories Press, 2004.

Soloman, Norman, and Reese Erlich, *Target Iraq: What the News Media Didn't Tell You* New York, Context Books, 2003.

Thussu, Daya Kishan, and Freedman, D., *War and the Media*, London, Sage, 2003.

Ministry of Defence. Operations in Iraq—Lessons for the Future, DGCC, December 2003. Available at www.mod.uk/publications/iraq_future-lessons/

*US Government The 9/11 Commission Report*

Watson, Bruce, George, Bruce, Tsouras, Peter and Cyr, B., *Military Lessons of the Gulf War*, London, Greenhill Books, 1991.

Woodward, Bob, *Plan of Attack*, London, Simon and Schuster, 2004.

*Articles and Internet sources*

Bowers, Faye, 'Al-Hurra Joins the Battle for News, Hearts and Minds'. www.csmonitor.com/2004/0224/p01s04-ustp.htm

Centre for Media Freedom, 'The Media Environment in Saudi Arabia', April 1998.

El-Farra, Narmeen, 'Arabs and the Media', *Journal of Media Psychology*, vol. 1, no. 2, Spring 1996.

Essoulami, Said, 'The Press in the Arab World: 100 Years of Suppressed Freedom', 3 May 2000. World Association of Newspapers, World Press Freedom Celebration.

Fuller, Graham E., 'The Future of Political Islam', *Foreign Affairs*, March April 2002.

Garden, Sir Timothy, www.tgarden.demon.co.uk/writingd/articles/2001/01103rusi.htm, London, RUSI, 30 Oct 2001.

Gerges, Fawez, 'A Change of Arab Hearts and Minds', 4 Feb. 2004, www.csmonitor.com/2004/0204/p09s01-cogn.htm.

Henderson, Simon, 'The Al-Jazeera effect'. http://www.washington-institute.org/templateC10.php?CID=18

Hroub, Khaled, 'Muslims in Europe post-9/11', www.sant.ox.ac.uk/main/princeton/pap_hroub.shtml

Human Rights First, 'Reported Iraqi Violations of Geneva Convention Rules on POWs', www.humanrightsfirst.org/media/2003_alerts/0327.htm

Indyk, Martin, 'The Post Gulf War Bargain', *Foreign Affairs*, Washington, DC, Jan./Feb. 2002.

Joffe, E.G.H., 'Relations Between the Middle East and the West', *Middle East Journal*, vol. 48, no. 2, Spring 1994.

Knights, Michael, 'The role of broadcast media in influence operations in Iraq', 19 May 2003 www.washingtoninstitute.org/watch/policywatch/policywatch2003/758.htm

Khoury-Machool, Makram, 'Losing the Battle for Arab Hearts and Minds', 2 May 2003. www.opendemocracy.net/debates/article.8.92.1202.jsp

Khurma, Merissa, *Al-Jazeera in English*, 7 Feb 2003, www.washington-institute.org/watch/policywatch2003/708.htm

La Franchi, Howard, 'Ways to Burnish America's Image Abroad', 3 Oct 2003, www.csmonitor.com/2003/1003/p02s01.ustp.htm

The Pew Research Center For The People and The Press. 'What the World Thinks in 2002'. http://peoplepress.org/reports/display.php3?ReportID=165

———, 'Views of a changing world 2003'. http://people-press.org/reports/display.php3?ReportID=185

Satloff, Robert, 'Wrong Answers to Al-Jazeera', *Washington Post*, 4 April 2003.

Schanzer, Jonathan, Al-Mirazi, Hafez, and Mouafac, Harb, 'Arabs View the War: Images, Attitudes and Opinions', www.washingtoninstiture.org/watch/policywatch2003/742.htm

———, 'A tale of two Qatars', 6 Dec 2002, www.washingtoninstitute.org/watch/policywatch/policywatch2002/685.htm

Sharabi, Hisham, 'The Political Impact of Arab Satellite Televison on Post Iraq War Arab World.' www.tbsjournal.com/hisham_sharabi.html

Sharp, Jeremy, 'The Al-Jazeera News Network: Opportunity or Challenge for US Foreign Policy in the Middle East'?, US Congressional Research Service. Available at http://fpc.state.gov/documents/organisation.

*Tension and Conflict or War* (the Green Guide) DGCC. Nd. www.mod.uk/new/green_book/index.htm.

# INDEX

## Revolt on the Tigris
*The Al Sadr Uprising and the Governing of Iraq*
Mark Etherington

'an extraordinary story, brilliantly told' — *Guardian*
'an important, detailed, evocative and revealing book' — *Sunday Times*
'a tour-de-force of war reporting; at times a comedy of errors and, at others,
a terrifying drama of suspense.' — *Publishers Weekly*, starred review
186x123mm., viii, 252pp. 2005 Hbk 15.00 1-85065-773-4

## Insurgency and Counter-Insurgency in Iraq
Ahmed S. Hashim

'Making sense of a seemingly chaotic situation, Hashim expertly illuminates the history,
motives and modus operandi of insurgents in Iraq. This ground-breaking book leads the
way in analysing the factors underlying the unremitting litany of violence in post-
Saddam Iraq.' — Gareth Stansfield, University of Exeter
186x123mm., 176pp. Oct. 2005 Hbk 15.00 1-85065-795-5

## Landscapes of the Jihad
*Militancy, Morality, Modernity*
Faisal Devji

'No political theorist, anthropologist or student of Islam will fail to be provoked and
inspired by this brilliant analysis of Jihadi discourse. ... Devji moves effortlessly
between theology, history and cultural studies to give us the first major English-
language interpretation of the moral world of contemporary Jihad.'
— Professor Arjun Appadurai, New School University
186x123mm., xvii, 185pp. 2005 Hbk 15.00 1-85065-775-0

## Globalised Islam
*The Search for a New Ummah*
Olivier Roy

'a new book by Roy [is] something of an event ... *Globalised Islam* is a highly original,
methodologically rigorous ... superb and complex sociological study.'
— *Washington Post*
xii, 352pp. 2004 Hbk45.00 1-85065-593-6 Pbk 16.95 1-85065-598-7

## The Search for Arab Democracy
*Discourses and Counter-Discourses*
Larbi Sadiki

'[Sadiki] avoids the simplistic black and white thinking that characterizes most public
discourse on this issue. He interrogates in a wide-ranging and subtle way a whole range
of Muslim thinkers, from medieval philosophers to nineteenth century modernists to
contemporary feminists and Islamists. This book is a key intervention in an increasingly
central public debate about Islam and democracy.'
— Juan Cole, University of Michigan
xii, 320pp. 2003 Hbk 39.50 1-85065-489-1 Pbk 17.95 1-85065-494-8